Gender and Caste Hierarchy in Colonial Bengal

Gender and Caste Hierarchy in Colonial Bengal

Inter-Caste Interventions of Ideal Womanhood

Deboshruti Roychowdhury

Stree

Gender and Caste Hierarchy in Colonial Bengal:
Inter-Caste Interventions of Ideal Womanhood
First published in January 2014 by STREE,
an imprint of Bhatkal and Sen
16 Southern Avenue, Kolkata 700026
email streesamya.manager@gmail.com
www.stree-samyabooks.com

ISBN 978-93-81345-05-4
93-81345-05-8

Rs 600.00

Design by Compuset International and STREE,
Typesetting by Compuset International, 85 Park St, Kolkata 700016,
and printed by Arunima Printing Works, 81 Simla Street, Kolkata 700006.

This book is a small token of gratitude to Debahuti Deb.
For being with me even when I am without you,
for cherishing my dreams,
and most of all for making me what I am today.

Contents

Preface

The anti-Mandal agitation aroused within me for the first time the realization that caste is not just pedagogic mumbo jumbo, which very conveniently and at times snootily ignores political and social issues that truly affect our daily lives. At a time when feminist scholarship began to explore the inextricable links between caste and gender and began to offer a terminology by which caste and gender could be understood on a comprehensible level, I wondered what made some women carry placards that read 'We do not want unemployed husbands'. As Uma Chakravarti asked, why wouldn't such women marry the bright low-caste lads who, according to the apprehensions of the upper-caste women post-Mandal Commission, were going to grab all the jobs offered?

Being introduced to terms like 'brahmanical patriarchy' in the aftermath of the Mandal agitation, I tried to comprehend why and how efforts to define and clarify these terms were (and still are) an aspect of contemporary feminist scholarship. The emerging body of scholarship gradually drew attention to the regional and nationalist dimensions of the workings of brahmanical patriarchy. However, during my campus life in Michigan, when I also watched several Bollywood movies, I realized how important it was for all Indian women to behave in a certain pattern that would fetch them the coveted title of 'ideal woman', which in turn would establish the husband or the father, the family, and the entire clan as honest, noble, sincere, successful, moral and, of course, pure.

I started wondering why it was so important for a family or a clan to make their women members behave in a certain manner and whether or not it was just for the sake of retaining property rights. An affirmative answer, although scholastically satisfying to the Marxist pedagogy, never left me satiated. *'Gandi aurat, gandi jaat'*, roughly translated as rotten woman, makes an entire caste or clan impure, made me question the purity factor involved with woman's existence in Indian society. This was the time when I got re-introduced and, eventually, hooked to the enigma called caste. Twelve years and three continents later, this very journey took the form of this book.

This book resembles my struggle and satisfaction of being an Indian woman, ironically upper-caste, but never an 'ideal' one. This fascinating journey would not have been possible without the support of the School of Oriental and African Studies' Research Fellowship Committee, which believed that research on caste and Bengali women set in a nineteenth-century background was worth pursuing; Dr. Julia Leslie, who inculcated the belief in me that I had the capability of pursuing my dreams; Dr. Sian Hawthorne for her constant guidance; Professor Abheek Banerjee, my first teacher in this epistemic journey, who persuaded me to fulfil my wish.

Without the staff of the various libraries and archives: National Library, Presidency University Library, West Bengal State Archives, and Anandabazar Patrika Archive in Kolkata; Nehru Memorial Museum and Library and the National Archives in New Delhi; The School of Oriental and African Studies and India Office Collection of the British Library in London, it would not have been possible to accomplish my work. I am indebted to my mother, Debahuti Deb, and Souryadeep Mukherjee for their unstinted support and reinstating my faith in life. I also thank Stree for its sustained cooperation.

All the translations from Bengali to English used here are my own, unless indicated otherwise.

A Note on the Bengali Calendar

The Bengali calendar or Bangla Shan (BS) is a traditional solar calendar formulated by Fatehullah Shirazi on the basis of the lunar Hijri and the solar Bengali calendars. Introduced in 1584, it was dated from the Emperor Akbar's accession to the throne in 1556. The Bengali year is always 593 years less than the year in the Gregorian calendar.

The Bengali months are as follows:

Baisakh (mid-April to mid-May)
Jaishtha (mid-May to mid-June)
Asarh (mid-June to mid-July)
Shraban (mid July to mid-August)
Bhadra (mid-August to mid-September)
Ashwin (mid-September to mid-October)
Kartik (mid-October to mid-November)
Agrahayan (mid-November to mid-December)
Poush (mid-December to mid-January)
Magh (mid-January to mid-February)
Phalgun (mid-February to mid-March)
Chaitra (mid-March to mid-April)

Introduction

> The result is that although I try to forget my caste, it is impossible to forget. And then I remember an expression that I heard somewhere: 'What comes by birth and can't be cast off by death is caste.'
>
> — Kumud Pawade (cited in U. Chakravarti 2003: 6)

> Marginality thus means something altogether different to me from what it means to social theorists. It is no metaphor for the power relations between one group of human beings and another but a literal description of where I stand (figuratively speaking): over here, on the edge, out of bounds, beneath your notice. I embody the metaphors. Only whether or not I like doing so is immaterial.
>
> — Nancy Mairs (1996: 59)

This book examines how high-caste hegemony as it developed and transformed during different phases of Indian history contributed to the formulation, adoption, alteration and reorganization of ideal womanhood[1] among the high-caste as well as the low-caste Hindus[2] in nineteenth-century Bengal. This ideal was constructed, criticized, altered, and emulated by agents, men with social agency within their castes and society, of almost all the caste groups of Bengali society during this period. Contrary to the common belief that it remained a prerogative of only the high caste is what this work demonstrates.

Bengal is the focal point of this discussion because colonial Bengal was the hub of British colonial activities and witnessed significant socio-political and economic changes,[3] subsequently becoming the experimental ground for the social aspirations of different social agents (see Chapter 1). The ambitious social targets of these diverse social groups challenged prevailing social norms, aimed to alter them, or in many cases remained loyal to them to meet different socio-political and economic objectives. This multifarious process of challenging, accepting, and reorganizing social norms to modify, improve, and stabilize social status in a rapidly changing social scenario was largely conducted on the basis of caste principles, notwithstanding other influences, for instance, the changing economic scenario of a colonized country, the effect of modernity, and so on. Moreover, contrary to the popular tendency of allocating to a caste ideology either an exclusively material status or an overpowering ideological positioning (such as one finds in Marxist or structuralist theories), the caste structure was a peculiar amalgamation of both. This complex nature of caste principles is elucidated by examining the notion of ideal womanhood insofar as it actualized the ambiguous nature of the caste structure. In this process the book shows the ideal of womanhood in its unique relationship with the caste system and how it manifests a dichotomy embedded in the material and ideological characteristics of the principle of caste.

This claim requires rethinking women's relationship with caste hegemony insofar as it determines gender relations and roles, and encourages the re-examination of women's roles and place in Indian society in terms of the gendered interaction between those designated as high and low. Thus the common representations of the well-known social symbol of the *adarsha nari* (the ideal woman) that are utilized to inform and justify caste/class ideologies at both national and local levels is examined through the lens of their examples in colonial Bengal. In this process the factors (for example, education, domestic virtues, and chastity) that played a decisive role in shaping this ideology and illustrate why the selection of certain values credited as 'ideal' need to be scrutinized discursively rather than accepted at face value. The book also reveals the strategically veiled relationships between caste and women within which women of all strata were arguably locked.

To validate this claim, close studying of the journals brought out by the so-called low castes, which represent an ostensibly marginal culture within nineteenth-century Bengal, shows how women in the lower strata of the society or, more precisely, a section of them, began to lose their autonomy and felt pressured to remould their identity within the normative structures of the high-caste culture. Women of the middle order also witnessed changes in their existence which was also remoulded according to a brahmanical model. All these changes took place within a carefully crafted ideal of women's existence, predominantly brahmanical in nature. Subsequently, similar to the high-caste imposition of normative womanhood, marginal groups also defined and limited the transformative possibilities that arose from strategic negotiations and competitive struggles between the high and low castes with respect to the position of women. In this process the resulting idea of womanhood became a kind of repository for the anxiety that arose from negotiations, not only between the high- and the low-caste groups, but also between old and new cultural norms. In order to track down these diverse courses of direction towards the formation, emulation, and resistance in relation to this complex notion of ideal womanhood are studies of class, caste, religious and gender identities in their shifting interrelations, rather than in isolated or essentialized ways. However, I readily acknowledge that intersections of these identities are very rarely of a neat or reductive kind.

Contrary to the structuralist model of caste, I argue that the caste system is a dynamic social structure that incorporates upward mobility and thereby attempts to absorb tensions from below (Sanyal 1982: 27; 33-64). I show how nineteenth-century colonial rule in Bengal opened up western education and created new opportunities in public employment and professions, rendering social mobility widespread and relatively easy. What became almost a universal tendency amongst the Bengali population was the desire to move up the social ladder and to consolidate the gains in status afforded by the decennial census survey.[4] This was the time when Indian nationalism began to proliferate with the specific purpose of self-improvement among the already privileged and heterogeneous power group known as the *bhadralok* of Bengali society, a product of British colonialism in the eighteenth and nineteenth centuries. In 1835 the British replaced the traditional Indian education system with a western one to educate a class of men who could serve as interpreters and work in the new government. The British wanted a group of men who were Indian in blood and colour, but English in education, taste and morals. As a result, Bengal saw the rise of a very western-oriented social group called bhadralok, which meant gentlemen known for their cultivation and courtesy, who had access to the best schools and colleges, at least in the form of western education.[5] This period, therefore, witnessed a re-invention of caste-based characteristics in order to assert caste-based superiority; different aspiring caste groups amongst the bhadralok aimed either to create or to legitimize their social standing, granting it a sense of permanence. The increasingly unpopular image of the colonial state among the bhadralok led the British administration to encourage this tendency among marginal groups for clear political purposes (Bandyopadhyay 2001: 52-84). J. H. Broomfield's work on the bhadralok domination on the sphere of nationalism (1968) has exposed Bengali influence in the formation of political ideology in the colonial period.

Various later works have demonstrated that throughout the nineteenth and early twentieth centuries, nationalist politics in Bengal were dominated by the bhadralok who belonged mainly, although not exclusively, to the brahmin and the kayastha castes along with the middle-caste baidyas, who were by this time enjoying kshatriya status in Bengal and therefore belonged to the upper strata.[6] Here it must be remembered that in the Bengali social order the kayasthas and the baidyas were also considered to be part of the shudra lineage. However, through different socio-political changes people who belonged to the *sat* shudra category produced groups occupying social ranks right below the brahmins, known as kayasthas and baidyas, and thereby created, a middle order in the caste hierarchy. In contrast the *asat* shudra groups remained at the bottom as the low-caste shudra and included many other social groups labelled as low.

The details of the caste situation in Bengal, insofar as it differs from the caste arrangements of central India, will be discussed in Chapter 2. I use the terms 'high', 'middle', and 'low' in the context of the caste structure of colonial Bengal since these contribute most to the analysis of ideal womanhood. Throughout this work the word 'high' is for the brahmins, both *kulins* and non-*kulins*,[7] 'middle' indicates the sat shudra—kayastha and baidyas—and 'low' refers to the remaining asat shudra and the dalits. By incorporating the brahmins into a single category I am certainly not denying the intricacy involved in the status of this uppermost caste group. For instance, the bharadwaj *gotra*[8] of a group of baidiki brahmins was well respected for their knowledge of the *Shastras* and *nabyanyaya* (S. N. Mukherjee 1975: 62-63), and *pirali* brahmins like the Tagores had to struggle to gain kshatriya social status on par with other brahmin groups.[9] However, that this caste group exercised significant social influence on the other castes is undeniable; I am designating a comprehensive high status to them.

The kayasthas and baidyas with their uniquely gained status parallel to the kshatriyas or vaishyas of central India are the middle group in my discussion. Unlike Inden (1976) who claimed that kayasthas and baidyas managed mostly a vaishyas status in Bengal, I argue that since at least the medieval period these two middle groups of Bengal occupied the second position in the caste order and never considered themselves in the third position equal to the vaishya category in the *varna* scheme, which is the four-fold division in Indian society, as it is defined in the ancient sacred texts. The four divisions are: brahmin (traditionally, priest and scholar), kshatriya (ruler and soldier), vaishya (merchant), and shudra (peasant, labourer and servants). The first three are called 'twice-born' *(dvija)* as the men who belong to these categories are entitled to don the sacred thread, while the shudra is not. In the varna scheme, the 'untouchable' is outside, that is, seen as the *panchama* varna. The varna scheme refers only to the broad categories of Hindu society, not to any functional and effective unit.[10] This might possibly be the reason why when the remaining asat shudra aspired to move up the social ladder in the colonial period they aimed for vaishya status, which was still unclaimed by other contenders in the caste structure of Bengal. Moreover, the occupations of the kayasthas and the baidyas were certainly not analogous to a vaishya identity, but which nonetheless did not correspond to a kshatriya status either. The trade and agriculture-centred lives of the asat shudra, however, were closer to a vaishya identity. In short, asat shudra and the dalits are considered 'low' in this discussion and the upward mobility of these lower orders and its repercussions for the women of these groups are one of the primary concerns of this work.

Returning to the discussion regarding bhadralok identity, it is likely that this was a culmination of changes in trade relations, agrarian policy, modernist influences, and the politics of caste-based identity formation influenced by socio-political and economic changes precipitated by colonial rule. The bhadralok redefined social power and authority by defying social norms and at the same time clung to the criteria of hierarchical social ranking. They were, as we demonstrate, a new power group in nineteenth-century Bengal, replacing the exclusive superiority of caste ranking prominent in medieval Bengal (from the early thirteenth century to the late sixteenth century) and at the same time remaining devoted to caste principles, indicating the ambiguous nature of the social situation that was undergoing rapid changes under colonial rule. In this context, it is also important to mention that bhadralok status had to be acquired since many high-caste brahmins and kayasthas did not belong to this category, in spite of their caste authority.[11] They were poor and uneducated, which were impediments in achieving the coveted bhadralok title. As a result, it is impossible to bestow an apparent homogeneous character to this identity. However, the varied nuances of this identity, stemming from the changing socio-economic relations of the nineteenth century and the aspirations of different agents who did not belong to the upper-caste group, have granted the identity certain uniqueness. This uniqueness is manifested in the invariable endeavours of the upper strata to close all the avenues of social mobility for the lower orders and the counter attempts of the latter to destabilize that attempt.

The resulting social skirmishes based on the contrary claims of superiority made by these groups in many cases invented auxiliary ideologies constructed out of basic caste principles (for example, the bhadralok ideology or the ideal of womanhood) which indicates the flexible and vulnerable nature of the caste structure. To deny the heterogeneous and ambiguous nature of caste identity and aspiration involved in these ideals would thus only give us a partial and distorted picture of social reality. Here we must mention that although colonial rule initiated a social situation where along with the possibility of the alteration of social standards in which upward mobility was relatively allowable, it simultaneously leant towards a hierarchical form of social order, privileging the high castes. As a result, the enthusiasm of the lower-caste groups in terms of social mobility was coupled with the trepidation of being mistreated by the colonial government, being misinformed and subsequently misled by influential high-caste native agents. These were certain male members of Bengali society with social agency, keeping in mind that the vast changes in the social, political and economic life of Bengal in the nineteenth century were mediated by a profound alteration in the social world of the Bengali elites, especially the intelligentsia. Their world-view, expectations from life and even their emotional responses were reshaped by the challenge of European dominance, encounter with western civilization and absorption into an international economy. In turn the Bengali intelligentsia, essentially a group of Bengali males, in terms of this process of transformation, the changes in outlook, concerns, attitudes and sensibilities, earned a certain amount of social agency otherwise unthinkable to the other members of the society surviving under colonial rule. These men were already a part of the colonial administration. At the same time colonial rule, which considered itself to be purveyors of the ideological pillars of democracy and equality, transmitted the hope of equality to low-caste groups who were certainly not a part of the colonial administration. This period, therefore, witnessed an arguably unprecedented form of organized movements against high-caste hegemony and/or structural attempts at becoming a part of the native power structure where the lower orders of society were encouraged to emulate or adopt high-caste norms and values.[12]

Questions could be asked on what the motivations really were behind these organized caste movements or emulation of brahmanical norms in order to move up the social order of the late nineteenth and early twentieth centuries. Were they driven by aspirations for high-status and power sharing? Or were they the consequence of protest, devoid of any such aspiration, against the inequity propagated by the caste ideology? One group of historians[13] suggests that specific caste agitations[14] were reflections of social and political aspirations of marginal social groups who used their caste identity to gain political advantage in the newly emerging socio-political situation. On the other hand, the privileged high-caste groups were also arguing in favour of their authoritative status in society, using their caste privilege. The result of this two-fold process of gaining social identity in terms of caste status was, however, in many ways the consolidification of the caste system. But others suggest that these caste movements aimed at subverting the ideology and monopoly sanctioned by the caste system, and thereby these movements were means of altering the status quo position of society in terms of caste status.[15] The popular tendency amongst historians is to follow the trend generated by the social mobility model inspired by Srinivas's well-known theories of Sanskritization and Westernization.[16] These theories suggest that as the changing social scenario in colonial Bengal allowed only restricted mobility, rather than total transformation of the discriminatory social order, as perhaps desired by specific influential caste movements; the marginal social groups aimed at less spectacular demands. They sought instead to legitimize or to enhance their position by publishing journals which advocated the necessity of refined social behaviour and the adoption of a ritualistic lifestyle, and also by claiming Census recognition that would give their social positioning an official status (see Chapter 4). The effects of such sanskritizing efforts were the imposition of greater restrictions on their women. Similarly to upper-caste women, women of the lower-strata now started representing the 'honour' of their community. The consequence was that even the lower castes now embraced a homogeneous brahmanic ideal of womanhood.

In the changing socio-political and economic scenario of the late eighteenth and nineteenth centuries, the middle order of society, which was positioned somewhere between the brahmins and the dalits, had also comprehended the benefits of emulating brahmanic hegemony. Accordingly, high-caste standards of socio-religious existence, especially with regard to controlling women, were now employed by the agents of the middle-order caste groups to bestow their newly earned social status an enduring nature. The absence of free choices for women thus became a ubiquitous phenomenon prevalent across almost all the social strata of colonial Bengal.

Here we must mention that marginal consciousness is not merely a structure exemplified by negativity; it is a historical process that is shaped and developed through a changing process of relations between the dominant and the subordinate (P. Chatterjee 1993). And instead of seeing in this marginal history a practical defeat of their status (ibid), we aim to illustrate the limits of resistance and the consequent or parallel emergence of standardized norms of existence for women by force or consent and/or both. Therefore, we accept that there were variations in individual situations where different marginal groups had different motivations to organize for social action,[17] and their emulative acts not only implied appropriation of high-caste norms; it also meant defying the brahmanic monopoly as it asserted its own symbolic and ritual priority.

The appropriation of brahmanic symbols, however, was not easy, and it was vehemently resisted by the upper order. For example, when the prominent agents of the lower castes started wearing the sacred thread as a mark of their respectability, the upper strata derided this attempt and began to ridicule the thread worn by the lower castes as nothing but a fibre worth a paisa of the lowest value.[18] The upper castes emphasized the lack of origin-based authority in these attempts that were associated only with hereditary social ranking. Subsequently, wearing a thread generated social status only to those who could boast of a respected origin. Appropriating brahmanic norms for women and claiming social authority by the virtue of the superior status of the women members of the community were, on the other hand, a relatively untroubled option. How this tendency prompted these marginal groups to embrace the brahmanic ideal of womanhood for their women will be discussed in detail in the following chapters; here it should be noted that it was not merely self-interest that encouraged these groups to sanskritize[19] and/or westernize their socio-religious existence by seeking acknowledgement from the colonial authority; on the contrary they were inventing a parallel ideology of their own history that represented a completely different picture of native identity in the colonial period. While high-caste nationalists were projecting the colonial period as a break with the 'golden era' of their ancient Vedic past, to marginal caste groups the colonial period was viewed as an improvement on their darker past when there was much less scope for any social mobility (Bandyopadhyay 2001: 250). Here the diversity in cultural use of language further explicates the point: the Bengali word *jati* in the charged political environment was being used to mean the 'nation' by high-caste nationalists, whereas oppressed marginal groups remained loyal to the traditional meaning of the word 'caste' (ibid: 155-56; 163-64), as the concepts of a nation-state or independence were less real to them than the reality of caste discrimination.

The complex connotation of jati and its ideological counterpart varna and the role that they play in developing and nurturing caste theory will be discussed later. 'Jati' is a Sanskrit word meaning a birth-based classification; a strict and firm system of classification of people in terms of activities they perform. The subsistence economy of rural India, dependent upon a jati-based division of labour, is the essence of *caste*. Jati used in the Indian subcontinent refers to 'race', 'breed', or 'lineage'. Accordingly, jatis are often demonstrated as the subdivisions of the four basic varnas, a formal demarcation on the basis of the type of profession or activity.[20] However, we would like to state that the existence of marginal groups negotiated the space for difference and identity not only for themselves but for the privileged high-caste groups as well. This was done by redefining and reorganizing their social existence in terms of the threats and aspirations of the lower order.

It is this process of negotiation and reconciliation in relation to the struggle of identity formation that establishes a tie between the opposing ends of high and low and redefines the definition of hegemony. As Homi Babha suggested, 'The work of hegemony is itself the process of iteration and differentiation [which] depends on the production of alternative or antagonistic images that are always produced side by side in competition with each other' (1994: 29). As we show in this book, in the context of nineteenth-century Bengal, this raises the issue of the ideological hegemony of caste being continuously reproduced and reinforced by the power groups of Hindu society. This includes not just the brahmins, but also the heterogeneous social groups who adopted brahmanical lifestyles and thereby enacted hegemonic authority being protected by the all inclusive ideology of the bhadralok. Thus keeping in mind the ongoing historical process of struggle and protest against brahmanic hegemony implanted in the caste structure, respecting the normative parameters of caste ideology became practically mandatory for almost all the social groups aiming for a change in status. This ensured improvement of social standing, or the cementing of newly accomplished authority, on a firmer basis.

The process of emulation and acceptance of brahmanical norms can also be interpreted as the marginal groups' strategic recognition of their subordination in order to break the brahmanical monopolization of the power structure. Therefore, early nineteenth-century Calcutta encounters power groups or *dals* dominated by members of diverse caste backgrounds representing varied aspirations of different caste groups. However, the prominence of a brahmanical code of conduct was rarely accidental among these multifarious power clusters. How the functioning of these traditional caste-based dals was replaced by the modernized bhadralok who although heterogeneous in nature still remained rooted to the caste order is discussed in Chapter 2. This shift exemplifies the versatile power politics emerging from caste-based authority that many agents of ordinary origins aspired for, and concurrently harboured the tendency of establishing a non-brahmin power core. The emergent print culture of the nineteenth century along with the unprecedented acceleration in educational accomplishments of the natives, however, shifted the spotlight from dal-based caste authority to the circulation and promotion of caste superiority through printed texts and journals. These journals were published by bhadraloks of different origins who exclusively worked as the mouthpieces of different caste groups. This tendency exemplifies how the colonial apparatus of modernization was ultimately channelled in order to contribute and intervene in the traditional debates of native society; in this case it was the longstanding debate over caste hierarchy.

As a result, in the second half of the nineteenth century, publishing a journal,[21] initially introduced as a high-caste phenomenon, by the turn of the century became a common activity shared by all other caste groups. The unique nature of caste hierarchy which, on the one hand, absorbed alterations as long as they were not damaging to the caste structure and, on the other hand, resisted any such harmful moves to destabilize the hierarchy is examined throughout. For example, social aspirants from the middle-caste groups like the kayasthas (for example, Deb, Dey, Mitra and Dutta) and baidyas (like Sen), were those who experienced prosperity in late eighteenth and early nineteenth-centuries, and accordingly entered the ranks of the bhadralok to enjoy the benefits of social authority. The rise of these groups indicates the changing social scenario and the inherent flexibility of the caste structure. It also confirms the fact that under colonial rule it was feasible for groups, even if non-brahmin in nature, to exercise almost the same authority in society, evidently without destabilizing the brahmanical power core. These aspirants belonging to the middle-order caste groups enjoyed their privileged status by running caste associations and dictating social norms along with publishing journals. By the end of the nineteenth century, the same trend was observed among the low shudra groups, for example, the mahishya, gandhabanik, subarnabanik, sadgope, and so on. They established their own caste associations and started publishing journals, disseminating their opinions about different social reforms, mostly referring to women's issues. I demonstrate that these attempts of the low-caste groups to achieve social authority in a caste-based hierarchy ultimately demanded the emulation and adoration of brahmanical hegemony. The book, accordingly, shows how the attempts to move up the social ladder led these low-caste agents to restrict their women's lives within an ideological boundary almost wholly brahmanical in nature. That women's status also became the benchmark of social status for these low shudra groups is well exemplified in their journals, which I argue articulated their social aspirations.[22]

Subsequently, I suggest that despite different attempts of diverse caste groups to topple the hierarchical order or to usurp the power enjoyed by a limited few, any challenge to the fundamentals of the caste structure was strongly resisted. The basic structure of caste domination was safeguarded cautiously by creating the fear of losing caste, which meant exclusion from the respectable world of social existence. The low-caste aspiration, on the other hand, could be recapitulated on the basis of three distinct agendas. Firstly, there was a willing submission to and imitation of upper-caste forms (Moffat 1979). Secondly, there were dissidence and rebellion against upper-caste norms (Bandyopadhyay 1997: 30-64). Thirdly, a quite unusual one, as Cohn (1987: 255-83) demonstrated in his study of low-caste chamars and dusadhis within the shivnarayani sect in Uttar Pradesh, low-caste groups could exist within a new sect, founded and led, of course, by upper castes, but which cleared a space, albeit on not so equal terms, for humbler communities.

At this stage, it is thus necessary to address the following questions: what constructs caste ideology? What does this ideology rely on? How does this highly discriminatory ideology manage to create such an irrepressible impact on the Hindu's existence? And, most importantly, how does this ideology succeed in maintaining its basic structure as unharmed in spite of consistent attempts to overthrow the hierarchical social order? I believe the answer to all these questions lies in the concern of male agents of different caste and class groups to regulate, organize and control their women on the basis of caste normativity. Thus I ascertain whether there is an inherent relation between caste and patriarchy, and at the same time establish the theory that an ideal of womanhood in colonial Bengal provided an almost homogeneous model emblematic of socio-political, religious, economic and, most importantly, nationalistic aspirations for nearly all caste groups, cutting across class lines. While illustrating the complex journey that this ideal took it is important to realize that caste identity co-existed with other competing religious, class, cultural, regional and national identities. As Nicholas Dirks states, 'Caste was just one category among many others, one way of organizing and representing identity' (2001: 60). Therefore, I am not ignoring the fact that at any particular moment of history any of these other factors could prevail over caste and/or other factors and become the main driving force. This does not make the other components of identity formation unimportant or displaced from any kind of social conjecture. For instance, in nineteenth-century Bengal taking part in the consecrated circle of education became the most valuable benchmark of native identity scoring over all other social symbols of respectability and authority. The implicit caste design, however, embedded in these educational endeavours once again refurbished the supremacy of the privileged (see Chapters 3 and 4).

Returning to the indistinct nature of identity and its imprecise liaison with caste hierarchy, I assert that it is the ambiguously transient nature of identity and the multifaceted nature of caste struggles and aspirations, rather than their assumed linear progress and homogeneous structure, which should be highlighted in any discussion of caste ideology. The focus on the ubiquitous presence of normative values and models for women in caste ideology, ultimately leads us to see how an ideal of womanhood applicable to women of almost all social strata was developed and imposed. In this process, however, the book also illustrates that it is the heterogeneous and continuing nature of the caste structure that gave rise to the ideal of womanhood, and this ideal is symbolic of both the high-caste tendency to attain social advantage through the imposition of ideological discourses and, on the other hand, the marginal groups' aspiration to subvert the iniquitous social order and taste for themselves the benefits of power.

Subsequently, this work also analyses why caste as a benchmark of status has always been seen as a special quality attached to men, making women's relation to this category uncertain.[23] Women were necessary in the promulgation of caste ideology but their own place within the caste system was irresolute. Thus the ideal of womanhood was a product of the recognition that men were dependent upon women to perpetuate the social and moral order as women held the reproductive power. At the same time, men had to confront the 'problem of women's sexuality' which posed a threat to the social order if left uncontrolled (Leslie 1996; U. Chakravarti 2003). For example, if high-caste women advocated social non-conformity then it would be relatively easy for low-caste men to have access to such women (U. Chakravarti 2003: 35) and thereby corrupt the hierarchical social order. The only way of dealing with this extremely important resource of reproduction was to exaggerate women's innate nature as dangerous and to equate it with lower-caste males' inherently sinful existence. Thus this dangerous sexuality could be channelled into legitimate motherhood within a tightly controlled structure of reproduction to keep the threatened hierarchical order unperturbed (L. Dube 1986: 24-30).

As the consent of women to secure the social norms was also necessary, the powerful ideology of womanhood was produced through the discourses of *patibrata* (a good wife who worshipped her husband as her God) and *stridharma* (the prescribed duties for women). Women, especially high-caste women, thus became the symbol of dangerous sexuality, which had to be controlled in a caste-based society to serve the social and political arrangements organized by male agents of a selective section. In a situation like this, women owing to their inherently dangerous and impure nature were always condemnable, but if they allowed themselves to be controlled by their ordained functions, then the condemnation was not applicable anymore (Leslie 1996: 247). Men at different stages of Indian history thus tried to control the dangerous sexuality of women by equating them with the low-caste members of society and simultaneously upgrading them to a venerated high status by transforming them or coercing them into the model of the ideal woman (U. Chakravarti 2003: 11-63). The subordination of women and the control of their sexuality were crucial to the maintenance of the caste order and contributed significantly to creating the ideal of womanhood. Moreover, this ideal, epitomizing the subservient nature of women, played a decisive role in controlling the aspirations of low-caste males. Consequently, there was an inbuilt conflict between the need to control high-caste women's sexuality and the aspirations of the lower order to break the social order by seeking sexual encounters with upper-caste women.

Accordingly, the ideal of womanhood became synonymous with wifely devotion, which, with all its material, social, and cultural connotations, allowed male control not only over wives, but also over widows, daughters, sisters, and mothers (see also K. Roy 1994: 33). In due course I will demonstrate that between worshipping the ideal woman and ridiculing the non-ideal, male elites and non-elites could measure all women through caste yardsticks and place them in their appropriate place. The sense of normativity attached to the process of measuring women in this way redefined womanly duties within caste. In other words, the process of resituating women within caste required the reinvention of new moral codes for women.

The ideal of Bengali (Hindu) womanhood as a selfless, ambitionless, ever-smiling good wife is of course expounded in range of religious texts prior to the nineteenth century and assumed in innumerable myths and traditional stories.[24] But rather than looking at the socio-historical factors contributing to this formulation, the temptation to look at this ideal as a normative essentialization of the orthodox Hindu tradition makes this ideal prone to caricature. The notion of ideal womanhood in the Indian context thus for a long time has been posited as a mysterious construct, a kind of curiosity which has limited attempts to examine the processes and contexts involved in the formulation of this notion in an inter-subjective framework.[25] Therefore the question to ask at this point is whether an ideology can express itself without the direct contribution of human beings? This question is important, I would contend, as certain carelessness has often marked scholars' work on studying pre-modern and 'traditional' Indian societies in which the members of society are generally characterized as unperceptive and unreasoning followers of ideologies without making any contribution to the development of those said ideologies.[26] This principle of typification denies a socio-historical view of social orders and instead directs analysis towards rigid and unyielding categories, which in turn only legitimize the ideological structure (Gupta 2000: 40).

In this book my task is to explain the different historical forces that have shaped the notion of ideal womanhood in a particular context rather than adopting an unquestioning attitude towards the 'traditional' Indian social structure. Chapter 1 therefore analyses the structural foundations of a caste-based social order that eventually gave rise to this gendered ideal by drawing in different socio-political theories as, in my view, sustained social experience and theoretical reflection are not mutually exclusive from each other. To introduce the ideal of womanhood is to imply a particular way of cutting up the world which relies on certain theoretical presuppositions based on caste.

NOTES

1 The ideal woman is the dedicated wife whose entire existence is dependent on her husband, and she is also the mother who gives birth to a male child. She is a selfless giver, someone who gives endlessly, gracefully, smilingly, whatever the demand, however harmful and unreasonable to her (Kishwar and Vanita 1984; Leslie 1989).

2 Terms like 'Hindu', 'Hinduism', and so on, have extremely debatable connotations and we would use these terms being aware of the disputes regarding improper usage. For the debates on the use of these terms see, eg, Carol A. Breckenridge and Peter van der Veer 1993.

3 See Bandyopadhyay 2004; Swapna Banerjee 1998; T. Bhattacharya 2005 for a discussion on the importance of Bengal in the British colonial administration.

4 The decennial Census of India is the primary source of information regarding the demographic characteristics of the population of India. The first Census in India in modern times was conducted in 1871. Since then, a population census has been carried out every ten years.

5 The bhadralok was a heterogeneous power group in nineteenth-century Bengal. However, the debate about the exact nature of their social grouping continues to be a major preoccupation amongst historians of Bengal. See, eg, Broomfield 1968; S. N. Mukherjee 1975; Baxter 1978; and T. Bhattacharya 2005. Consequently, I devote a substantial part of this book to demonstrate the incongruous and still extremely influential nature of the bhadralok as it played a decisive role in shaping the notion of ideal womanhood in nineteenth-century Bengal.

6 See, eg, S. N. Mukherjee 1970; T. Bhattacharya 2005; Swapna Banerjee 1998, Bandyopadhyay 2004.

7 The term *kulin* has its etymological origin in the term *kul.* Along with the general sense of a clan or lineage, the term *kul* had an additional, unique meaning in Bengal, in that *kul* status was indicative of an elite position within the caste system. A person possessing this elite status was described as a *kulin,* literally, one who belonged to a high-status kul. This elevated status was believed to derive from spiritual and ritual purity, as reflected in the practices and inner qualities of those who were deemed to be qualified to be kulin. The kulin status was thus the benchmark of the special position enjoyed by a certain cluster of people within a specific caste group that made them different not only from people belonging to other castes but also drew a line of difference between them and their fellow caste members. Thus, there were kulin brahmins and kulin kayasthas radiating special glory apart from their privileged caste status. *Kulinism*, in short, needs to be understood in the context of the same varna and jati arrangements and hierarchies that had characterized the caste system in India. See K. Chatterjee 2005 for a detailed discussion of kulinism and its significance in pre-colonial and colonial Bengal.

8 People belonging to the same lineage, supposedly descended from a common ancestor.

9 S. N. Mukherjee has shown how the Tagores in order to be recognised as kulins asked for the support of the maharaja of Krishnanagar. This clearly shows the insecurity involved with the Tagore's social status because of their pirali origin, which was considered to be a brahmin group of tainted status. See S. N. Mukherjee 1975: 63. The problems that the Tagores faced because of their pirali status in getting their daughters married to eminent brahmin families are discussed in Deb 2004: 3.

10 The *varna* is only a reference category not a real group (see S. Dube 1990: 48; Srinivas 1962). In the varna model of caste, there is a single pan-Indian hierarchy without any variation between one region and another, in the sense that the brahmin is placed at the top and the criteria of ranking are based upon the ritual purity given in religious texts. But, in the matter of spread of these varnas and caste compositions within the varna model, there is a variation from region to region. In South India, it is said, there are no indigenous and authentic kshatriyas and vaishyas (see S. Dube 1990: 49;

Srinivas 1962: 66). In these areas, these two categories refer to the local castes which claim the status of kshatriyas and vaishas (varnas) by the virtue of their traditional occupation and their dominant positions. In this scheme, the category of shudra subsumes the majority of castes (jatis) which have little in common. It includes, at one end, a rich, powerful and highly sanskritized group while at the other end the tribes who submerged and assimilated into the Hindus marginally (see ibid: 65).

11. S. N. Mukherjee 1987, citing the Census report of 1921 has shown that a bulk of brahmins and kayasthas in nineteenth-century Bengal were not educated in English and hence were not a part of the elite bhadralok circle.
12. See, eg, Bandyopadhay 1997, and Swaraj Basu 1994 on the low-caste protests in the colonial period and the politics behind it.
13 That caste movements in the colonial period were the result of the socio-political aspirations of the marginal groups are illustrated in the works of a large number of historians, eg, Bailey 1957: vii; Zelliot 1973: 39; Washbrook 1975: 176-77.
14 The lower-caste movements from the last decades of the nineteenth century were organized and largely led by the namashudras of East Bengal and the rajbangshis in the north. They organized and led two of the most powerful movements among the scheduled castes of Bengal. In fact, when scheduled caste politics emerged in the province in the 1930s, they provided it with both leadership and a popular support base. Moreover, these two communities by and large remained aloof from the nationalist movement. The namashudras (2,087,162 as per Census 1911) constituted the largest agrarian caste in East Bengal and their alienation from the Congress led anti-British agitation weakened the nationalist movement. Similarly, the rajbangshis who were also a dominant caste in north Bengal exhibited apathy for the Congress-led freedom movement and this possibly explains much of the weaknesses of the nationalist movement in this region. It also says something about the high-caste politics of the Congress. See Bandyopadhyay 1990: 1-123.
15 The proponents of this argument are Gough 1963: 174-75; H. Jha 1977: 56; Pandey 1983: 71-74; Omvedt 1994: 14.
16 This is true for the works by Taniguchi 1994; Swaraj Basu 1994, and Bandyopadhyay 2001; Srinivas 1962.

17 The variation in individual caste situation is analysed by Smriti Kumar Sarkar 1994: 64-89. Sarkar has shown how the prosperous kañsari were threatened by the coming of new cheaper mass-produced colonial products and how that threat led them towards a solidarity movement rather than any other social or cultural influence.

18 The bhadralok ridiculed it as *'siki paishar suto'*, a thread so cheap that anyone could buy and wear it. See Bandyopadhyay 1994: 48.

19 There is a conflict between the usage of the two terms 'Brahmanization' and 'Sanskritization', which originates from the mistaken association of sanskritic culture exclusively with the brahmin castes. As Milton Singer has suggested, Sanskritization may follow the kshatriya, vaishya or even the shudra models; see Singer 1964: 84-119. Srinivas (1966: 20), in his account of Sanskritization, has also pointed out that sonar brahmins of western Uttar Pradesh in India do not follow a culture that is sanskritic in nature. Although Brahmanization in the widest sense of the term cannot be universally equated with Sanskritization, in this book we use the term 'Brahmanization' as a useful term for sanskritic Brahmanization to denote the particular and most influential species of 'Sanskritization'. We would, however, acknowledge the differences involved between Sanskritisation and Brahmanization as in many cases the latter is the imposition of brahmanical culture whereas the former is the emulation of brahmanic forms by non-brahmin groups.

20 There are around 25,000 jatis in India, each associated to a specific occupation and lifestyle. 'Anthropologists use the term to refer to a social group that is endogamous and occupationally specialized; such groups are common in highly stratified societies with a very low degree of social mobility.

21 For example, *Bamabodhini Patrika, Samachar Chandrika*, *Bharati* and many other newspapers and journals published by the native enthusiasts were emblematic of their caste status or the brahmanical caste principles that were religiously endorsed by these elite groups.

22 For a general discussion on caste associations and social mobility see Bandyopadhayay 2001: Chapter 3.

23 For a detailed discussion on the ambivalent relation between caste and women see L. Dube 1986 and 1988; U. Chakravarti 2003; Uberoi 1994 and 2006; Inden 1976; Bandopadhyaya 2004; O'Hanlon and Washbrook 1994; Prem Chowdhry 1994.

24 Here we are using the Bengali ideal of womanhood focusing only on

Hindu religious norms since the factors that gave rise to the Bengali ideal were in many senses analogous to the situation that gave rise to the concept of a Hindu state. A detailed discussion on the historical process using Hindu and Indian identities interchangeably is available in Inden 1990; Stietencron 1997; King 1999; and Smith 1919. The term 'Hinduism' is used in the process of searching for, arranging, and interpreting data about the religions of the Hindus, but in such a manner that these fit into a preconceived notion of what a coherent religious system constitutes. It is indeed the notion of the homogeneity of Hinduism, which finally leads to the production of highly complex explanations or theoretical constructions in order to confirm the postulated unity in spite of so many inherent contradictions. For further discussion on this issue see Marshall 1970; Radhakrishnan 1927; Rukmini 1999; Raychaudhuri 1988; Savarkar 2003; Thapar 1985 and 2000.

25 We are borrowing this idea from Gupta's discussion of caste (2000) where he criticizes the tendency to project the caste system as a monolithic ideological formulation to which all Hindus necessarily acquiesce. What matters, then, in terms of history, is when the caste system came into being and began to exercise its unchallenged authority over society. The specific historical conditions that account for its growth, transformation, and contemporary status are often kept out of purview. The case with the ideal of womanhood is similar, where it is assumed that the ideal expounded in a range of religious texts, myths, and epics are unquestionably held by Indian women, without any attempt to focus on the historical, and socio-political factors contributing to this ideal.

26 See, eg, Dharmapal 1983.

I

Introducing the Ideal: Caste and Gender

IMAGINATION AGAINST TYPIFICATION: STRUCTURE AND SUPERSTRUCTURE

In the caste system, people as social actors/agents (see Introduction) played their respective roles in the formulation of hierarchical stratifications. Caste practices in everyday life, and at various levels, were never, and still are not, unquestionably preordained by what brahmanical texts have had to say. It should also not be assumed that the ideology of caste was a creation of brahmins alone, or that it was thrust on others, either completely against their will, or that the low castes were ideologically enslaved to the upper castes such that their economic exploitation was justifiable (Gupta 2000: 182). While the brahmins did indeed play an important role in the codification of the caste system, it was not as if they were the sole agents (ibid). Moreover, while upper castes attempted to justify economic and other kinds of exploitation on caste grounds, this was not blindly accepted by the lower castes. Had that been the case, then there would have been no caste dynamism, nor mobility or transformation of any sort in Indian history. It is certainly true that the caste system rests in part on the basis of the myth of natural superiority but each caste expresses that superiority in its own way and to its own advantage.

This position is not contrary to the Marxist position, which seeks to locate ideological formulations and political expressions in relation to social practices and struggles for dominance. In fact, Marx believed that it is from material foundations that specific ideas, values, beliefs emerge.[1] He claimed that the superstructure of ideology does not have an independent existence, but grows out of the material relations people enter into in concrete historical situations. In other words, elements in the superstructure are not outgrowths of the pure mind, but of the mind contemplating and inferring on and within given social conditions. That is to say, the ideology of the caste system exists at the level of material relations between different social agents (Godelier 1972: 275-76). Taking this point further, Louis Althusser claimed that ideological elements and ideological systems are, necessarily, the outgrowths of the material world, yet at no point can they become autonomous. They can, however, live beyond the conditions that gave birth to them, but these elements keep living on and are structured and restructured, built and disintegrated to express and articulate the lived-in conditions of people in society. This is why Althusser (1969: 209) suggested that ideological elements are not univocal; they have many voices, but are not equivocal either. Accordingly, we show that in the context of understanding the development of the ideal of womanhood a further error occurs in assuming that this ideal has had a clear run. There were, and still are, social agents constantly struggling against the social constraints they were forced to contend with, but at the same time they applied and reapplied ideological elements to express themselves, their ambitions, desires, and of course fears. But how does the human spirit work in diverse social situations? Under what circumstances does a particular social situation give rise to a caste-based society which is pre-eminently patriarchal, and consequently how does that society construct an ideal of womanhood?

In an attempt to answer these questions, following Lévi-Strauss, we might search for the apparently common properties of social structure.[2] Lévi-Strauss's object of analysis is to study the social structure via the human mind, which in turn is influenced by a variety of customs, institutions and practices, and not to demonstrate or emphasize either that the structure of the human mind determines concrete socio-economic environs, or that myths, customs, rituals constitute the social structure. His search for the deep structure behind the superstructure explains the universal attitudes of mind, and also the principle that keeps ordering and reordering the cultural world with its great diversity (Lévi-Strauss 1969: 21). All this is extremely important if one is to understand the methodological foundations of Lévi-Straussian structuralism, in which there is a continuous flow of the contribution, assembly, distribution and organization of the universal and the particular, in other words, between the ideals and the real components that conceived these ideals. This structuralism that acknowledges the mutual contributions of the universal and the particular, the ideal and the real, is essentially different from the popular form of structuralism. The latter has generally contributed to the formation of the notion of ideal womanhood as a homogeneous identity growing out only of lofty ideals.

The second type of structuralism posits a perennial empirical separation between binary opposites; the ideal and the real/actual are thus fixed empirical stations incapable of any structural transformations that might bring about different combinations. However, according to Lévi-Straussian structuralism, what is important in analysing binary pairs is the relations among these pairs, which can be expressed in algebraic formulae or in ratios: A is to B as C is to D (ibid). According to this view, there is no perennial separation between binary oppositions (between the 'ideal' woman and the 'real' woman); they are, in fact, capable of different structural transformations that bring about different combinations (of womanhood). That is why the ideal keeps altering and accommodating different real factors that are its essential ingredients, and at the same time it struggles to safeguard the homogeneous effect of the model against any resistance and animosity. All of this can happen and does happen, but the typical or at least traditional structurization of the ideal of womanhood cannot accommodate them as this model assumes that what exists at any point of time is because of a grand ideological design, and that each such design is always deliberately arrived at, and unquestionably followed by social agents.

What also escapes the attention of the typical model of womanhood is that the superstructure, in this case, the ideal of womanhood, is a vast storehouse of ingredients that play a decisive role in the formulation of the ideal. There are far too many elements in it to make an empirical inventory possible. Perhaps this is the reason that it is an extremely difficult task to pinpoint when and how some specific factors make one an ideal woman, and this is precisely why it is not those elements that make an image an ideal one but rather the politics involved in the selection of those elements that need to be looked at. As the following chapters are primarily concerned with the characterization of the ideal woman and the conscious design and politics involved behind it in nineteenth-century Bengal, I will not go into detail here. But what I want to emphasize is that only certain elements of the superstructure of ideology are more directly related to the basis, the material factors of the infrastructure, than others. For example, in the case of the ideal of womanhood the basic components are the chastity and fidelity of women. These most relevant components must combine with other elements borne more directly out of mundane experiences (for example, education and other effects of modernity in colonial Bengal). These experiences in turn have the mnemonic effect of revitalizing certain other items from collective memory (for instance, the 'revival' of ancient Indian womanhood in the formulation of the ideal womanhood against the background of colonialism and burgeoning nationalism in Bengal), which also go into combination to form an ideological structuralization. The order of the formation of the ideal, we just mentioned, might not remain the same. It could always be reversed, or could also be a 'mix-and-match' of diverse experiences in different historical moments, giving rise to particular requirements of a heterogeneous group of social agents that ultimately pave the way for a new articulation of ideology.

In short, the governing elements of the superstructural theme of ideal womanhood are an outgrowth of specific material conditions. At no point can this ideal become autonomous, as has been claimed in the popular construction of this concept and reproduced by many scholars of Indian culture.[3] Rather, this ideal can live beyond the conditions that gave it birth. These varied components of the ideal are the caste dynamics that live on and are continuously structured and restructured to fit into the lived reality of the social actors concerned. While making this claim I am not ignoring the contribution of other factors like class and geographical variations of customs and traditions in shaping the ideal of womanhood, and, as already acknowledged, very rarely is this ideal the outcome of any neat composition.

PUTTING CASTE IN PLACE

Let us unravel the power structure of Hindu society in pre-colonial and colonial Bengal,[4] which, although protean insofar as it reflected the continually changing power relations in Indian society, was never wholly unsettled. This was because the brahmanic hegemony it enabled was maintained both by ideology and imperatives of structure; in other words, by both coercion and consent. In this process of hegemonization, the space for contestation was certainly not foreclosed, but the fact that the upper castes always managed to insulate or protect themselves from threatening social situations could happen only because of their clever manipulations of systems of production blanketed by lofty ideals. These were customarily based upon marriage exchanges and rules of reproduction by which high- and low-caste ranks were maintained and altered. Thus, caste in reality is an extensively constructed gender system that cultivates and sustains the material dreams of aspirants from different social backgrounds.

Colonial observations of India were dominated by discussions of caste at the onset of colonial rule.[5] But the more these contributors struggled to grasp its complex nature the more tempting it became to yield to the popular notion that privileged its religious aspects (P. Chatterjee 1993: 12-38; Sharma 1994: 1), an emphasis which follows from the colonialist stress on the 'difference' or otherness of the colonized inhabitants (Béteille 1991: 33). It was an emphasis shared by a wide range of observers from Alfred Lyall to Max Weber, who claimed that it was predominantly religion that incorporated all different social groups into the great circles of castes (Stokes 1978: 20-23). The caste system has long been subject to such 'typifications' (Gupta 2000: 227) primarily because it is postulated as such an alien and exotic construct that 'there is greater purchase in stocking curiosity than in examining data in an intersubjective framework' (ibid),[6] thus forcing a discontinuity between socio-political and economic systems and preventing a contextualized, historicized examination of human activities.[7] Even recent academic debates have revolved around the same tendency,[8] presenting a stereotypical image of Indian society and viewing the caste system as an idealized structure which has always had an unmodified and unchallenged character based on the ideological rationale of scriptural laws (Habib 1995: 165). The theoretical intervention of Louis Dumont's *Homo Hierarchicus* (1970) has added to this particular way of conceptualizing India with great sophistication. Dumont thus deserves special and detailed mention here, since I want to explain how in *Homo Hierarchicus*, as the title itself suggests, he shows the hierarchical ideology to be the very core and heart of the caste system; devoid of this hierarchy, there would be no caste.[9] I will outline Dumont's principle positions in his own words, since critical refutation as well as analytical absorption of his theory lays down the foundational presuppositions of this book.

For Dumont, 'a hierarchical relation is a relation between larger and smaller, or more precisely between that which encompasses and that which is encompassed' (ibid: 24). With this definition of hierarchy Dumont proposes to shift the focal points of his account that deals with the caste system. In place of the isolation and the separation of castes from one another, which is essential in the caste system, Dumont's theory of hierarchy must be brought to the forefront. But the principle of the system still remains to be ascertained. In this regard Dumont's view is that 'it is enough to observe that actual men do not behave simply: they act with an idea in their heads, perhaps that of conforming to custom' (ibid: 40). He then claims, 'the caste system is a state of mind, a state of mind which is expressed by the emergence, in various situations, of groups of various orders generally called "castes"' (ibid: 71).

This state of mind provides the orientation towards the whole 'which in the eyes of those who participate in it legitimizes their respective positions' (ibid: 149). Moreover, Dumont adds, 'to adopt a value is to introduce hierarchy, and a certain consensus of value, a certain hierarchy of ideas, things and people, is indispensable to social life' (ibid: 54). It is therefore only through ideology that one can embrace the essence of castes and comprehend the true principle behind the caste system. And that 'single true principle' is 'the opposition of the pure and impure' (ibid: 81). Dumont claims that only this opposition between pure and impure can be construed into the superiority of the pure over the impure, and it governs the separation between the two. It also influences the division of labour because pure and impure occupations must similarly be kept separate (ibid). This hierarchical principle, Dumont deduces, is responsible for the 'linear order of castes from A to Z . . .' (ibid: 96). Caste A and Z must exist empirically for the 'two poles are equally necessary, although unequal' (ibid: 93). As Dumont declares, 'the decisive step is accomplished once a quality like impurity is attributed in a permanent manner to certain people. There to a great extent will be found the clue to Indian complexity' (Dumont and Pocock 1957: 16). For Dumont, therefore, in a true hierarchy 'that which encompasses is more important than that which is encompassed' (ibid). And, most importantly, he claims, 'for pure hierarchy to develop without hindrance it was also necessary that power should be absolutely inferior to status' (ibid). What follows from all these assertions is that caste hierarchy is not merely a linear order but a 'series of successive dichotomies and inclusions' (ibid: 106).

For example, the shudra is opposed to the block of the first three castes; vaishyas are opposed to the block of brahmin and kshatriya, which finally divides into two (ibid). Here again, Dumont demonstrates the relationship between the high and low, pure and impure, and encompassing and the encompassed in the order of hierarchy.[10]

Irfan Habib has criticized the Dumontian trend of elaborating caste hierarchy on the basis of the ideology of purity, without any reference to material phenomena by saying that if Dumont is right then we have to accept that the economic impulse within Indian society must have been very weak (Habib 1995: 161-65). But does Dumont really deny the presence of material hunger in the development of the caste ideology? I believe, on the contrary and to his credit, Dumont has raised the problem of the relationship between religious principles and politico-economic ones in the caste system very forcefully. As he said, 'This unresolved duality, which has not even been properly characterized, hangs like a millstone round the neck of the contemporary literature' (Dumont 1970: 75) However, the question of the relationship between ideology and social interaction is not fully faced by Dumont; it is, he says, 'a methodological problem'. And then again he asserts that ideology is 'central' because 'man acts consciously and we have *direct* access to the conscious aspect of his action' (ibid: 263-64). Otherwise 'there is complementarity between the two, a relationship which is variable' (ibid). Here once again anti-Dumontians could argue by raising the point that Dumont fails to give us the 'access to the conscious aspect' of the Hindu mind. He, in fact, asserts that venerable ideas in brahmanical holy books explain contemporary Indian peasant life (Kolenda 1976: 596), which assumes a monolithic status in his theory. He has not analytically explored the ideologies of living Hindus either (ibid); subsequently, the very influential conscious ideology of the lower castes in refuting caste hierarchy is not one of the things that Dumont's theory offers us. Moreover, the problem of the relationship between text and context, ideal and real, remains unresolved.

Moreover, adding more discomfort to Dumontians, empirical studies of power relationships suggest that economic power plays a very important role in ascertaining socio-political and religious status. Dumont mentions the contention between the ideological and the politico-economic that appears to be the familiar argument between the ideological determinism of Hegel, Durkheim and Weber, on one side, and the materialistic determinism of Marx and his followers on the other (ibid), but he never fully relates the predicament with respect to caste in this debate.[11] He only indicates these two opposing positions by labelling them as 'ideology' and 'materialism' (ibid). Yet materiality and ideology in the Indian caste structure are both unavoidable and complementary to each other in developing and maintaining caste arrangements.

Notwithstanding the materialistic design lurking behind caste ideology, in spite of the severe criticisms offered to Dumontian caste analysis by historians[12] one can hardly ignore the value-based ideology ingrained in this system to which Dumont points. It was this ideology that generated an almost inviolable authoritarian status for high-caste groups in Indian society despite the frequent attacks against the discriminatory social structure. In fact, it was frequently the invincible nature of this authoritarianism attached to caste status that allured people of different social standing to emulate caste-based socio-cultural performances, to cling to different caste symbolisms and, most importantly, to resist others who sought to achieve the same. That people of low social origins could consider or seek to achieve social mobility denoted the flexibility of the caste structure. Nonetheless, the tendency to emulate brahmanical social standards by almost all the caste groups indicated the robust nature of the ideological superiority that this system generated in spite of the marginal groups' contestation of the hierarchy that it advocated. Here by 'brahmanical social values' I will demonstrate the socio-cultural and religio-material outcome of the two-fold process of imposing high-caste standards on the lower castes and the emulation of the upper-caste norms by the people at the bottom in respect to the hierarchical caste structure in which every caste aspired to achieve the status enjoyed by the group above them. In many cases, the emulative impulse aimed at a two-level advancement, and people belonging to the shudra category attempted to raise their status to the kshatriya rank and refused to be recognized as vaishya, a tendency we will discuss below. We use the term 'brahmanical social order' as a largely symbolic or, at least, organizational phrase, indicating the omnipresence of hereditary authority endorsed by the varna system, something that the people of different strata in different phases of Indian history aspired to achieve despite their discomfort with the discriminatory social norms that resulted from the system.

This complicated process of emulation and imposition of brahmanical social order underwent a significant transformation in nineteenth-century Bengal. The caste structure in Bengal was different from the social scheme followed in central India, and consequently there was no recognizable vaishya caste in Bengal where the people who earned their living from trade and agriculture were known as shudra. In the colonial era, however, against the backdrop of massive social change when social mobility seemed to be a moderately realizable endeavour, people belonging to different trading and agricultural communities strove for vaishya status, specifically the kayastha and baidya ranks, who were by that time enjoying social prominence similar to their kshatriya counterparts in central India. This proved, however, in many cases to be an excessively ambitious project, whereas aiming for vaishya status would not have harmed the present social state of affairs and at the same time would have incorporated the people devoid of *dvijatva* into the coveted circle of the brahmanical social order. *Dvija* in Sanskrit means 'twice-born', someone who is a male member of the first three varnas in the brahmanical social order: the brahmins, the kshatriyas, and the vaishyas. The person undergoing dvijatva secures second birth; the first birth is physical, while the second birth is a 'spiritual' one. The second 'birth' occurs when one takes a role in society, at the time of the upanayana or initiation ceremony. For example, a brahmin is initiated into the ultimate pursuit of life, *Brahmapadesa* (preaching or advising in the matter of the nature of Brahman, the Ultimate Reality). Traditionally, a kshtraiya would start learning the use of arms, while a vaishya would start a trade apprenticeship.

A proper assessment of the extremely tangled social stratification systems of India would disclose the true nature of the caste order as a cautiously crafted ideology motivated by material greed or ambition. However, the idealized scheme of supremacy ingrained in varna-based authoritarianism ultimately manifests it as something clearly more than mere materiality, although undoubtedly motivated by tangible benefits. The basis of caste in this view, thus, is not just class defined by economic criteria with the requirement of endogamy added to it. Accordingly, economic groups should not be confused with status groups, although these two categories have a propensity to merge; in relation to the caste structure they have the unique ability to operate separately; for instance, in colonial Bengal the newly emerged status group, the bhadralok, did not always have a linear equation with monetary power. There were many people from high-caste backgrounds, who, although poor, still belonged to the bhadralok circle because of their indisputable social status. But there were social agents of lower castes who owing to their financial authority commanded access to the consecrated bhadralok circle, eminently brahmanical in nature. The enigmatic interaction of both materiality and ideology in the development and maintenance of the caste structure gradually unfolds in this theory, which will ultimately reveal how the material nature of the caste structure owing to its ideological foundation demands a unique kind of social authority that transformed the bhadralok of nineteenth-century Bengal into a tacit custodian of caste ideologies. It is no exaggeration to state that the bhadralok of Bengal, who comprised different members from diverse caste backgrounds, remained truthful to high-caste ideologies, since adherence to high-caste norms was always more beneficial for material purpose rather than their renouncement.

A JOURNEY FROM *HOMO HIERARCHICUS* TO THE HETEROGENEITY OF THE CASTE STRUCTURE

So where does *Homo Hierarchicus* take us? Any attempt to define the Indian caste system raises more questions than it resolves. As a result there emerge tendencies, as mentioned earlier, to conform to the 'state of mind' theory and to disapprove of any examination of ideology on the basis of different socio-economic formations. Defying this 'state of the mind' theory by contributing to the Indian caste system, the historical development of an economic structure of localized exploitation within the village nexus brought about the elaboration of the jati, or what is popularly known as the Indian caste system.[13] The dependence of the exploited lower groups on each other and on their masters in a close society necessitated greater elaboration of the rules of exchange and interaction that ultimately made jati an endogamous unit of social operation. It is impossible, however, to ignore the rationale of 'natural superiority', as highlighted by Dumont (1970), which validated the claim that the varna scheme was not abandoned either, as it served effectively to strengthen the regime of jatis on an ideological basis. Therefore, a summary of this complicated process might go like this: the varna system that initially played an important role in the ideological integration of the different regions and sub-regions in India later evolved as an indigenous ideological scheme which merged castes into larger status categories or classifications.

To elucidate further, in the code of Manu, the four varnas are given as brahmin or priest; kshatriya or warrior chief; vaishya or merchant; and shudra or menial servant (Manu 6.21.25). These four groups are described as arising respectively from the mouth, arms, thigh, and feet of Brahma (ibid); the different points of physical origin of the varna reflect the different status accorded to them in sacred Hindu literature. The brahmin, kshatriya and vaishya were considered twice born and entitled to wear the sacred thread as a mark of their special status. The shudra was considered low and the servants of the other three varnas. Throughout the sacred literature of Indian tradition, distinctive behaviour patterns, ritual acts and moral codes were prescribed for each of these varnas. There have been tendencies to project the caste system as solely representing the varna scheme (de Bary et al. 1988: 15). Nowadays, most anthropologists agree that the varna scheme refers at best only to the broad categories of society (see Srinivas 1962: 65 for an early example of this tendency) and not to real categories that are reflected in the endogamous localized jati pattern. The varna system, however, is applied to groupings of jatis (Hutton 1963: 66) and thereby operates to classify categories of castes broadly on the basis of shared status, historical origins, lifestyles and ritual behaviours. The varna scheme is therefore the indigenous elite model which makes explicable on a pan-Indian basis the extreme localisms of jati-based custom and behaviour. As Srinivas points out:

> [Varna] systematizes the chaos of jatis and enables the sub-castes of one region to be comprehended by people in another area by reference to a common scale. Further, the [varna] system represents a scale of values, and jatis occupying the lower rungs have throughout tried to raise their status by taking over the customs and rituals of the top jatis. This has helped a uniform culture throughout the Hindu society. (Srinivas 1962: 25)

Srinivas thus emphasizes how the pan-Indian varna scheme counteracts the provincialism of the jati system and represents a scriptural and popular model for supra-local interaction. Dumont, however, takes exception to the claim that the classical varna scheme offers a uniform culture throughout India (Dumont and Pocock 1957: 51). Acknowledging the existence of unresolved conflict about status in the varna scheme in a single region, Dumont argues that it is difficult to believe that the varna scheme successfully solves variations between regions. According to Dumont, rather than spreading a uniform culture the varna scheme demonstrates the prevalence of certain values in Indian society. Here, despite the problematic nature of the claim that Indian society accepted the hegemony perpetuated by the normative values ingrained in the caste structure indisputably, we cannot ignore the significant influence of the ideological pattern propagated by the varna system that promoted common behavioural norms for caste groups, notwithstanding the diverse nature of social behaviours practised in India depending on local customs, economic situations, religious influence, and so on. The varnas thus do promote homogeneity. But this homogeneity emerges from the common ideological acceptance and frequent mechanical duplication of the varna models in different regions, rather than as a neat organizational homogeneity practised at a pan-Indian level (Fox 1993: 27-45). This homogeneity follows a norm and at the same time encourages diversity. Thus conflicts among castes still exist as does an ideological distinction promoted by the varna ideals. As a result, the attributional uniformity of belief or action that characterizes the local jatis said to be brahmin or kshatriya stems from their ideological adherence to a common model expressed in the varna scheme and it is this ideological eminence that constructs a continuous hierarchical social structure comprising the struggling existences of the local jatis striving for the ideological superiority enjoyed at the top.

I believe that this elusive nature of ideological superiority, which emanates from caste hierarchy, that every other jati aspires to achieve, is arguably provoked by a desire for material gain. Therefore, the association between varna and caste can best be described as the interplay between the elitists' scripturally endorsed ideology and the grassroot level material realities of the jati. However, to see this interplay solely between the pan-Indian varnas and the local forms of jati in order to comprehend the Indian caste structure comprehensively would be an over-simplification. Historians and anthropologists have successfully related varnas and jatis to their respective epochs, the diverse forms of modes of production and the ideological drive to which the systems of stratification have corresponded historically. Instead of allocating the caste structure a materialist or a structuralist status, I would endorse the recognition of both materiality and ideology in practising this hierarchy.

Since the Dumontian brahmanical model of caste stratification actually developed through history, and history is impregnated with the contrary, often conflicting, economic and political tendencies of different social groups, the evolution of the caste system cannot then be separated from these tendencies. In addition, if this system has absorbed these contradictions and still successfully masqueraded as a unitary social system, then it must assert the universality of the hierarchical social structure by covering up the ground force of these contradictions. It is precisely in order to fulfil this function that the ideological rationale behind the caste system has been developed, which according to Lévi-Strauss bridges the unhappy contradiction on which the society rests (Lévi-Strauss 1966: 16; Glucksmann 1974: 80), which are in this particular case, different conflicting power aspirations of different social agents. So it is just not the rationale behind the social stratifications elaborated in the brahmanical texts and unequivocally followed by different social groups that gave rise to the caste system; the direction might be quite the converse, insofar as it is the method of manufacturing an ideology that productively conceals the exploitation, suffering and discrimination involved in the historical journey of the Indian caste system. This, however, does not undermine the importance of ideology in developing and maintaining the caste system since it is ideology that exercised an undeniable influence in maintaining and safeguarding the oppressive tendencies of the caste hierarchy and at the same time enticed various social agents to aspire for caste-based authority as apparently unquestionable in nature.

At this juncture the important functional significance of the caste structure as signifying an association with a hereditary traditional occupation indicative of the social division of labour (Bandyopadhyay 2004: 13) might lead us to compare caste organization with class structure, perhaps described in terms of the forces and relations of production and ownership of property (Habib 1995: 164-65).[14] But the main problem with this kind of caste-class continuum arises from the supposed difference in the nature of inter-group relationships in these two systems of social organization (Bandyopadhyay 2004: 13). For example, in the caste system, this relationship is viewed as one of 'economic interdependence' (Leach cited in Bandyopadhyay 2004: 13), resting on the 'bonds of cooperation' (ibid); the hierarchy, according to this view, is thus never dissolved, as the 'functional specialization and hierarchy are organically linked in this system' (ibid). The relationship between the classes is, on the other hand, one of competition, and there are opportunities for the members of different class groups to reduce ultimately the discrepancy between the classes of the haves and the have-nots. According to Bailey, the caste system is better described as a 'closed organic stratification' and the class as 'segmentary stratification' where there is more scope for competition among the group members (Bailey 1957: 35).

Here again we witness the attempt to represent inter-caste relationships as devoid of conflict or opposition, a tendency which has indeed been 'overdrawn',[15] and once again is the result of an excessive reliance on the scriptural view of caste, a tendency that is a legacy of colonial ethnological discourse.[16] If there was cooperation at the economic level among different caste groups, it is not perhaps wrong to suppose that it was more imposed than spontaneous, as was the acceptance of the cultural attributes of rank and the social roles associated with it (Gupta 2000; Habib 1995). This is also to suggest that the class situation in India is very often expressed through religious idioms of caste (Mencher 1974).[17] Nonetheless, scholars challenging the Dumontian view[18] of caste rigidity have shown, more than enough, how occupational mobility, no matter how impracticable it may sound in an apparently closed system of stratification, has always been present in the Indian caste system at every period of history (Silverberg 1968).[19]

Similarly, as in other phases of Indian history, colonial rule facilitated the dispersal of wealth and power across caste lines, cutting through class status. Members of the lower strata of society at the same time also reinforced the traditional conservatism following high-caste ideology to achieve socio-economic fortune amidst the changing face of the composition of the society. Simultaneously, there were traces of resistance against the dominant order, and all these diverse tendencies provoked social mobility although restricted in nature. Focusing mainly on the Bengali bhadralok in the nineteenth century, it can be seen that caste-ascribed status (ritual ranks) and caste-free roles (economic or political) of different social groups were gradually resolved under a caste ideology that determined the wealth and power pattern of society. This was possible as the caste system was never a static or rigid system of classification to be distinguished from the class structure of society, which was supposed to be fluid and open (D'Souza 1969: 35). However, to underplay the role of ideology in motivating the social aspirants of diverse origin to embrace brahmanical norms and thus to achieve social authority would be an error of judgment in apprehending the very complex nature of the caste philosophy that has successfully maintained the balance between the functional and ideological aspects of this system.

The balance between the ritual character of caste stratification and secular nature of class division in the Indian social system is often, if not always, harmoniously maintained as there is a 'dynamic equilibrium' (Lynch 1969: 12) between ritual and secular status. But how was this so-called equilibrium maintained? Nicholas Dirks has attempted to answer this question in terms of the power aspects of caste society. In his study of pre-colonial South India he showed that caste was never just a religious function, and the king was never just a pawn in the hands of the priests; in fact, the caste system was always consolidated through an alliance of both Brahmanism and state power (Dirks 1987).[20] However, instead of solving the puzzle of the social equilibrium maintained between the ritual and secular aspect of the caste society, Dirks only bestows another perplexing effect upon it. Instead of investigating the material aspect of this so-called equilibrium,

Dirks provides an explanation for the material aspects of caste status. However, the maintenance of this equilibrium is not just about controlling the material power embedded in the systems of production in society either. Had it been such a simple phenomenon based on material exploitation then the apparent spiritualistic nature of the caste structure would not have had such a sustained impact, neither would the ideology of heredity-based superiority become almost impossible to overcome for the lower-caste groups.

Caste is thus an intricate system of social stratification in which secularism and spirituality (or at least spiritual legitimization of its structure and order) go hand in hand. Moreover, in this social stratification the material aspects of the ideological structure are blanketed by its cultural importance. But then the secular nature of the cultural aspect of the caste structure is appropriately undermined by drawing inspiration from the spiritual approach already present in the system, thereby once again masking the material character of exploitation buried under spiritualism. This criss-crossing of materiality and spirituality, or in other words, the overlapping of the ritual and the secular aspects of the caste system, no matter how complicated, is successfully maintained by ritualizing the systems of reproduction and production through a prearranged system of matrimonial bonding that ensures a programmed set of reproduction and control over social authority involving financial gain. The most important prerequisite of having a guarded system of reproduction is controlling the reproductive power of women, which in turn demands controlling their entire existence. Thus lofty ideals are conceived to restrain women within a confined lifestyle, which are very often complacently followed by women themselves because following these norms ensures them a venerated status which is no less than the status enjoyed by the goddesses. Similarly, to keep them confined within the boundaries of their home, domesticity is ritualized and embedded in differences between purity and impurity, morality and immorality and, most importantly, the high and low nature of existence. All these are cleverly organized in the name of tradition, thus veiling the caste structure enduring in this scheme, granting the lives of women with tremendously influential reproductive power. The control of women's lives and their reproductive power in the name of a spiritualistic tradition thus works as a perfect tool for maintaining a balance between the material aspect of the social structure, with its emphasis on stratification, and its secular/cultural features. The cultural aspects of the social order, although apparently secular in nature, are heavily saturated in religious materiality, perpetuating a discriminatory social existence, both secular and spiritual in nature.

This nearly impossible and perplexing balance between religiosity and secularity, or spirituality and materiality representative of the caste structure in India is maintained by control over women, where the restricted status of women works as a 'gender fulcrum' that maintains the balance between the opposing ends of religiosity and secularity, spirituality and materiality by restricting women's sexuality. In the course of the following chapters we suggest that the constituent elements of ideal womanhood, for example, education and reformed nature of domesticity, had not only material roots but also material functions blanketed by high-caste ideals. Here, once again we reiterate that the attribution of high- and low-caste rank to persons or groups is necessarily a subjective concern held by persons inside a given social system, whereby the brahmins claim their innate superiority. Kshatriyas and many other groups are simultaneously able to belittle the brahmin's status and occupation, and, most importantly, the low castes are able customarily to deny their low pedigree. The complicated material account of caste ranking, masked by various ideological aspects of the Hindu social system is actually based on two features: shared or inherited natural substance like blood or semen and a particular code of conduct. According to the standards proliferated by the caste system, all living beings are organized into castes, each of which is defined by its particular bodily substances and moral codes that are inseparable from each other. Thus no distinction is been made between an order of 'nature' (read 'secular') and an order of 'supernatural' (or 'sacred') (Inden 1976). The unity between the sacred and the secular is maintained by proper marriage and reproduction, as only proper marriage ensures the sharing of the same coded bodily substance and the birth of proper offspring. The threat to caste hierarchy on the basis of natural substances has been resisted by the proper enactment of marriage and reproduction. The woman, as the central character in this performance, has to be kept under constant guard so that no norms are defied that result in detrimental social situations infested by social groups of mixed origins and impurely coded bodily substances. Then all these actions against women would evolve naturally being influenced by an idealized existence.

Scholars studying the rise and development of Indian nationalism in the colonial period have demonstrated how the indigenous elites resorted to 'rediscovering' and 'rewriting' a 'tradition' faced with a colonial aggression that taunted their cultural conditions by construing their women's lives in such a way that they became emblematic of the 'tradition' (Mani 1989; U. Chakravarti 1989; T. Sarkar 2001). Many have examined the range of attitudes that surfaced in the process of imagining and inventing a 'golden age' in which women were supposedly enjoying venerated goddesses' status, clearly a constructed ideal in need of re-adoption.[21] These studies have proven that re-thinking women's sexuality becomes necessary whenever the existent social order is under threat and the arrival of British imperialism was no different. The difference in the colonial context, perhaps, lay in the fact that for the first time the need to sort out questions regarding women's untamed sexuality along with projecting the same women as symbols of respectability, tradition and modernity were addressed decisively as the colonial period showed prospects of endowing the latest ideal of womanhood with a pan-Indian effect.

A number of scholars have argued that the colonial period marks a decisive moment in understanding caste and in the shaping of its contemporary manifestations, for instance, the image of native women.[22] Many others see the pre-colonial indigenous social structures as equipped with an auto-corrective mechanism, which ensured the non-oppressive nature of the structure.[23] As a natural consequence of this understanding, feminists, Marxists, and other secular thinkers, who are critical of the pre-colonial past of India, are positioned as products of western education by the traditionalists, which again is a consequence of the colonial impact on India.[24]

Taking this point further I want to show that such a pervasive social institution like the caste system could hardly have been imposed by only administrative measure. It had to be organic rather than artificial, which in turn highlights the importance of ideology in developing and maintaining caste order. To comprehend the organic nature of this social stratification, patriarchy and high-caste dominance must be granted not only a historicity but also a common lineage because of their close interaction (U. Chakravarti 2003: 37).[25] According to Nur Yalman, the fundamental caste-based social organization in the Indian subcontinent was dependent on a neat structure supported by three factors: preserving land-based property, women and the purity of ritual activity (Yalman 1969). These three are structurally linked and it is impossible to maintain all three without forceful control over female sexuality. The purity of caste, depending heavily on the factors of preserving land ownership and ritual activity could not be maintained without guarding women who were in a constitutive position for the entire structure by virtue of their reproductive power. The fear of mixed marriages illustrated in Manu, which was nonetheless a social reality, and the attempts to prevent its occurrence by placing an ideological ban on it, thus continued to be a concern through the early centuries of the first millennium CE (U. Chakravarti 2003: 49-56).

The collapse of an earlier tribal/clan-based society and polity in the post-Vedic period, and especially the establishment of familial control over land consumed within a patrilineal succession to kinship ordained that the sexual behaviour of certain categories of women needed to be closely guarded. Within the category of women, wives in particular had to be under male control, as the emergence of private property required a sharp distinction to be made between motherhood and female sexuality (Tambiah 1973: 223). The latter had to be channelled into legitimate motherhood within an extremely tightly controlled reproductive structure, which would ensure patrilineal succession. Once the caste system was systematically consolidated, sexual intercourse had to be restricted only to prescribed partners to secure caste hierarchy. Motherhood was thus idealized, ritualized and sanctified to ensure the purity of the reproductive system. Furthermore, reproductive power was the only power that women still possessed in this social structure and one of the most effective ways of dealing with this asset for women was to project untamed female sexual power as terribly dangerous.[26] Thus the normative (as well as the narrative) literature of ancient and medieval India is full of references to the inherent wickedness of women and their uncontrolled lust.[27] And the most interesting feature of this 'innate' nature of women, known as the *strisvabhav*, unlike that of the shudras or other low-caste people, was the representation of the conflict between the nature of women, and their duty or the *dharma* (the consciousness of forming an ordered universe, and hence the moral duty of accepting one's station in life). The innate nature of the lowest caste was in harmony with the nature of actions prescribed for them by the brahmins, whereas the innate nature of the women was in direct conflict with their duties as chaste wife. As strisvabhav was thought to entice women away continuously from their *stridharma* (see p. 16), it was thus necessary to transport women from the domain of an untamed environment to the systematic world order controlled by brahmanical ideals. Significantly, some myths clearly suggest that a 'demonic' strisvabhav was the maternal heritage of women whereas the stridharma was their paternal heritage, given to them by the brahmins (Leslie 1989: 251).

The general subordination of women became essential at this stage because it was only then that the method of controlling women's sexuality could become operative. This method of controlling women operated mainly through three devices:

ideology, discipline and power (U. Chakravarti 2003: 73). Accomplishing the ideological goal of controlling women's dangerous sexual power was made possible by disciplining them through discourse on, or through, the imposition of, stridharma and *patibratadharma* (the ordained duties of a good wife), and if they did not obey these social codes there was the threat of harsh punishment for their aberrant behaviour. In most cases, wifely codes were internalized by women with a good deal of complacency as the *patibrata* (see p. 16) concept was successfully constructed by the Hindu patriarchal order as something in which women themselves controlled their own sexuality and believed they gained power and respect only through the codes that they adopted. Hindu wives' chastity and fidelity in accordance with high-caste values came to be regarded as the only means of their salvation.[28] The patriarchal norms and institutions of controlling women's sexuality were thus successfully masked and so was the attempt to establish high-caste hegemony. High-caste supremacy channelled through patriarchal norms as an ideology subsequently became ritually naturalized.

The role of mythology in naturalizing this patriarchal ideology is of key significance. While the *Dharmashastra* texts are straightforward in claiming the need for women to be dominated and controlled, myths are much more subtle, and thus more effective in constructing the patibrata ideal. Sita in the *Ramayana* epitomizes the patibrata ideal. She is a beautiful and dutiful wife, the chaste and passive archetype of womanhood in Hindu mythology. There are several other powerful models of wifely virtue (such as Savitri, Damayanti) and the power that they acquire through their devotion. But the myths also make us aware of what happens when aberrant women do not follow their wifely duties. When women are chaste and dutiful they need no protection, as their patibrata ideal ensures their safety, but when they are errant the use of force by kinsmen is legitimate to keep the social order intact. Texts and mythological literature are full of stories of the use of violence by kinsmen to keep women in control (Bhattacharji 1994: 16-41). Here again, high-caste hegemony reserves the severest punishment for women who engage into sexual relations with men of the lower castes.[29] The purity of women ensured the purity of the caste system and thus the social order, as a very close link was established between caste, class, state and patriarchy. Together they provided the ideological framework of womanhood. The roles that were played by mythologies and the prescriptive sacred texts to guide and restrain women's lives were subsequently taken up by different domestic journals in nineteenth-century Bengal to advise women on how to make their family life a success (Walsh 2005). In the colonial context, the domestic arena became the only area where native males could exercise their authority, and all these advice manuals asked women to make the domestic terrain the haven of their life. Accordingly, advice was given on how to cook sumptuous and healthy food, how to scour plates, how to stitch, how to clean and, most importantly, how to satisfy the male members of the family by becoming a good daughter, daughter-in-law, wife and a mother (ibid). This emphasis on domesticity turned out to be a covert method of refurbishing the caste order via the idealization of women's existence (see Chapters 3-4).

CONTROLLING WOMEN: RECREATING THE 'IDEAL WOMAN' IN THE COLONIAL ERA

In the early nineteenth-century, Hindu nationalists deployed an idealized presentation of womanhood to counter British colonialism. At this stage, almost all arguments about the inherent incapability of Indian society to acquire the virtues of modernity and, most importantly, nationhood tended to converge upon the supposedly 'unique' institution of caste. According to Partha Chatterjee, in responding to this charge Indian nationalists adopted mainly two strategies (1999: 173). The first was to deny the claim that caste was essential to the functioning of Indian society. In the nationalist framework this position was identified as left-wing nationalism, more precisely as Marxism. As Chatterjee notes, according to this view, caste is a feature of the superstructure of Indian society, the existence and adequacy of which is to be understood in terms of the ideological products of the 'specific pre-capitalist social formations that have made their appearance in Indian history'.[30] This view claims that with the suppression of the pre-capitalist formations caste would also disappear (ibid). The advantage of this argument is that by refusing to give the caste system any special status it is able not only to dispute the rule of colonial difference in the public sphere but also to uphold the indigenous project of modernity at the same time. However, when the nationalist claim of self-governance was attaining its peak, this argument was not useful as it appeared to accept all the claims made on behalf of western modernity and advocated them for modern India (ibid). In doing so, there was no room left for challenging the colonial criticism of India as a debased, caste-ridden society. To avoid this difficulty, a second strategy was preferred where caste was retained as an essential element of Indian society, making it necessarily different from western society. What this strategy denied, however, is that the caste system was fundamentally contradictory to, and incompatible with, a modern and conscientious society.[31]

Partha Chatterjee argues that well before demands for self-determination and political freedom began to define nationalist activity, it was in the arena of culture that Indian nationalism established its claims of sovereignty. This was affected by developing a separation in the domain of culture between the provinces of the material and the spiritual (ibid); these were then linked with another set of binaries, the outer and the inner. This distinction enabled Indian nationalists to come to terms with the very conspicuous material success of the West, identified as affairs of the 'outer', while simultaneously staking a claim for the superiority of the East in matters spiritual, the 'inner.' Extending this analogy, the inner/outer split was then transferred to the spaces of social activity. The 'inner' was linked to the private, the domestic sphere (*ghar* = home), and the 'outer' with life in the public sphere (*bahir* = the world) (T. Sarkar 2001: 1-68). From there, establishing an analogy between the public/private distinction and the separation of roles along the lines of biological difference was but a short step. If native domesticity needed modernization, a modernity defined within an Indian idiom, it was to be performed from within the national tradition and therefore to be essentially different from that of the West. The modern woman would 'have to display the signs of national tradition' (ibid: 9); improved and reformed through education, she was to be refined and different, not only from previous generations and lower-caste, lower-class or uneducated women, but also from westernized Indian women. Women complied, or were forced to accord with this patriarchal nationalism, which professed to recall them to their sacred responsibilities. As carriers of tradition they owed it to the nation to preserve (and even restore) its pristine and original standing. If the native man was obliged to submit to the demands of modernization imposed by the colonial state, this was counterpoised by the woman's firm allegiance to her inner, essential, national self. Partha Chatterjee further contends that once high-caste women acknowledged the protocols and definitions of social comportment fixed by nationalism, it made possible their mobility outside the home because their bodies were encoded with the 'spirituality' of a 'superior' tradition (ibid: 125-27).

Accordingly, at the interface of Indian nationalism's challenge to colonialism, women's sexuality was made a critical site for the symbolic economy involving the nation, one that functioned to mobilize an embryonic, collective political identity via the route of an altered version of tradition that upheld an updated model of living for native women. This new ideal of womanhood embraced modernity, but altered it by drawing from superior indigenous traditionalism and thereby upheld a social structure, the caste system. As a result it was in this period of early nationalism and high imperialism that the figure of the chaste, upper-caste, upper-class Hindu woman emerged. In her role as wife (and mother) such a figure functioned as the supreme emblem of a consolidated Hindu nationalist selfhood.

This process of repatriation objectified women's bodies, which were seen to be marked by religious affiliation, and placed them under the protection of the nation-state (T. Sarkar 2001: 1-76). The ideological construction of women's bodies as symbolic booty and the direct correlation established between women's purity and the vulnerable nation (chaste woman's body = uncolonized, sacred, national space) were common to several anti-colonial nationalisms.[32] Since a woman's body constituted the specific site for the exercise of native control, women's lives were thoroughly probed and programmatically elaborated by their male counterparts. The single largest area of discursive production and regulation was women's sexual purity over which strict supervision was exercised, and its place established by defining it as the prerogative of the husband or the future husband. As a result, the life of upper-caste, chaste Hindu women, although exposed to western education and western lifestyles, turned out to be a state of perpetual bondage continuously monitored by their own people. And subsequently women of other classes and castes almost vanished from nationalistic discourse as the educated, chaste, high-caste and class *bhadramahila* could only represent the true picture of Indian tradition to counter the colonial hegemony. The bhadramahila was projected as the ideal counterpart of the bhadralok, although endowed with the dual responsibility of safeguarding the home and the nation. The bhadralok failed to protect the nation and their control over the home was heavily dependent on their women.[33]

I am aware of the non-linear nature of the responsibility shared by the bhadralok and their women and refuse to designate the term 'bhadramahila' as the ideal counterpart of the bhadralok since the perfect equivalent of the native elite was much more than a gentlewoman. She was the model of virtue, both modern and traditional, safeguarding the native's precious existence against colonial aggression and also encouraging their nationalist aspirations. The bhadralok male agents proved incapable of protecting their women, tradition and the nation, whereas their women were endowed with the responsibility of rescuing their men, tradition and the nation by virtue of their qualities of chastity, fidelity and amenability. The term *bhadra* that means 'gentle' in Bengali extended its usage indicating the modern, educated and aristocratic nature of this male power group largely following a Victorian notion of respectability, although not attaching any normative worth to their existence that were the foundational factors of their women's lives.

The historiographical account of nineteenth-century Bengal shows corruption and adultery were permissible to the bhadralok whereas their women were required to lead a life of both physical and mental virtue.[34] The etymological meaning of the term 'bhadralok' was quite similar to its actual manifestation whereas the term 'bhadramahila' widely used as the counterpart of the bhadralok clearly meant a lot more than just the gentle, accommodating and sophisticated existence of these women. These women were expected to lead perfect lives devoid of any imperfection at all. For example, they had to be perfect in cooking the most complex cuisine, nursing ailing members of the family in a most critical situation, satisfying the husband by engaging with him in academic discussion as well as sexual intercourse, and so on. And all the while they must never forget that the greater virtues of chastity and fidelity were prerequisites for attaining a respectable social status, clearly an idealized existence that was much more demanding and complicated than their men's pursuit of respectability. Keeping in mind that the role and responsibility of the bhadramahila[35] was not analogous to the situation of the bhadralok, we do not use the term 'bhadramahila' as the emblem of nineteenth-century Bengal womanhood. Rather, we propose to use the term *adarsha nari*, literally, the ideal woman facilitating an ideal existence for her menfolk by propagating the superiority of native culture.

Here I must mention that if pro-women activism and social reform projects as part of a broader anti-colonial struggle made a singular contribution towards ameliorating the condition of women, it was only by way of a secondary consequence.[36] 'Woman' in the male nationalist discourse was an empty signifier tethered to social and political contingencies. And 'tradition', the catch-all term for things pre-colonial, constituted a significant part of the politics of resistance and represented to the native a discursive space over which colonial control was not to be endured. The crucial changes that this phase subsequently witnessed were:

(i) 'Tradition' was reconstituted under colonial rule and in different ways women and brahmanic scripture became interlocking grounds for this re-articulation. Women became emblematic of 'tradition', and the reworking of 'tradition' was largely conducted through debating the rights and status of women in society.

(ii) Despite the intimate connection between women and 'tradition', or perhaps because of it, these debates were in some sense not primarily about women but rather about what constitutes authentic cultural tradition.

(iii) The privileging of brahmanic scripture and the equation of 'tradition' with scripture was, as Lata Mani has suggested, an effect of a 'colonial discourse' on India. By colonial discourse Mani means a mode of understanding Indian society that emerged alongside colonial rule and over time was shared to a greater or lesser extent by officials, missionaries and the indigenous elite, although deployed by these various groups to different, often ideologically opposite ends. This discourse did not emerge from nowhere, nor was it entirely discontinuous with pre-colonial discourses on India. Rather, it was produced through interaction with select natives, although the officials had power over the natives in question (Mani 1989: 48).

(iv) The production of tradition had several consequences. It meant that officials could insist, for instance, that brahmanic scriptures were prescriptive texts containing rules of social behaviour, even when the evidence for this assertion was problematic. Further, they could institutionalize their assumptions as Warren Hastings did in 1772, by making these texts the basic of native personal law (ibid).[37]

As a result, the process of establishing the superiority of Indian 'tradition' anchored deeply in the brahmanical base and furnished with the elements of high-caste hegemony was pushed forward as the sole aspirant of the inheritance of indigenous 'tradition' and clearly as an essential element in the still developing nationalist identity (Thapar 1985: 21).

It was the high-caste Hindu woman in her identity as the wife (and later the mother) who in the early days of cultural nationalism stood under the fairy lights of the modernization project. The home was her preserve and her functions were the continuation of her husband's line, nurturing the future (male) citizen-subject, and the reproduction of male labour-power needed for the newly emergent capitalist economy. As mentioned earlier, the agenda of cultural adjustments formulated by the native intellectuals aimed at creating an enlightened domesticity without transforming its sacred Indian (read Hindu) character or effecting a re-distribution of power in interpersonal relations. It was an assumption of the willing subordination or loving surrender of the Hindu wife to the authority of the husband, as opposed to the repressive colonial power which the Hindu man encountered everyday that an initial nationalist critique of the coercive colonial state formulated. Tanika Sarkar notes that for the Hindu man 'the only sphere of autonomy and free will was located within the Hindu family, to be more precise with the Hindu woman, her position within an authentic Hindu marriage system and the ritual surrounding the deployment of her body' (2001: 98). Hemmed in within the domestic sphere, the chaste body of the Hindu woman, 'pure and unmarked, loyal and subservient to the discipline of the *Shastras* alone' (ibid: 65), represented the only national space so far un-contaminated by colonial contact, and was thus considered the repository of authentic Indian values. Mandatory monogamy and chastity for women constituted the bulwarks of tradition and were, in consequence, pivotal to the self-definition of a culture that considered itself spiritually free (and superior) but nevertheless held subject to another culture that was materially more advanced. The sanctity and exclusivness of the high-caste household were ensured by upholding taboos against contacts with other castes and religions as part of a series of purity rituals that applied only to women. The potency of both caste and religion as centripetal forces in organizing community identity is evident even in the post-Independence era, when the secular state legislated on affirmative-action policies to end discrimination in the public sphere, but these factors still continued to shape the socio-cultural practices that structured everyday life.

I am, however, not suggesting that reformist and revivalist brands of nationalism invented chastity. The discursive production of sexual purity as part of a political ideology dates back to the time of the *Dharmashastras*. But the political privilege, the immense prestige and visibility that the concept of chastity acquired as a prerequisite for achieving self-governance was indeed novel during the colonial era. It was the location for a struggle of discourses on manhood, nationhood and ideal citizenship, the site on which Indian identity was itself poised. The development of the idea of an inviolate (and inviolable) national space around the purity of the new ideal woman simultaneously enabled the colonized Indian man, nettled by criticisms of incompetence and effeminacy from the colonizers (aimed especially at Bengali men), to recuperate in some measure his threatened masculinity (A. Nandy 1998; T. Sarkar 2001). It was by extending a pledge of fierce protection and regulation of women's chastity, so went the logic, that they would be able to exercise a guardianship that they had failed to maintain over the country.

Although the approaches to the history of ideal womanhood discussed above have probed the politics behind this construction of the ideal, they have failed to reveal how this politics representing high-caste ordering of social norms was actually executed. This trend in historiography, for example, the works of Ghulam Murshid (1984) and Jasodhara Bagchi (1985), do not question how high-caste hegemony was manifested in different layers of the society through an ideal representation of native womanhood, which also symbolized the self-respecting and virtuous image of the male members of a subjugated society. That this process entailed a reaffirmation of the prerogative of the high-caste members of the society is reflected in the historical literature but the method of this performance that restated brahmanical social values in almost all the layers of the social order is not sufficiently analysed and they thereby in turn fail to throw light on the gendered nature of caste aspirations in relation to the ideal of womanhood.

Moreover, historians, for example, Partha Chatterjee (1993) and Tanika Sarkar (2001), draw attention to the process of relocating the domestic arena as the only area of autonomy for colonized male agents and the ensuing control over their women's lives that let them to regain their lost sense of power since in all other battles they proved to be losers against their colonial masters. But, then again, they do not highlight how the increasing male control over domestic life and the subsequent ritualization of almost every aspect of domestic existence to keep women engaged with household duties and, more importantly, to prove the superior and spiritual nature of the inner domain of the native world ultimately reinforced the ritual-based brahmanical form of life. The work of Walsh (2001; 2004) highlights the importance of domesticity as a discourse in nineteenth-century Bengal but while attempting to record the middle-class nature of Bengali domesticity she ended up highlighting only the high-caste nature of native domestic life. Moreover, while Walsh's work draws attention to the fact that even the most insignificant features of domestic existence were brought to attention during the last half of the nineteenth century, she does not establish the necessary connection between maintaining an untainted domestic life, the situation of women placed at the core of that domesticity, and the safeguarding of the caste structure. Borrowing from Partha Chatterjee (1993) she explains this emphasis on domesticity as the natives' attempt to regain their lost authority but does not illustrate how these reflected the imposition of brahmanical standards on low-caste domesticity. As a result, she portrays the native domestic order in an almost monolithically high-caste manner.

Similarly, Partha Chatterjee (1993) declares that the sudden disappearance of the 'woman question' from the agenda of public debate in colonial Bengal lies in nationalism's success in situating the 'woman question' in an inner domain of sovereignty, far away from the arena of actual political contest against the colonial state. In this process Chatterjee practically bestows a totalitarian structure on the social arrangement of nineteenth-century Bengal devoid of any diversity, ambiguity and/or antagonism, ignoring the layered existence of the social order accommodating people of different strata. Consequently, he fails to notice the significant preoccupation with the 'woman question' among the low castes. As a result, much of this scholarship on this period reflects and contributes to a form of 'high-caste solipsism' that is a tendency to think, imagine, and speak as if Brahmanism adequately describes the world. Thus, 'high-caste solipsism' is not the consciously held belief that brahmins are inherently superior to all other castes, but a form of myopia which simply does not see the experience or existence of the other castes as significant, unless in spasmodic, impotent forms, which have little or no long-term momentum or political usefulness.

Since domestic existence is the basic unit of social life in a caste society, by conquering the domestic world through reaffirmation of brahmanical norms, high-caste customs prevailed not just over the household existence, but extended their boundaries to the local and, against the backdrop of the demands of the emergent nation state, to the national level. We thus want to resist the universalization of the construction, modification and reception of the ideal of womanhood in colonial Bengal only in terms of high-caste existence by recognizing the contribution of the middle and lower orders in the forms of acceptance and/or rejection or alteration of this model womanhood. This guides us to explore under what socio-political compulsions the middle and lower orders of the caste structure approved of the brahmanical form of gendered norms and domestic rules and to ask whether this process of brahmanization was hegemonic in nature or whether the aspirant caste groups managed to preserve their individualism by accepting standardized brahmanical norms only strategically. The participation of these aspirants and struggling castes in their modification, construction and acceptance of the ideal of womanhood implies diverse socio-political and economic objectives and compulsions of different social groups. In doing so I moderate the high-caste approach in criticizing the very high-caste dominance in Indian society replicated in the scholarship, which only ensures a false consciousness of the discriminatory social structure.

Contrary to this familiar tendency, Partha Chatterjee shifts his gaze away from high-caste historiography and focuses on the conscious process of identity formation at the grassroot level. By unravelling the story of the hari community's religious insubordination against brahmanical hegemony he uncovers the hollowness of the Dumontian claim that the ideological force of dharma eternally binds individual caste groups to the system (P. Chatterjee 1993: 180-81). Ratanlal Chakraborty's work on bhuimalis of the Mymensingh district of earlier East Bengal (1994: 120-34), Swaraj Basu's work on the rajbangshis (1994: 43-64), and Bandyopadhyay's work on the namashudras (1997) also illustrate the relevance of these social protests against high-caste hegemony. It is Bandyopadhyay who in his impressive work on the low-caste groups' diverse and indistinct form of aspirations has pointed out the incontrovertible participation and contributions of these marginal groups in the high-caste Hindu chauvinist formation (1997 and 2004). We too establish a coherent link between caste discrimination and the construction of an ideal of womanhood, and subsequently reveal the aspirations of members of the different strata of the society to emulate this ideal in re-manufacturing brahmanical patriarchy. The emulation of brahmanical norms for women could also be considered to be a tool for attacking high-caste supremacy by ascending the social ladder. The emulation of brahmanical guidelines for controlling female sexuality by agents of different caste groups gave rise to an almost homogeneous ideal of womanhood, cutting across different caste positions and class alignments and, more importantly, affirming, altering and integrating the nature of this discourse in which participations, contributions and competitions of agents of different strata of society were taking place, and it was hardly unequivocal in nature.

NOTES

1 See Godelier 1972: 1; 96-97; 275-76 for a helpful summary of Marx's thought in this regard.

2 Lévi-Strauss' structuralist analysis offers a chance to discover the 'timeless universal human truths' so beloved of the humanist perspective, but using a methodology that seems much more 'objective' and 'scientific.' For Lévi-Strauss in particular, such universal human truths, what all humans share by virtue of being human, exists at the level of structure; all signifying systems, all systems of cultural organization, share the same fundamental structures, regardless of their particular content. So the motive for using structuralist analysis is, in this sense, the same as the motive for using a humanist perspective: to find out what we all have in common, or what 'the human condition' is (as many of us have asked). Poststructuralists, by contrast, reject the whole idea of anything being universal or timeless or essentially 'human' as homogenizing. On the other hand, it is argued by some that it is falsely construed that for Lévi-Strauss the social structure is derived from the structure of mind (eg, see Glucksmann 1974). According to this view such misinterpretation occurs because insufficient attention has been paid to the methodological principles of the Lévi-Straussian method. For example, if one looks closely at his study on kinship it will be noticed that what he is actually doing is using linguistic theory, and the theoretical insights of linguistic theory, the distinction, for instance, between *langue* and *parole,* to bear upon the ordering of authority and joking relationships in kinship studies. See Lévi-Strauss 1969: Chapter 1.

3 The number of western academic and indigenous writings on Sita and Savitri and their enormous power to sacrifice and suffer do not focus on the reason behind the social constructions of these images and a similar approach by Indian scholars to portray these characters as emblematic of Indian tradition is a clear case here. For a stereo-typical image of ideal Indian womanhood through the portrayals of

these mythical characters, see Nagar 2006 and Menon 2003.

4 By 'putting caste in place' is not denying its importance but rather trying to identify its importance relative to other aspects of social life, which although considered as axial to Indian society have so far not been highlighted enough in terms of the relationship of this hierarchical set up to women's place in Indian society.

5 This is, however, not to deny that socio-religious identity based on caste principles could be seen as an equally dominating perception among the natives. Nonetheless, it was colonial rule that gave this notion of caste-based socio-religious identity a pan-Indian form. To gain an understanding of the colonial preoccupation with caste see, eg, the works of Charles Grant collected by Ainslie Thomas Embree 1962). See also Cohn 1987 for Grant's analysis of caste. Cohn has shown that there is considerable literature by evangelicals and missionaries on the Indian caste system. Cohn mentions the works of William Carey (1801), William Ward (1822), William Robertson (1828) in their assessments of the Indian social order. In fact, Cohn has provided an extensive list of works based on the caste system starting from the third century BCE when scattered accounts of Indian society were starting to be written by travellers. Cohn's list particularly takes note of the evangelical, Orientalist, and missionary preoccupation with the Indian caste system.

6 This tendency also summons the ways in which caste ideology has been seen as an unchallenged authority in both political and economic matters. The fact that the ways in which this ideology can be muted and transformed to justify political and economic ambition has nothing to do with an eternal ideology.

7 For example, see Milner 1994; Madan 1992.

8 T. N. Madan, eg, specifies, that in Indian cultural traditions any 'search for secular elements' is a 'futile exercise' because in this culture the power of the king is subordinated to the authority of the priests (1992: 402). For a detailed discussion of this tendency see also Senart 1975.

9 Dumont is not only the most systematic exponent of the dominant conceptual view of the caste system but he also attained this distinction by undermining almost all the established conceptual views on the subject, either in terms of detail or in terms of conception and methodology (Dumont 1970: 66).

10 Dumont proposes that the principle of hierarchy, as manifested in the caste system in India, is based on notions of purity and pollution. Célestin Bouglé (1870-1940) at the beginning of the twentieth century had enumerated three essential features of the caste system: separation, interdependence and hierarchy: separation, in matters of marriage and contacts; interdependence, since each group is assigned a specific profession and depends on the services of other communities; and hierarchy, which ranks the groups as relatively superior or inferior to one another (Bouglé 1971). Dumont insists that these three characteristics are reducible to a 'single true principle', namely, the opposition of pure and impure. He argues that the principle of hierarchy pivots on the opposition between purity and pollution, which corresponds to the notions of superiority and inferiority (Quigley 1994). According to Dumont, the opposition between pure and impure is sustained by the disjunction between the ritual status of the brahmins and the secular power of the kshatriyas. Dumont argues that in the ideology of caste, though the kings are politically dominant, their temporal authority is subordinated to the spiritual authority of brahmins. This disjunction between power and status is implicit in the hierarchical opposition of pure and impure: 'Thus in the theory of varnas one finds that status and power are differentiated, just as the general consideration of hierarchy seemed to require' (Louis Dumont cited in ibid).

Based on the principle of purity that Dumont's theory of caste elucidates, brahmins were accorded the highest status in the caste structure. The politically dominant kshatriyas were ranked next in order. Other ranks in the society were also segregated according to the hierarchical principle of purity and impurity. Those who dealt professionally with natural, impure substances like dead bodies, cutting hair and removing night soil were designated the lowest position. Those who were neither specialists of purity nor impurity were ranked along this pure-impure axis where brahmins formed the apex and the untouchables, the bottom (ibid: 26-30). Dumont rightly asserts that similar to the phenomenon of the brahmins and the king assuming supremacy in the varna system, the brahmins and the dominant castes exerted their supremacy over other castes in the jati model.

11 Both Yalman and Marriott have so characterized it in their reviews of Dumont's *Homo Hierarchicus*. See Yalman 1969 and Marriott 1970: 66-75.
12 See Gupta 2000 as an example of criticism of Dumont.
13 See, eg, Srinivas 1962; Tambiah 1973; Gupta 2000; Habib 1995; Dirks 1987; 2001; P. Chatterjee 1993; S. Bandyopadhyay 1997; 2004; and U. Chakravarti 2003.
14 For example, D. D. Kosambi's dictum that 'caste is a class on the primitive level of production' offered the view that caste did not arise out of any internal and unchanging divisions of varnas in Indian society. See Kosambi 1985: 25.
15 See, eg, Yogendra Singh 1997.
16 For a further discussion, see Cohn 1968; Mani 1989; U. Chakravarti 1989 and Dirks 2001.
17 See also Claude Meillasoux 1973.
18 See, eg, Gupta 2000 and Habib 1995.
19 In an open system of stratification internal mobility is an accepted property of the system. On the other hand, in a closed system of stratification, mobility is strongly discouraged. In such cases determined ideological wars have to be waged by the aspirants in their bid for upward mobility. In doing so the basis on which low-ranked caste was accorded earlier has to be delegitimized. This would imply that a hitherto low-ranking caste must necessarily step out of its location within the ranked hierarchy and energize an ideology of difference in order to justify and legitimize its urge for upwardness. By the same token, closed systems of stratification have always witnessed tremendous upheavals and dynamism which have usually gone unnoticed as there are always attempts to protect social authority from any challenges, and attempts are also made to ensure a closure against any openness. Here we also have to keep in mind that open and closed systems of stratification are not always discrete historical stages but can closely be intertwined at the empirical level, simply because in every system of open stratification there is a point beyond which mobility is made unachievable, and on the other hand it is often believed that a closed system of stratification gives way to open ones. See Gupta 2000 and 1997 for a detailed discussion of this. See also Quigley 1994 and Fuller 1984.
20 See Dirks 1987 and 2001. See also Lynch 1969: 12.
21 In their struggle against colonial dominance Indian nationalists

strategically invented a national history and argued that it was interrupted by colonialism. Accordingly, they described ancient India as a golden age of great prosperity, cultural vitality, civilization, spirituality, in which women had high status devoid of any cruelty performed against them. These projects allowed them to create a romanticized alternative to what they perceived as the social chaos of industrializing Europe and its over-emphasis on materiality and technology.

22 Nicholas Dirks, one of the most prominent upholders of the colonial creation of the caste system, argues: 'It is increasingly clear that colonialism in India produced new forms of society that have been taken to be traditional, and the caste system itself as we know now it is not a residual survival of India but a specifically colonial form of civil society' (1993: 59). See also Naidu 1996 and Bandyopadhyay 1997.

23 For instance, Dharmapal, an important scholar representing this position, sees these indigenous structures as having an in-built self-correcting mechanism, which ensured that these structures were never too oppressive. For a detailed discussion see Dharmapal 1983.

24 For a discussion of the impact of 'westernization' on the Indian past see Thapar 2004; Niyogi 2006; and Dilip Chakrabarti 1997.

25 Also, acknowledging this connection that developed over centuries is useful because it helps to connect the two most important phases of Indian history. The first phase is contained in the changes from a pre-Manu social arrangement, from the fifth to the third centuries BCE, to the arrangement depicted by Manu in the first and second centuries CE; the second phase is from Manu's systemized arrangement to the contemporary social context of caste and gender in India. In the context of these two phases the prescriptive nature of brahmanical texts of the Rig Vedic and pre-Vedic era must be confronted with lived social reality, which is most often accessible. Nineteenth-century Hindu nationalist leaders, predominantly male and high caste, romanticized this period in order to establish the superiority of their tradition over their European counterparts (P. Chatterjee 1998; Murshid 1984; and T. Sarkar 2001). Vedic society, which was barely subjected to historical analysis, was made the 'golden era' as far as women's existence was concerned (K. Roy 2002). However, recent scholarship has begun analysing the textual, and to some extent the archaeological evidence in order to map the

economic and social history of that period. Although a detailed analysis of this era is still to be undertaken, whatever little evidence we have today does not support the claim of 'golden past' of Indian womanhood made by the orthodox nationalist leaders (ibid).

26 For a discussion of the idealization and systematization of womanhood invested in the concept of motherhood, see Kosambi 1962; L. Dube 1986; K. Roy 2002; and U. Chakravarti 2003.

27 The *Ramayana* and *Mahabharata* are full of these examples, as are *Manusmriti* and *Satapatha Brahmana.* See Bhattacharji 1994.

28 For comprehensive analyses of the construction of an ideal of womanhood through the patriarchal ritualization of women's sexual identity during this period, see Bhattacharji 1994 and Leslie 1989.

29 Violence was intrinsic to the working of patriarchal norms. The husband, and the clan or community to whom the woman belonged, had the authority to punish the errant wife or women in general. In the *Ramayana*, Lakshman mutilates Surpanakha for her sexual overtures to the princes of Ayodhya. The cutting off of the nose is a metaphor for genital mutilation for her disobedience (U. Chakravarti 2003). For violence on women as a tool for controlling their errant behaviour see Bhattacharji 1994; Leslie 1989; L. Dube 1986.

30 For a discussion of the Marxist approach to caste see Habib 1995.

31 For a discussion of this strategy see Radhakrishnan 1927; Ghurye 1932.

32 The female characters like Shanti in Bankimchandra Chatterjee's novels are emblematic of the equation between the purity of the woman's body and the uncolonized nation. For a detailed discussion see J. Bagchi 1985; T. Sarkar 2001; Murshid 1984.

33 For a discussion of this gendered discourse of power and agency in the native domestic arena see T. Sarkar 2001. See also Sumit Sarkar 1992 and P. Chatterjee 1993.

34 See Kaliprasanna Sinha 1991 [1862] *Satik Hutum Pyachar Naksha*, Arun Nag, ed. (Kolkata: Ananda: 2004) for the deteriorating moral standards of Bengali bhadralok; trans Chitralekha Basu, *Sketches by Hootum the Owl: A Satirist's View of Calcutta* (Kolkata: Samya, 2012).

35 Generally used as a counterpart of the term 'bhadralok'; in other words women endowed with all the qualities that any bhadralok possessed were referred as bhadramahila. However, they had the

added responsibility of acting as a pativrata.

36 Lata Mani argues, in the context of the ban on widow burning, that the anxiety was not so much about women as it was about civilization, religion and culture. Love, intimacy and women's lives were subjects of intellectual debates conducted entirely in the idiom of religion in the public sphere. Unsurprisingly, men, who mainly belonged to the high-caste groups exclusively, dominated this public sphere, and consensus on these issues was discursively developed and decisions taken followed a brahmanical pattern. See Mani 1989.

37 Under the governorship of Warren Hastings, Bengal witnessed the production of Orientalist knowledge to serve the interests of the colonial government. In fact, it was Hastings, who initiated the study and translation of a series of Hindu texts in the belief that an accurate knowledge of India and Hindu manners and customs could only be grasped through these ancient records. See for example, U. Chakravarti 1989: 30; King 1999: 63. Hastings had specific plans regarding the governance of the natives, which strongly suggested that the natives should be governed by their own laws and influenced by a textualized form of Christianity. Hastings and his contemporaries comfortably presumed that these laws could only be found in the sacred texts rather than in diverse local customs. As Rocher states: 'Society was made to conform to ancient *Dharmashastra* texts, in spite of those texts' insistence that they were overridden by local and group custom. It eventually allowed anglicist administrators to manipulate the porous boundary between religion as defined by texts and customs they wished to ban' (1993: 215-49). Also see Thapar 1989: 220-21 and Balagangadhara, 1994: 16-17. Here it may be argued that as the local customs were so diverse, the colonial administration was basically presented with a situation that could only be faced by one standard law everywhere. According to this argument the 'practical necessity' of the colonial rulers cannot be underestimated. But the fact that the colonial administration never openly declared the 'practical purpose' behind choosing Manu, and rather projected the *Dharmashastra* literature as the only window through which India's glorious past could be accessed.

2

Gendering Caste: The Bhadralok and Social Reforms

CASTE IN NINETEENTH-CENTURY CALCUTTA: NEW SOCIAL STANDARDS

In the colonial social milieu of eighteenth-century Calcutta the apparently inflexible caste hierarchy of the Hindu social system went through a series of alterations as the arriviste of low- and middle-caste groups succeeded in gaining positions of power and authority, previously unimaginable in what had appeared to be a closed social system. In the new social setting of late eighteenth-century Calcutta, wealth began to prevail, to a degree, over conventional caste rules as a marker of status. This change was temporary, ultimately relapsing into a system where lineage prevailed over other measures of social status through the renovation of the high-caste model of womanhood. Moreover, the efforts of upwardly mobile lower-caste groups who were the beneficiaries of colonial reformative policies in the end aligned themselves with the institution of caste so that they could supplement their financial status with the high social status only afforded to brahmins. The main means of doing so was through the creation of an ideal of womanhood derived from the brahmanical model of the pativrata, an ideal, which cut across the caste lines, both high and low.

In the early days of colonialism British traders and rulers still unfamiliar with the indigenous forms of commerce had to depend on interpreters and mediators, a role that became a profitable profession for a diverse group of Bengalis from different social standings. Apart from the original merchant families of Calcutta like the Sheths and Basaks, many others who came to the city from outside to earn their fortunes made their way to the top by working closely with the British merchants and rulers in their capacities as *baniyas* or brokers to the British traders, or as *dewans* (intermediaries) in the judicial and revenue sections of the administration; there were many others playing the role of interpreters and junior assistants to the foreign traders and rulers.[1] The new situation opened up unique opportunities even to those from the lower classes to improve their social standing by the virtue of their close proximity to the foreign rulers. Thus because of the new foreign administration there were gradual changes in the orthodox social rigidities of caste and ancestry; the conventional norms and standards that used to connect different strata of society in a hierarchical order also began to collapse. It was thus that the washerman Ratan could transform himself in to Ratan Sarkar, a prominent member of Bengali elite society.[2] Similarly, Jayaram Tagore, ancestor of the renowned Tagore family, once looked down upon as a 'pirali brahmin'[3] (see also Chapter 1) according to the orthodox brahmanical standards, received enormous respect when son Darpanarayan established himself as a dewan to the then acting Governor General Mr. Wheeler. Henceforth, the position of the Tagore family in Calcutta became incontrovertible (Sumanta Banerjee 1989: 25).

That conventional caste rules were eclipsed by economic power during this period is well illustrated by the story of one Kaliprasad Datta, a successor of a wealthy kayastha family. Kaliprasad was threatened with social exclusion by a faction of the Hindu parvenu of Calcutta on the grounds that he had a Muslim mistress. Warned by this unexpected development Kaliprasad approached the leader of another privileged faction, Ramdulal Dey, who himself rose from a lower background to the position of a baniya of a private English merchant company and accumulated huge wealth through independent dealings with

American business firms (ibid). Ramdulal advised Kaliprasad to appease the city's prominent brahmin fraternity, who were still indispensable for any religious occasion in Hindu households and whose stamp of approval was absolutely compulsory for a lower-caste Hindu to ensure upward mobility (ibid). Accordingly, Kaliprasad showered money and gifts on the brahmins and his efforts bore fruit—Kaliprasad emerged as a winner and Ramdulal fittingly summed up the situation with a sarcastic comment: 'I keep caste in my coffers!'[4]

Since affluence became the order of the day, the new Bengali hopefuls from humble background seemed obsessed with making their fortunes, and in so doing established themselves as successors to the previous social order where only men of distinguished birth could achieve social status and exercise authority. There was thus an undeclared competition among the parvenu to obtain honorary titles by engaging themselves in close dealings with the colonial rulers who could bring them the social repute they always longed for (ibid).

The efforts of these nouveau riche groups to raise their social status were predisposed to caste bias. These arrivistes recognized that the only way to guarantee their newly earned social status in the long term was to bolster their social location. This was to be coupled with traditionalistic elements, the primary means of which was to turn to the customary social system based on caste principles. Thus the parvenu, although not upper caste by birth, adopted brahmin lifestyles, proclaimed their privileged status by virtue of their wealth and at the same time increasingly disassociated themselves from their ambiguous background, as that would prove to be unprofitable for their long term strategy of maintaining their newly earned status on a permanent basis; a surreptitious weapon so far only used by the people of higher origin by virtue of their dignified birth. A few events of this period will suffice to show how the nouveaux riches disregarded their previously ordinary social rank and embraced traditional brahmanical social regulations. Raja Nabakrishna Deb (1733-1797) was a typical representative of the new political norms and social aspirations of this period. Nabakrishna, a man of obscure origins, started as a Persian teacher to Warren Hastings as early as 1750 (ibid: 28). As a loyal ally to the British, he was rewarded when the British occupied Calcutta. By 1767 he was appointed as the political intermediary to the company, serving mainly as an agent between native aspirants and the company (ibid) and his constant faithfulness to the company also secured him the coveted title maharaja,[5] an honour previously unthinkable for a man of ambiguous origin. The new raja started enacting the role expected of kings or zamindars, the new metropolis being his chiefdom.

Nabakrishna's grandson Radhakanta (1784-1867) was arguably the most prominent orthodox leader of nineteenth-century Bengal, upholding social conservatism by following brahmanical social standards. He became the leader of a party of orthodox Hindus that acrimoniously opposed liberal-minded Hindus like Rammohan Roy (1774-1833) who advocated social and religious reforms.[6] Although a loyal supporter of the British government, Radhakanta was opposed to any interference by the government in the social and religious life of the people and struggled to preserve the orthodox social order by upholding brahmanical social principles and maintaining the abject condition of women. Thus although *sati* or widow burning was not practised in his own family, he came forward to defend this inhuman custom when the government contemplated its abolition.[7]

A list of rich Bengalis in Calcutta prepared in the 1820s[8] further demonstrates the social authority enjoyed by the people of unassuming background merely by virtue of their financial prowess. It mentions that most of these men became rich in the late eighteenth century when social changes made their efforts to ignore the venerable caste hierarchy relatively unproblematic. The ten men in the list are: (*i*) Nimai Charan Mallik, trader and baniya who established the Mallik family of Burrabazar; (*ii*) Raghu and Abhay Charan Mitra, sons of Gobindaram Mitra who in the 1720s was appointed deputy zamindar of Calcutta by the English East India Company and virtually ruled Calcutta and amassed a huge fortune; (*iii*) Madan Mohan Datta, a trader who established the Datta family in Hathkhola; (*iv*) Ramkrishna Mallik, a trader and the founder of the Mallik family of Pathuriaghata; (*v*) Lakshmikanta (Noku) Dhar, the founder of the Posta Raj family, a banker to Clive and other important Britons in Calcutta; (*vi*) Nabakrishna Deb, founder of the Sovabazar Raj family, was the baniya of both Clive and Verelst; (*vii*) Ramlochon Ghosh, the baniya of Warren Hastings and his wife, the founder of the Ghosh family of Pathuriaghata; (*viii*) Gokul Ghoshal, trader and baniya; (*ix*) Darpanarayan Tagore, trader and the *amin* of the Company; and (*x*) Nilmani Tagore, *amin* of the Company.

This list shows that none of these parvenus belonged to any esteemed origin. That this group largely followed the brahmin ideology to sustain their social claims is clarified by accounts of the elaborate patronage of brahmanical ceremonies that these men sponsored. In the *shradhha* (ritual offerings after death) of Nimai Charan Mallik, Rs 15,000 was donated in addition to gold, silver, horses and the feeding of 200,000 beggars. Each of the beggars received two rupees. The total expense was estimated to have been Rs 1,800,000. At his mother's shradhha, Nabakrishna Deb was said to have spent around Rs 900,000. The eldest son of Madan Mohan Datta of Hathkhola was Ramtanu (known in the city as Tanubabu) whose entire house was washed every day with rosewater and *attar* (perfume oil). He banned the entry of brass or bell metal utensils in his house. Members of the house and guests ate off gold and silver plates (a hundred of these were used every day). The dhotis he wore came specially ordered from Dhaka and cost Rs 45 each. He wore a dhoti only once and would tear off the border so that it did not rub against his waist. His lifestyle became the byword for luxury (ibid). People used to say '*babu to babu Tanubabu*' (if you want an example of a *babu* that would be Tanubabu). The word 'babu' used to denote affluent and indolent gentlemen given to a life of luxury.[9] However, affluence was still not considered to be the only yardstick of good taste and ensuing social eminence.[10] A description of Dwarakanath's palace in Belgachia in north

Calcutta, where he used to entertain his European and Indian guests, provides a typical example of the aesthetic sensibilities (or lack of them) of the nouveaux riches of Calcutta (ibid).[11] Mere opulence did not lessen the requirement of genuine social status along caste lines. Thus the humorous doggerel about the city's lack of untainted honour that could only be found in the lifestyles of high-caste individuals and which was considered absent in the wealthy social representatives of ambiguous backgrounds went like this:

> *Pirali kayet tāti aar sonar bene korle abad tara desh boye dhon ene.*[12] (Seth 1934: 318)
>
> A group of people from tainted origins like the *pirali*, kayastha, weavers, and traders started habitation in this new place only by virtue of their money.

Another ballad on the changing social scenario that was taking place in the new metropolis in which legitimacy based on one's origin was losing significance and where money was becoming the crucial factor in determining social status scorned the propensity thus,

> *Dhanyo he kolikata, dhanyo he tumi/jatakichu notuner tumi janmobhumi/ratarati barolok hoibar tore/ghar chere kolikata giye bas kore.* (ibid: 314)
>
> The great city Calcutta is unique indeed: it is the origin of all that is new/only those who want to become rich overnight rush here, abandoning their homes.

The intrinsic worthlessness of the money-based culture that was booming in the city of opportunity was criticized relentlessly in humorous doggerel, proverbs, jokes, and rhymes of contemporary society. The nouveaux riches were severely condemned for their attempt to emulate the lofty traditions of the people of authentic origins, many legendary proverbs of the nineteenth century point out the triviality of the new social scene:

> *Ghare nai sambhabona, bahire tai babuana.* (Dey 1952: 317)
>
> The lack of prosperity at home but flaunting their 'wealth' outside.

or,

> *Ghare nai asthorambha, bahire tai kocha lamba.* (ibid)
>
> Sheer fiasco at home makes these upstarts indulge in ludicrous foppishness.

As the new social milieu of early Calcutta granted people from humble backgrounds the opportunity to attempt modifications to orthodox social norms regarding caste and ancestry, the conventional values that used to bind society began to break down. During this period, bribery, embezzlement of funds and forgery of documents became the order of the day among the new Bengali elite as they were motivated by making their fortunes as fast as possible (Sumanta Banerjee 1989: 25) and thereby attain the social status and authority that they coveted. At the same time, the leisurely and elaborate lifestyle of these baniyas and dewans, quite frequently based on corrupt behaviour, became the means of drawing the attention of their new rulers and thereby achieving honorary titles which would help them establish dynasties that could be regarded as successors to the old Hindu maharajas and 'rajas' (ibid).[13] A popular song of the mid-nineteenth century sums up the social mores thus:

> *Ajab shahar Kolketa/Randi bari juri gari michey kathar ki keta.*
> (Sinha [1861] 1977: 46)
>
> A strange city Calcutta is, where whores, houses, carriages, and cars abound/And how stylish it is to tell lies here.

For the poorer classes, however, social change was of little concern, since the practice of the arrivistes was always beyond their reach, as was the lifestyle of the high-caste groups. Subsequently, the expensive habits of the nouveaux riches to throw parties were often the target of the urban humorists. For example, in the 1840s when Dwarakanath Tagore gave extravagant dinner parties for the top English administrators in north Calcutta, the lower orders used to go around the streets singing mockingly about these parties:

> *Belgachiar bagane hoy chhuri-katar jhonjhonani/Khana khaoar koto moja/Amra tar ki jani?/Jane Thakur Company.*
>
> (Soudamini Debi 1912: 232)
>
> Knives and forks are clattering in the Belgachia garden house/ How delightful with all that food around!/But what do we know about it?/It is all an affair of the Tagore Company.

This verse also indicated the arrivistes' violation of social norms by sharing food with the foreigners only to gain economic benefits. This was considered a disgusting disregard of the norms of purity usually only confined to people of lower origins. The competition among the city's arrivistes to rise in the social order by disregarding their social origins or norms earned the contempt of the lower orders who unlike the newly wealthy agents of disputed origins, had no prospect of economic gain in the new metropolis, and thus were not a part of this social race (Sumanta Banerjee 1989: 86). The mockery of the attempts by the nouveaux riches to move up the social order in the songs and poems of the lower orders exemplified their frustration of not being able to achieve the same status. When Pritiram Marh, the low-caste millionaire, like many of his contemporary low-caste arrivistes, desired to buy his way to the upper strata of the society and failed, the city of Calcutta hummed the following verse composed by the humorists of the lower order of the society:

> *Dulal holo Sarkar, Akkur holo Datta, Ami kina thakbo je kaiborta sei kaiborta!* (Seth 1934: 314)
>
> If Dulal (Ramdulal Dey) has earned the reputed title of 'Sarkar', and Akkur (Akrur Datta who accumulated wealth as a contractor of the Company) has managed to achieve a reasonably high caste status, why should I remain the same 'kaibarta' (the lower caste groups comprised of the fishermen and agriculturists) as I was before?

The leisurely and improper lifestyle of these groups stood in sharp contrast to the standards of the authentic and ideology-based brahmanical socio-religious order. The emergence of Bengali babus, claiming social clout only on the basis of their opulence, thus viewed as representatives of degenerate lifestyles, smoking hemp, accompanied by expensive meals, visiting *baijis* (north Indian dancers whose *nautch* performances became a mark of aristocratic leisure in nineteenth-century Bengal).[14] A rhyme in the form of a street-guide for pilgrims to the holy places of the new metropolis illustrated the rapidly changing social standards:

> *Bagbajare gaajar adda, gulir Konnogore,*
> *Battalai moder adda, chandur Bowbajare.*
> *Ei shab mahatirtha je na chokhe heray,*
> *Tar moto mahapapi nai trisangsarey.*
>
> (ibid: 133)
>
> Bagbazar is the hub of hemp-smoking, Konnagar of opium pills. Battola is the centre of drinking, and Bowbazar of opium smoking. If anyone fails to visit these places there cannot be a worse sinner than him in the three worlds of heaven, earth, and hell.

But who were these often ridiculed but mostly respected group of people generally termed as the bhadralok during late eighteenth- and nineteenth-century Bengal? The term *bhadralok* is quite frequently used in the discourse of the Bengali intelligentsia during this period to illustrate the fragmented antagonistic and ambiguous social relations between the different castes and classes during this period. In this book the term 'bhadralok' is used as a generic term to indicate the families who moved into Calcutta during the latter half of the eighteenth century and the early part of the nineteenth century (see also Chapter 1). They emerged as a very large body of a hierarchical, heterogeneous, upwardly mobile community of professionals, bureaucrats, businessmen, and civil servants under colonial rule. In their attempts to fulfil their own socio-political aspirations, they acted as intermediaries between the British rulers and the common people. The term is also used as a useful analytic category to describe the distinct group that was formed out of the social challenge to brahmanical caste supremacy where changing one's social status depended on acquiring wealth in a new metropolis. The word '*bhadra*', a Sanskrit term, usually denotes many values including property, particularly homestead property. It is also used to refer to gentility. From the early nineteenth century other than the much criticized babus[15] a bhadralok group began to emerge as a social category and became practically an institution in the mid-nineteenth century. In its institutional sense the term was first used by Bhabanicharan Bandopadhyay (1787-1848). Native clerical and petty officials serving the British colonial state, the nouveaux riches, new zamindars, and the entrepreneurs were made the themes of satirical works of Bandyopadhyay like *Kolikata Kamalalay* (1823), *Naba Babu Bilas* (1825), *Naba Bibi Bilas* (1831), and he ridiculed this group by coining the new term 'bhadralok'. The *nabya-bhadralok* or the new gentlemen, according to him, amassed wealth after coming in contact with the Europeans, and being influenced by them, they became indifferent to the religion and culture of their ancestors.

By the mid-nineteenth century, the bhadralok seemed to have gained social recognition. From this time onwards, the administrative and the landed middle classes of the nineteenth century came to be known in general as bhadralok, whose hallmarks were education and wealth.[16] Their aspirations were to make their newly earned social status permanent by aligning themselves with hierarchical social rules based on caste ideology. Thus the more orthodox attitude of the bhadralok marked them as different to the defiant babus. The reason for this apparent difference between the two social groups emerging almost during the same period is well illustrated while discussing the bhadralok

The bhadralok were a heterogeneous urban community of different castes and classes that described themselves on the one hand as separate from the feudal aristocracy and the peasants of the rural areas and on the other hand distinct from the English administrator and the native low people of the new city. A brief discussion on the foundation of the *Gourdeshiya Bhadraloker Sabha* or 'The Society of Bengali Bhadralok' on 16 February 1823 at Hindu College will help to clarify the social structure of this multifarious group. The Sabha clearly divided the new Bengali urban elites into two categories: bhadralok and *abhadralok,* or *itarlok* or *chotolok*, literally meaning people of low origin (S. N. Mukherjee 1975: 62). The bhadralok included the *madhyabitta* or middle-ranked group of distinct culture and taste, and for the abhadralok[17] to achieve the coveted bhadralok title that might establish desirable origins adherence to upper-caste social norms was compulsory. In conformity with what S. N. Mukherjee claims, 'the bhadralok status was not ascriptive, it had to be acquired' (ibid). The acquisition of high status hinged on achieving a respectable place in the hierarchical social order based on caste dynamics. The caste-biased nature of the bhadralok showed a concern to establish a sustainable social authority based on traditional brahmanical norms, in contrast to the more rebellious attitudes of the babus who thought themselves to be triumphant against social disparity solely by virtue of their material success.

The bulk of the group named bhadralok, however, was hardly composed of brahmins. The social leaders of the bhadralok belonged to all three of the upper castes of Bengal: the brahmins, baidyas and kayasthas. That membership was open to people of all backgrounds is clear from the fact that Radhakanta Deb's first list of 'Principal Hindoo Inhabitants of Calcutta' in 1822 included at least seven families who came from disputably low origins—they were the subarnabaniks, tili, and members of the weaver castes.[18] People of these caste groups who acquired bhadralok status imitated high-caste values, flaunting their newly earned wealth. The Sheths of Calcutta, although a merchant group, opened reading rooms for the educated young natives of Calcutta, as education had always been considered a forte of brahmins; they also acted as justice of peace in many social scuffles in order to establish their social authority. But their most distinguished attempt to achieve social status based on brahmanical activities was the supply of holy water to the images at Somnath and Dwarakanath. Imitating high-caste brahmins they established their family deity 'Radhakanta Jew' in Calcutta (L. N. Ghosh 1983: 155-57).[19] Nabakissen Mitra, a moulik kayastha (not a kayastha of high origin) by virtue of his immense wealth modelled himself after traditional rajas and patronised kulin brahmins settled in Calcutta with funds. Notable brahmin pandits like Jagannath Tarkapanchanan, Baneshwar Vidyalankar, and Radhakanta Tarkabagish were all indebted to Nabakissen Mitra and helped him in establishing his social authority (N. N. Ghose 1901: 171-234). He patronised *ghataks* (matchmakers) and with their help married his grandson Radhakanta Deb to a kulin kayastha family thereby raising his social status (ibid).[20] The subarnabaniks of Pathuriaghata and Chorabagan were equally powerful (L. N. Ghosh 1983: 51); the subarnabanik leader of Burrabazar, Nimai Charan Mullick went on to become the chairman of the Dharma Sabha in 1830 (ibid: 68).

The power structure of indigenous society were distributed amongst various *dals* or factions and although it is not possible to get the exact number of dals in the Calcutta of that period, it was generally agreed that between 1820 and 1850 there were five major dals in the city. These most important dals were led by Radhakanta Deb, Ashutosh Dey, the Tagores, Bishwanath Motilal and Kalinath Munshi.[21] Of these only the Tagores were of brahmin origin but, as mentioned earlier, their status was a tainted one. All these dals were open to membership of people of different origins as long as the dals benefited from the members' financial prowess or other social influences but all the dals practised social rules based on strict high-caste values.[22] When the Dharma Sabha almost became a caste tribunal in the 1840s, Deb's newspaper *Samachar Chandrika* published the proceedings of his dals on a regular basis. It seems that in every meeting of the dals the *dalpati*, that is, Deb, used to pass judgments on about 200 petitions on caste cases and *dans* (gifts to brahmins), drawing inferences from caste-based customs.[23]

The chief function of each dal was to preserve the caste, social status, and religion of each member. It was suggested that heads of different dals, like real kings, should use their utmost power to keep all the members within the orthodox tradition which was indisputably brahmanical in nature so as to maintain the social order. For example, if any man through vicious inclination ate what he was not supposed to eat or drank what was inappropriate for him to drink, the leader of the dal immediately served notice to all its other members that such a person had fallen and no one was to have any social intercourse with him.[24] Thus the threat of erosion of the ideological basis of Hindu social order, in a new social environment, was not a crisis just for the brahmins or people of other upper castes; people of ambiguous origins who made it into the elitist circle of the bhadralok were in many senses even more protective of the native hierarchy based on brahmanical norms to maintain their own social ranks.

In a situation like this, along with the threat of erosion of the ideological basis of the Hindu social order, there was simultaneously the attrition of disaffection of the younger generations under the influence of Christian missionaries. Western culture exercised a tremendous attraction on the youth, and it led to a subsequent aspiration to modernity among the western-educated natives. Between 1827-1828, Henry Louis Vivian Derozio, a young lecturer of Presidency College, exposed his students to European history leading them to react against the native orthodox social order and subsequently to challenge British colonization in India.[25] He encouraged their attempts to attack conservative native habits by eating beef and taunting the image of goddess Kali with the greeting: 'Good morning Madam'.[26] Danger also loomed in the form of a proposed alteration to the orthodox ideological basis of native existence from the Brahmo Samaj.[27] Together these events reinforced the traditional conservatism of native agents, but not all of them were men of reputed births. Thus a group of men from ambiguous backgrounds vouched for traditional conservatism to eradicate the societal split between them and their distinguished counterparts. The permissiveness of the eighteenth century that allowed people of low-caste backgrounds to raise their status consequently evaporated. Thus we see a tendency to protect traditional caste hierarchy revived both by high-caste upper-class people as well as those of ambiguous origins who managed to secure a higher social status during the rapidly changing period of early colonial Bengal. It was thus not surprising that Ashutosh Dey, whose father Ramdulal Dey, mentioned earlier, had scoffed at caste minutiae, turned out to be one of the most prominent leaders of the orthodox Dharma Sabha, imposing sanctions on anyone violating the traditional caste norms. He forced one Madhusudan Mitra to forsake his daughter-in-law as the son had married her in violation of caste norms. Madhusudan's son was required to do penance in order to gain re-entry into the Dharma Sabha, an icon of social authority during the colonial era.[28]

THE CURIOUS CASE OF THE BRAHMINS

The city of Calcutta enjoyed two-fold economic predominance in colonial India: both as the hub of British commerce, shipping, finance, and investments in the east in general, and also as the city where British capital was in command more overpoweringly than anywhere else in India (Sumit Sarkar 1997: 164). Just before the First World War, about three-fifths of the total British capital invested in India was based in Calcutta (R. Ray 1984: 14-16). Calcutta was also the centre of the vital British dominated import-export trade,[29] which successfully paid for

British trade deficits with the rest of the world. The growing interests of the British managing agencies in Bengal's economy ultimately led to a collective British monopoly in the field of commerce, finance, railways, tea plantations, coal mines, and jute mills, a trend that ultimately changed the status of Bengal owing to the significant changes in socio-political and economic areas. Thus the city of Calcutta placed at the heart of all these activities became a flourishing symbol of majestic grandeur, power, and profit (A. Bagchi 1972; Sumit Sarkar 1997). In the early days of the pre-eminence of the city it was mainly inhabited by British traders, poor whites and Eurasians, and a large number of Muslim service groups,[30] and the migrants from villages of poor areas of Bengal, who were, in most cases, men of ambiguous origins,[31] who in seeking good fortune headed for Calcutta.

The members of the upper strata of society on the other hand, did not require any effective change in their livelihood, and nor were they convinced of the prospect of a profitable and reputable lifestyle in the new metropolis. Instead they were content with the patronage that they received from the maharajas and rajas in the form of land donated to them, and from gifts and fees from local notables and from householders with whom they had hereditary *jajmani* associations (Sumit Sarkar 1997: 222).[32] However, this relatively easy existence had come to an end by the early nineteenth century due to various socio-political events. For example, there had been Maratha raids, affecting parts of the south-west and the west in the eighteenth century followed by the devastating famine of 1770 in which Midnapore, Hooghly, Burdwan, and Nadia were the worst-affected districts (P. Sinha 1965: 50-53).[33] The rapid changes in land rights through company revenue experimentations which crystallized in the Permanent Settlement of 1793 further exacerbated the situation (ibid: 223). The new sunset laws[34] must have also changed the flow of allowances to the brahmins which now seemed a prohibitive extravagance for the landed gentry (ibid). Moreover, the decline of traditional crafts under the colonial regime of one-way free trade could also have intensified the financially depressing situation for the rural brahmins surviving on this expertise.[35] And, eventually, there were the decisive consequences of the change in the flow of the Ganges eastwards, sending the old heartland of brahmanical culture of the delta region irrevocably into decline, a process quickened after the mid-nineteenth century by railway embankments blocking old drainage patterns (P. Sinha 1978: 224).[36]

In sharp contrast, the growing metropolis of Calcutta emerged as a place of new opportunities for a significant part of the traditional upper-caste coterie. Arrivistes of low origins who accumulated massive wealth through beneficial alliances with the early British traders and administrators initially dominated native life in Calcutta. This faction increasingly experimented with independent private enterprise and then subsequently settled down as urban real estate owners and zamindars proclaiming social authority, a trend previously unimaginable for people of their background. Most of them were from non-brahmin, and at times from traditional low-caste groups (ibid). The opulence and subsequent social authority that this group commanded must have caught the attention of the upper-caste coterie, especially at a time when their assured sources of income were under threat, and they eventually decided to adorn contemporary city life with their traditional presence. This change was welcomed by the people of ambiguous origins as well as by the colonial masters as they needed direct help from the brahmin literati for administrative purposes. This was a trend that became necessary in 1780 because Hastings had decreed that matters of inheritance, marriage, caste and other religious issues or institutions of the Hindus were to be administered according to the laws of the *Shastras*.[37] Consequently, judge-pandits had to be appointed to assist Englishmen in settling issues at the civil courts of the company,[38] a preference reinstating the status of the brahmins even in the less socially stratified context of the new metropolis.[39] But the window of opportunity for the traditional literati was restricted in nature; it did not last long with the triumph of Macaulay's anglicization policy which was much more compatible with the colonial course of action as the British did not have to rely on the native literati to run the administration anymore.

In the interaction between the colonial rulers and the brahmin pandits (and later on Hindu liberals and Hindu conservatives too) what was gradually and carefully constructed was the myth of a golden past of the native existence via the ideal of high-caste traditions (see also Chapter 1). This myth successively constructed a new ideal of womanhood, and colonial rule reinforced the early notion of ideal womanhood on an unshakeable basis, representing an amalgamation of brahmanical values. This ideal necessarily presupposed that there was a specified Hindu identity, which essentially belonged to the high-caste people and in the traditions of that group the image of ideal womanhood functioned as a historical truth. The link between Hindu identity and a belief that the 'authentic' representation of that identity could only be found in influential Hindu texts was established.

THE 'BRAHMANIZATION' AND 'WESTERNIZATION' OF HINDUISM

Western colonization contributed to the modern construction of Hinduism in two important ways, which ultimately consolidated the social stratification of the caste system. Firstly, the core of Indian religion was located in certain Sanskrit texts (the selection of which was, in most cases, devoid of any deep social or religious thought concerning India's diverse cultural tradition),[40] a practice which can be termed as the 'Brahmanization' of Hindu religions. Secondly, there was an implicit (and at times also explicit) tendency to define the Hindu religion in terms of a 'normative paradigm of religion based upon contemporary western understandings of the Judaeo-Christian traditions' (King 1999: 101). The second endeavour can be considered to constitute the 'westernization'[41] of the Hindu religion, which was focused mostly on Hinduism. These two processes are closely interrelated and in due course solidified the hierarchical social order.

The western attempt to locate the core of the Hindu religion in ancient texts, a tendency already mentioned in reference to Warren Hastings' endeavour to coordinate colonial administrative policies derived from scriptural laws, started with the western literary bias towards textualisation[42] (Breckenridge and Van der Veer 1993: 23-44). Thus, significantly, this process of colonization limited itself in the process of textualising native culture and engaged in the strenuous process of forcing these texts to provide evidence that they originally did not contain (ibid: 23-44). This is not to claim that before colonization Indian culture did not have its own literary traditions; rather I want to emphasize that the way in which western presuppositions about the role of sacred texts created an Orientalist bias towards focusing upon such texts as the only locus of Indian religiosity was unprecedented.[43] This over-emphasis on sacred texts was an easy process for academics and highly educated western administrators, because as a result of their training and background, they were already inclined towards prioritising literary forms of expressions. Importantly, some of the early European translators of sacred Indian texts were also Christian missionaries, who in their translations decisively constructed uniform texts and a homogenized written canon through their imposition of western philological standards on Indian materials (King 1999: 101-03). As Frykenberg argues, 'Indeed, perhaps no single set of movements did more to further the growth of modern Hinduism in its corporate and its revivalistic forms than missionary institutions' (Frykenberg 1989: 39).

In the eighteenth century, when through this process, the colonial power was becoming instrumental in facilitating the rise of a centralized and modern Hinduism; the new Hinduism increasingly became a comfortable vehicle for the privileged coterie.[44] At the beginning of the process of integrating a vast collection of myths, beliefs, rituals, and laws into a coherent religion, and of shaping an amorphous heritage into a rational faith known as Hinduism, it never became a representative of the majority community, that is, the Hindus, of India. Even at the end of this process when this Hindu identity was transformed into a national identity to fight against the colonial rulers it did not become a representative of the majority community of India. Throughout this process the oral, popular, or, the non-brahmin, lower-caste (and class) aspect was either ignored or derogated as evidence of the degradation of Hinduism into superstitious practices that had no link with Hindu sacred texts.[45] The reliability and the range of the source material available to them by the end of the nineteenth and early twentieth centuries when they were engaged in writing Indian social history is another question, which needs to be considered. In most of the cases the interpretations were highly coloured by the dominant intellectual presuppositions of European scholars at that time. As Thapar (1993: 27) has pointed out the transcreation of non-European concepts through European lenses resulted in grave misunderstandings.

At another level, the sources on India available to those who were not professional Indologists were generally limited but equally misleading. The primary sources in this case became the Census Reports or available translations of the *Dharmashastras* (T. Sarkar 2001: 83). The abortive move by the Deputy Census Commissioner Gait in 1910 to exclude castes not served by brahmins, kept out from temples, or suffering from similar disabilities from the category of Hindu is a clear case of colonial contribution towards the intensification of social stratifications (ibid: 84).[46] A major reason for this bias is what became well known in the nineteenth century as the Aryan theory. The basis of this theory was the equation of language and race. In Europe a division was forged between the Aryan and the Semitic races based on the Indo-European hypothesis and in India it became that of the Aryan and Dravidian, with the upper castes been seen as the descendents of the Aryans (Thapar 1993). This theory became hugely popular among the native elites as they could differentiate themselves from the lower castes believed to be non-Aryans.[47] For a European audience there were also the translations of the texts and works of Indologists such as, William Jones (1799) and Henry Thomas Colebrooke (1895) or historians such as Vincent Smith (1919) and Grant Duff (1832) with their eurocentric biases towards the interpretation and understanding of these texts. In all these works it was argued that Aryans were implicitly superior to the non-Aryans as they were the initial conquerors who had founded civilizations in both Europe and Asia (Thapar 1993: 29). In India, the arrival of the Aryans was associated with the compilation of the Rig Veda and this was believed to be the starting point of Indian civilization.[48] Caste society was explained as being based on racial segregation with the Aryans forming the higher castes and the system was defended as a scientific division of society based on racial groupings to preserve identity.[49]

It would, however, be partial not to reiterate the fact that long before colonial rule caste hierarchy played an important role in establishing brahmanical privilege in the Indian social system. Over decades in different regions the questions of caste and caste practices constantly surfaced and the judicial powers had to arbitrate in many cases to settle them. The attempts of low castes to move up were also a familiar aspect of the caste system and were widely documented during the pre-colonial period (Srinivas 1962: 91). Similarly, in the colonial period the increasing upward mobility of mixed social groups was looming large and, more dangerously, a foreign administrative power was taking over again, signalling serious social and moral corruption within the brahmanical ideal social order. Here again the brahmins used these events as an opportunity to revamp the social order in their favour by minimizing the significance of other social groups to the foreign rulers through their interpretation and transcreation of a select number of sacred texts.

Nonetheless, the colonial era was different because for the first time the scale on which the social authority could be negotiated, arbitrated or changed was much wider, as it operated on a pan-Indian basis. Most importantly, the influence of the colonial administrative system was much wider. For the colonial rulers it was not possible to avoid dealing with caste as part of their governance (U. Chakravarti 2003: 116-17),[50] and this was bound to make a difference to the way caste was understood and measured. The colonial officials involved in recording caste status in different regions[51] often took 'knowledgeable' and 'authentic' opinion from the Sanskrit scholars. The result was again the production of an elitist, brahmanical view of social stratifications. For example, in Bengal the Sanskrit scholar Rajendralal Mitra (1823/24-1891)[52] was made the arbiter by the Lieutenant Governor of the social position of different castes. Mitra predictably, argued that caste questions should be settled by the Census authorities by following the ancient scriptures of the Hindus, and not by conceding any particular claim of any particular caste or class (ibid: 117). Mitra, a kayastha bhadralok, was perhaps more brahmin than a real brahmin in his clinging to traditional social norms. However, the representatives of the lower castes were determined to use this trend of relying on Census reports based on caste hierarchies to change their social status in terms of appealing to the colonial authorities. They provided evidence of unlawful torture and dominance of high castes to the British rulers (Srinivas 1962: 90-110). This evidence was mostly an inversion of the brahmanical theory of the debased origin of the low castes (ibid). Colonial rule gave the low castes one more opportunity to break out of the caste 'prison house' and this was the possibility of conversion to Christianity. Armed with their new identity the low castes could challenge the symbolic world order of the caste system (U. Chakravarti 2003: 119). As a result of this substantial social transformation, the colonial era marked a continuous struggle for both the high and low castes to gain socio-political authority and acceptability, however, on a more encompassing level than in the pre-colonial era.

Understanding the severity of the situation in which an alteration of the hierarchical social order was once again threatened, a group of elites in their attempt to restrict social mobility deliberately omitted the differences between the brahmanical form of religion and local forms of Hinduism. Strategically their main advantage was the colonial bias towards a text-based, monolithic form of religion, which the rulers considered to be the only way to comprehend the multifariousness of Indian culture. On the other hand, there were other groups of elites to whom the brahmanization of Hindu culture was the only plausible way to undertake the reformulation of Hinduism in order to challenge colonial superiority.[53] An amalgamation of both these tendencies culminated in the most notable propensity to emphasize Vedic brahmanical texts, upper-caste beliefs and customs as central, essential, and foundational to Hinduism. As mentioned earlier, Bhabanicharan Bandyopadhyay candidly expressed his disgust at the attempt to devalue the brahmanic bias in indigenous life;[54] on the other hand the emphasis on caste-based structural and normative-aspects of Hinduism was also the contribution of people like Rammohan and Vidyasagar who, coming from the established power structure of Hindu society and its teleological boundaries, did not confront the inequitable power structure by prescribing reformative social actions, nor did they offer any fundamentally opposite ideological alternative.[55] Similarly, the elaborate ritualistic observance of Maharaja Nabakrishna Deb's mother's shraddha, Ramdulal Dey's shraddha held by his son Ashutosh Dey (Mullick 1935: 28) exemplified the inclination of people of humble origin to emulate rigid norms of behaviour in order to firmly establish their social status. As a result pro-brahmanical activities still remained the most effective index of social status in the charmed circle of the bhadralok, and the brahmanic model continued to be one of the most important reference points for reputable social behaviour.[56] In this process the most common ground shared by Rammohan, Vidyasagar, Bhabanicharan, or Radhakanta Deb was the tendency to universalize the conditions and problems of native women in order to construct a national identity in resistance against colonial aggression, and thereby ignore the significant differences in the status of women across the different levels of the caste hierarchy. Thus the 'woman question' of this period not only remained closely associated with the caste question; it also gave rise to a monolithic ideal of native womanhood unlike that of any other phases of Indian history.

We are not trying to suggest, however, that the process of Brahmanization was placed in a cause and effect relationship with the colonization of the Hindu religion. In fact, as we have already noted, the caste-based brahmanical religion was active in its own way in the transformation and appropriation of non-brahmanic religions long before the Muslim and European invasions (King 1999: 98-108). By Brahmanization we mean a process in which the sanskritic culture absorbed and appropriated the non-brahmanical (at times the 'popular' and even the 'tribal') religious forms, which was an effective means of assimilating different and diverse cultural strings and imposing social, political and religious authority on them. Conveniently for the British rulers the brahmin caste represented itself as a self-defined cultural elite that was extremely cooperative with British ideology. Here, it would not be an exaggeration to maintain that in the process of brahmanizing Hinduism the privileged high-caste groups benefited most, as it legitimized their triumph over the tribal, local and lower communities. Moreover, with colonial support high-caste domination resulted in a comprehensive and organized form of religion like never before. As Frykenberg (1989: 89) points out:

> Highly placed and influential groups of Brahmans, supported by Brahmanized non-Brahmans, did most of the defining, the manipulating, and the organizing of the essential elements of what gradually became, for practical purposes, a dynamic new religion. Moreover, this process of reification, this defining and organizing of elements which they did, occurred with the collaboration, whether witting or unwitting, with those who governed the land. What were produced were a centralization, rationalization, and bureaucratization of information. Brahmans have always controlled information. That was their boast. It was they who provided this on a scale so unprecedented that, at least at the level of all-India consciousness, a new religion emerged the likes of which India

> had perhaps never known before. In other words, those who ruled over the executive, judicial and legislative functions of the state and who exercised authority in the administration of state decision were influenced by the hosts of officials who worked with them every day. The hosts handled most of the paperwork.

The sanskritic 'Brahmanization'[57] of the Hindu religion, filtered through colonial discourses, remained a profoundly anti-historical approach as it postulated an ahistorical essentialism to which all forms of Hindu religion were forced to relate. But the surprising element involved in this process is the strategically active participations by the upper-caste colonized people, who saw this process of Orientalization as an opportunity to revive brahmanical superiority. Thus, as Romila Thapar suggests, this new Hinduism, anchored deeply in a brahmanical base and furnished with the elements of upper-caste belief and rituals, was pushed forward as the sole claimant to the inheritance of indigenous Indian religion and clearly as an essential element in developing nationalist identity (Thapar 1985: 21).

Accordingly, the invention of Hinduism as a single 'world religion' also coincided with the rise of a nationalist impulse in India from the nineteenth century onwards. The modern nation-state, undoubtedly, was a product of European socio-political and economic developments from the sixteenth century onwards and the introduction of the nationalist model into Asia was a further product of European imperialism in this area. It is ironic that the Hindu nationalists who fought so strongly against British imperialism accepted notions of 'nationhood' and Hinduism that were ultimately acquired from their imperial rulers.[58] But perhaps this is all that the opponents of colonialism could do under circumstances where the concept of the nation-state essentially provided an archetypal model for all aspects of social, economic and political advantages for the indigenous people. Romila Thapar points to the logic behind the construction of a common Hindu identity thus:

> Since it was easy to recognize other communities on the basis of religion, such as Muslims and Christians, an effort was made to consolidate a parallel Hindu community . . . In Gramsci's terms, the class which wishes to become hegemonic has to nationalize itself. (Thapar 1989: 230)

In the hands of British Orientalists, missionaries and colonial administrators the heterogeneous aspects of a complex tradition came to be treated in a monolithic and linear fashion. In other words, Orientalists and missionaries were largely instrumental in transforming a disparate tradition into a uniform and manageable system, predominantly brahmanical in nature, or at least to retract their own biases of what a religion should look like mainly to serve their own purposes. In doing this they were assisted by native pandits of reputed origins who were in an advantageous position to interpret issues of important social significances according to their convenience.[59] The scheming moves of the brahmin pandits were however restricted within the parameters set by their colonial masters to complement their requirements.[60] India was to be governed by its own laws which were to found only in its ancient texts, but these laws were to be ordered in a scientific and rational way for the benefits of both the rulers and the ruled (King 1999: 108-16). The investigations of the Indian past thus became necessary and became known as the Indo-European Hypothesis. The basis of this hypothesis was the equation of language and race and the association of the theory with India had its genesis in the philological relationships noticed between Sanskrit and Greek, Latin and other European languages (Thapar 1985: 28).[61]

Because within the Orientalist project various western scholars contributed in producing a monolithic, textualized version of Hinduism and eventually a text-based Indian past that would fit well with the western Christian theological structure, the perception of the Indian past was influenced in two contradictory ways (U. Chakravarti 1989: 29). One strand was represented by the Orientalists whose reconstruction of the glory of Indian civilization in the ancient past was accepted in totality by nineteenth-century Indian writers and nationalists, mainly to regain the self-esteem that was lost following the establishment of colonial rule. The other strand was the Utilitarian and Evangelical attack on contemporary India, especially on the visibly low status of women. The degeneration of Hindu civilization and the abject position of Hindu women as requiring the 'protection' and 'intervention' of the colonial state were the two most important aspects of colonial politics. On both grounds British rule in India could be justified by claiming moral superiority. Interestingly, Orientalism and Utilitarianism coalesced in the works of early nineteenth-century nationalist writers[62] who constructed a successful and enduring image of ideal womanhood in the lost past to counter the oppressed accusations regarding the existence of Indian women in the present (ibid: 30). However, these trends relied on an archaic patriarchal, caste-based and class-based treatise on the Indian/ Hindu way of life, ignoring diverse regional voices. The result was a homogenized patriarchal and hierarchical form of religious tradition and cultural identity. In part the production of this may be due to the fact that status distinctions were deeply ingrained in British society, but the lack of concern for low-caste ways of life may also be explained as a natural consequence of a heavy reliance on the conservative indigenous elite, the brahmin pandits.

Because the colonial tendency to reconstruct the Indian past gradually assumed a practical and utilitarian function, the main concern no longer remained one of discovering the treasure of Sanskrit literature, but rather of stratifying the ancient texts to establish colonial authority (ibid). The social stratifications based on ancient literature were consequently on the debates about the present. Uma Chakravarti (ibid: 32) further points out that

> What was of lasting significance from the point of view of historical consciousness was the fact that the reconstruction of the past was no longer confined to the pages of Asiatic researches, read by a select few. The reconstructed past was increasingly appearing in pamphlets and vernacular journals,

> made possible with the introduction of printing, and the participants in this were the newly emerging intelligentsia, composed of both traditional and modern elements who perceived themselves as interpreters of tradition in a changing situation. This intelligentsia could regard itself as a product of an 'exhausted' culture but, through the work of the Orientalists, could simultaneously feel optimistic that, despite the present circumstances, they were representative of a culture which had been originally disrupted by historical circumstance but was capable of revitalisation.

Rammohan Roy who among the indigenous intelligentsia epitomizes this dominant trend of restoring the golden past of Indian traditions, is best known for his battle against sati, although his writing and thinking covered plenty of other issues related to Hinduism.[63] Rammohan's predisposition to gender-related issues in reviving the indigenous glorious past concerned the essential correlation between the pre-eminence of a tradition and the status of woman in that traditional arrangement. Rammohan was perhaps the most prominent individual among the reformers who started searching for an alternative version of Hinduism, which eventually led him to the search for non-superstitious and non-ritualized strands in the glorious past of Indian culture, providing an indigenous alternative to degenerate Hinduism in the form of Vedic Hinduism. Disregarding everything except the Vedas and the Upanishads, which he identified as the only authentic core of Hinduism, the golden age of Hindu tradition, was thus conceived as suggesting the period when the Upanishads were composed (Mani 1989: 102-18).

Furthermore, for the colonial masters the superior status of their morality was easy to ascertain by highlighting the low status of woman among the native population. Simultaneously for the subjected natives it was important to show the purity of their women in order to demonstrate the superiority of their tradition, as tradition and the status of women were interchangeable. In an attempt to initiate this venture, attention to high-status women was an obvious focus.[64] The 'woman question', that is, questions concerning women of the higher stratum thus became a concern for both the ruling powers and the colonized agents in the reconstruction of the past, although for completely different reasons (U. Chakravarti 1989: 32-35; Mani 1989: 102-18) and in that process high-caste agendas regarding the issues of caste and gender were once again invigorated.

HEGEMONIC SOCIAL REFORMS AND THE CASTE-BASED PATROLLING OF NATIVE PATRIARCHY

Via the path of the abject conditions of native women British colonialism sought to legitimatize itself and legislation pertaining to social reform marked the legitimization process (Cohn 1983: 165-210). This legislation involved personal and private aspects of life such as marriage, motherhood, and women's relationship to their bodies, sex, and sexuality. These laws subsequently influenced less intimately, but more essentially, property laws and the social hierarchy that enabled the colonial state to ascribe moral identities to the indigenous population (Swapna Banerjee 2001: 1-73).[65] Here, the reformist endeavour of the colonials in their attempt to provide a set of ideals and norms also reformulated the hegemonic nature of native social stratification produced through the passive pathologization of the indigenous female body. The state posing as the guardian of native morality, claiming to be the protector of Bengali women, and making charges of immaturity, brutality, and incompetence against male native agents unsettled native life by interfering in the intimate sphere of Bengali homes and sex lives. Accordingly, the home and the world split, which became the basis for native nationalist agenda (P. Chatterjee 1989: 233-52), was severely challenged by reform proposals, precipitating both moral contestation and political commotion. Interpreted as a direct attack on Indians' residual right to self-definition, objections were voiced not only from *shastric* traditionalists but also from liberal reformers, asserting a principle of non-interference.

The difference between these two groups did not lie in the fact that the former was more rooted in indigenous tradition and the later in westernized notions of democracy and utilitarianism. Their difference, in fact, stemmed from two different readings of the same Hindu custom. While *shastric* injunctionists described Hindu domesticity and customs as unchangeable sources of native identity, any distortion of which would generate devastation of the social order, the liberalists celebrated those changes with the hope of returning to an earlier purity and identified the current situation as arguably the chief source of present decay. They both flaunted brahmanical learning.[66] Moreover, as the state granted relative autonomy to religious beliefs and customs, allowing legislative intervention only if those customs could be shown to violate scriptural injunctions, the reformists and the conservatives shared similar discursive methods and practices to establish their programme. Because of their own training and association in turn this trend was also adopted by people of ambiguous origins, the bhadralok, in fighting their own causes. The pro-hierarchy bias of the colonial rulers, the native elites divided between traditionalist and liberalist camps, and the aspiration of the people of lower origins ultimately resulted in a more intense social discriminatory policy, a development not always intentional but given the nature of the socio-economic and political changes during this phase, it was an inevitable consequence of the British administration in India.

Let us scrutinize two related acts of legislation: the Act of 1829 that abolished the custom of burning alive of Hindu widows and the Act of 1856 that addressed the remarriage of Hindu widows. These two acts illuminated the nature of reformist actions from different angles, and further helped to explain how the uproar that erupted from these reforms were in effect an indigenous reaction to the threat that this legislation posed to native patriarchy, and thus to upper-caste norms and practices. These two legislative acts highlight the fact that behind the reformist legislations and contestations over their *shastric* implications there was a discursive notion of a pure female body which represented an unmarked site that signified not only self-determination for the natives, but also exemplified upper-caste social norms. The precise source of grace for a Hindu woman, who became the repository of power and honour for otherwise defeated Hindu men, was her body. It signalled her unconditional chastity, extending beyond the death of her husband, through an indissoluble, non-consensual infant form of marriage, through her ascetic widowhood, and through her self-immolation.[67] This discourse imposed a disciplinary regimen upon her that controlled and defined her from infancy to death and simultaneously secured the social status of her man as the superior counterpart. Crucial to the understanding of these laws is the division between the reformists and the liberals, already mentioned, against the colonial legal realm. Each was diverse and yet authentically hegemonic in its own analysis of the reformative actions. Each of the legislative laws analysed here related to the mandatory relationship between the compulsory chastity of the native female body and the lineage system resulting from the strict observance of reproductive laws that essentially preserved the hierarchical social structure.

In nineteenth-century Bengal the new urban middle classes or the bhadralok were an internally discriminated group, heterogeneous in its caste composition through which different members had achieved and then subsequently consolidated their socio-economic status.[68] This heterogeneous group in its role as the middlemen of the East India Company's revenue and commercial transactions, benefited immensely from opportunities afforded by colonial rule, but ultimately remained constrained by the conditions of colonial subjugation (Raychaudhuri 1988: 21-56). This in turn gave rise to a new set of socio-moral values combining the bhadralok's material and traditional interests. Consequently, the historiography of nineteenth-century Bengal suggests that the bhadralok encountered a series of struggle between 'tradition' and 'modernity' as a battle between orthodox forces and agents of progressive reforms. This battle was arguably prompted by the scuffle over the legality of widow burning which inaugurated the contested area of the 'woman's question' in colonial India and became the focal point of the conservatives or the reformists. The enthusiasm of both the reformists and the traditional factions of the bhadralok over issues of tradition and modernity, although tied to the economic transformations of the period under colonial rule, was not completely dominated by it.[69] The land reform and trade policies wrought by the East India Company introduced the notion of the private.[70] Furthermore, the subsequent emergence of the bourgeoisie was fundamentally to shape the nature of socio-economic transformations that ultimately emerged as the key to the self-representation of the nascent nation-state and the ideological formation of the native elites (Mani 1998: 42-45; T. Bhattacharya 2005: 1-108).

According to Marxian historians, it was the economic flux of this period that produced conservatism from those with investments in landholdings, and following the same logic a progressive stance from those with investments in the commercial sector. However, the example of the elites of Calcutta does not confirm this scrutiny.[71] Rammohan Ray and Radhakanta Deb, for example, both based in Calcutta which represented anti-sati and pro-sati lobbies respectively did not confirm to such scrutiny. Rammohan Roy's financial status was based initially in money-lending and in his connections with the East India Company, and then consolidated through purchase and management of lands. Radhakanta also was a wealthy landowner and his family's prominence could be traced back to his grandfather Nabakrishna Deb's appointment as the company's interpreter. Radhakanta's stance is difficult to categorize neatly as either anti-reform or pro-reform as he was pro-sati and anti-free trade, but also pro-western education and pro-education for native women (Mani 1998: 46). He approved of widow burning, although sati was not practised in his family, unlike in Rammohan's case.[72] When Rammohan started advocating the abolition of widow immolation and the colonial government finally attempted to abolish the practice, the conservative section of the Hindu community led by Radhakanta Deb strongly opposed any interference by an alien government in the social and religious life of their community. Their primary tactic was to send, through the Dharma Sabha, a petition to the Privy Council in England, urging repeal of the anti-sati regulation. The Sabha also took upon itself the task of defending the traditional Hindu religious and social system against onslaughts from various quarters. It received support from many wealthy Hindu zamindars who held orthodox views and who were for various reasons dissatisfied with the government's revenue policy (Swapan Basu 1978: 91-111). The chief public organ of the Dharma Sabha was the Bengali newspaper *Samachar Chandrika,* whose editor Bhabanicharan Bandyopadhayay was the secretary of the Dharma Sabha. Other than Bhabanicharan, the members of the Sabha were all people of non-brahmin origins who had achieved success in the changing metropolis. These were Radhakanta Deb, Gopimohon Deb, Tarinicharan Mitra, Ramkamal Sen, Kashinath Mullick, Ashutosh Sarkar, Gokulnath Mullick, Baishnabdas Mullick, Nilmani Dey and Harimohan Tagore (ibid: 132) whose pirali origin indicated a lower status than the eminence of pure brahmins. The members of the Sabha were more brahmanical than brahmins and austerely inflexible in terms of any alteration of orthodox Hindu customs which they clung to guarantee their own respectability.[73]

Even Rammohan, who although campaigning vehemently against sati and arguing passionately against orthodox rituals, never relinquished various high-caste practices.[74] All these events suggest that instead of grouping these people as pro-modernity and anti-modernity or conservative, their nature as competing groups represented different phases of modernity or reformism based on their respective socio-cultural needs. This classification did not require consistent reactions from the native participants, but nonetheless it expressed the terms and contours of the discussion of the battle between this 'competing versions of modernity'[75] and how by the involvement of both the colonizers and the colonized, the teleological construction of the 'woman's question' which was mainly the chronicle of the upper-caste subsequently preoccupied the lower-caste people. The resistance of the native agents with respect to questions of gender in the colonial reformist agenda, however, as mentioned, was divided in terms of their dispositions. To make our job straightforward we would rather refer them as liberals/reformers and traditionalists while acknowledging that their outlooks were often obscure and interchangeable.

It is noteworthy that although liberals frequently criticized the sexual duplicity observed in the domestic arena, in real life they did not entirely fight for equal rights for their women (T. Sarkar 2001: 551).[76] Rather, they took two apparently different but inherently similar approaches according to the extent to which their own socio-economic purpose coincided. In the initial stage of the liberal reform movements they based their argument on the hypothesis that it was custom that harmfully circumscribed native domestic life and subsequently rendered the native male agents incompetent compared to their colonial masters. The British goal of creating a 'class of persons Indian in colour and blood, but English in tastes, in opinions, in morals and in intellect'[77] to serve the British administration, began to falter as these groups demanded a share of the privileges enjoyed by the colonial elites (Raychaudhuri 1988: 21-56). Consequently, during the rise of a more nationalist tone the liberal argument, with respect to their claims for the right of self-rule, took a different turn in so far as it was now argued that it was only the erroneous application of native customs and traditions, and not the customs themselves that constricted native women and rendered men incapable of self-governance. So the claim of self-rule based on the superiority of custom-based traditions remained unscathed as did the concept of superior Indian womanhood as emblematic of the custom-driven tradition (P. Chatterjee 1993: 116-35).

Conservative arguments went through similar changes. Tanika Sarkar (2001: 551) shows that the earlier justification of custom-based lifestyles had to draw its strength from a scriptural foundation as well as the larger humanist project involved in it. Both widow immolation and celibate widowhood, they claimed, were based on consent and at the same time elevated the status of ordinary women to goddesses; a status otherwise impossible for ordinary women. But between 1870 and 1880 nationalist elements penetrated this discourse which, although not always contesting political subjugation, claimed complete *cultural* autonomy and protection from foreign intrusion (ibid). The men were already polluted by their close contacts with foreign masters, whereas the women, still mostly untouched in the domestic arena and thus more governed by custom-motivated rituals and norms, embodied the actual freedom that nationalist elements yearned for. Women thus represented cultural authenticity and, more importantly, the future of the nation (ibid). If traditional norms valorized the death of women, then that death would only enlarge their political function; once again faith and custom were more significant symbolically than the actual sacrifice of native women; moreover, a strong emphasis was placed on the women's consent and loyal acquiescence with the customs (ibid). The stress on consent was, however, often beleaguered with dilemmas.

Liberal reformers like Rammohan Ray either eulogized the valour involved in the process[78] or became engaged in detailed interrogation of traditional customs. Women, as a result, remained a discursively minor theme in both the situations (Mani 1998: 65-82). The conservatives, on the other hand, projected the consent of native women as an absolute pronouncement about the entire procedure and eulogized the political function of her death (T. Sarkar 2001: 23-52). What lay between the liberals and the traditionalists was the chaste female body, and the indissoluble marriage that was performed right after a girl entered puberty. Once puberty set in, she had to go through a life cycle of ritual cohabitation with her husband since otherwise her womb would become polluted and the sons of that impure womb would not be able to make offerings to ancestral spirits.[79] Ensuring the proper functioning of ancestral rites to release forefathers from their past deeds, the maintenance of *dharmik* marriage at early infancy was essential. Even if marriage was unconsummated or even after women were widowed, they needed to remain absolutely chaste, since the performance of the marriage sacrament made her the half-body of her husband. Thereby, the alternative of the valorous act of widow immolation was celibate widowhood, which was bounded by ritual prohibitions and deprivations that signified a life of permanent inauspiciousness. This facilitated the widow's task of remaining resolute in her pledge to be the living half-body of her deceased husband (ibid: 546-52). If she lived by those regulations the social order remained undamaged and she in return offered power and honour to the household. Accordingly, by valorization and the aestheticization of orthodox disciplinary norms the patriarchal and hierarchical social order was firmly maintained (U. Chakravarti 2003: 25-66).

The nineteenth-century reform laws I have chosen to discuss here were given particular attention by all sections of Bengali society because they addressed the core area of Hindu hierarchical social existence, their conjugal system. When the Widow Remarriage Act of 1856 was introduced, it specified: 'In the case of a widow who is of full age or whose marriage has been consummated, her own consent shall be sufficient to constitute her remarriage lawful and valid' (Clause VII of Act no. XV of 1856 cited in T. Sarkar 2001: 554). This law not only denied the control of the husband over his wife even after his death, it also gave women the right to self-determination. This clearly endorsed the nullification of the eponymous law-giver, Manu, who had declared that a woman must never acquire rights in her own person and that she must, rather, be ruled by father, husband and son at the different stages of her life (Manu, trans. 1991: Chapter IX, 1-10) The act thus violated the basis of patriarchal orthodoxy in which a girl was traded as an object of exchange between two lineages to maintain the purity of the social hierarchy, a transaction for which the consent of the girl was immaterial. Moreover, the Widow Remarriage Act exacerbated the risk of a husband's loss of exclusive control over his wife's womb. In addition, the consent of the widow opened up the possibility of an entirely different kind of a conjugal relationship, based on premarital love and romance. Tanika Sarkar has pointed out that a widow was the only adult woman who now became available for a romantic and yet licit relationship (ibid: 554) and her presence legalized availability that became a potential danger to society. This trend potentially questioned a lineage pattern based on conjugal relationships where uniformity between comparable caste groups was the primal condition of marital bonding so that the caste structure and lineage system remained protected. At this stage by altering and extending the archetypal equation between women and tradition the discursive breaking down of the equation looked like this: women=tradition=property; moreover, in such a hierarchical social structure the equation emerged like this: (the body of) women=tradition=property=preservation of social hierarchy.

The nineteenth century was thus a period that saw the re-evaluation of the Hindu conjugal system and the laws involved in this reconfiguration were related to the mandatory deaths of Hindu women: first, their physical death through the custom of widow immolation and then a second death through the denial of social and/or sexual rights by virtue of her 'crime' of remaining alive after her husband's demise. The physical death of Hindu women after the demise of their husbands was regarded as a moral virtue (Leslie 1992: 173-89); their sexual and social death was thus associated with ascetic widowhood. However, banning widow burning in 1829 and the Widow Remarriage Act of 1856 arguably threatened to alter the orthodox treatment of Hindu women's physical and sexual deaths upon which native domesticity and social order were wholly dependent. Tanika Sarkar has pointed out that widow immolation was the absolute proof of native women's virtue, an inimitable quality that placed them on a high pedestal and at the same time the courage involved compensated the much criticized effeminacy of their male counterparts. But the act of 1829 criminalized this morally superior act, whereas widow remarriage, a moral sin, was legalized by projecting celibate widowhood as cruel and symbolic of the deprecating status of native womanhood. As a result, the normative arrangement between absolute female chastity and wifehood was shattered, and this also threatened to rupture the material fit between female chastity and material arrangements reflective of the social hierarchy (T. Sarkar 2001: 551-59).

According to Rammohan Ray the nineteenth-century Dayabhaga law was accountable for the greater incidence of sati in Bengal compared to areas where the Mitakshara law prevailed (Mani 1998:59).[80] The Dayabhaga law gave widows limited rights over a husband's property upon his death (Carroll 1989: 792). In doing so, it made the widow a danger to the designs of surviving relatives and thus disposed her to the menace of widow immolation in the name of the orthodox Hindu tradition. The significance of material interest involved behind the scheme of widow immolation is given credibility by a remark made by G. Forbes of the Calcutta Court of Circuit in August 1819. After recommending the prohibition of widow immolation, Forbes said, '[I]t may be worthy of remark that there are no less than 57 civil suits involving property amounting to four lakh of rupees [400,000], now pending in the court in which Hindoo widow ladies are parties' (Mani 1998: 59). Moreover, the parliamentary records of 1821 show that the cases involving families were predominantly from brahmin background (Parliamentary Paper on Hindu Widows 1821: 243). However, there are records of widow immolation taking place among the lower caste groups as well, for example in 1823 out of 575 cases of sati in Bengal there were 234 brahmins, 49 of other castes, and 292 shudras (ibid). But women of low-caste background who eventually became sati did not come from wealthy environments, and, arguably were killed instead to get rid of an otherwise worthless female member of the family using the upper-caste norm to justify the action (Swapan Basu 1978: 31).

It was perhaps not mere coincidence that as landed property was still a prerogative of upper-caste groups the occurrence of sati among the castes was highest among the brahmins as a single caste group (ibid: 32-33). More significantly, the presence of young widows was a threat to the social order which could be eliminated by their traditional deaths. Even the educated and aristocratic circles of Calcutta expressed the same concern for public morality (Bandyopadhyay 2004: 108-42). The alleged growing sexual anarchy in society that was offensive to the high moral standards of the Hindu social system was exclusively attributed to the sexual frustration of Hindu widows and their subsequent inability to restrain their libido. The progressive newspaper *Tattvabodhini Patrika* asked: If men could remarry after the death of their wives, why could the widows not do the same? In the same breath, however, the journal observed that in fact widow remarriage was all the more necessary as the libidinal urge of women was eight times greater than that of men. (There was, of course, no explanation of this calculation in the article. As it seems, this statement only specifies the social trend of portraying women as non-trustworthy in terms of their insatiable sexual appetite.) It was because of them the paper argued, that notoriety was brought into society.[81]

It is necessary to examine Hindu women's rights to property under both the Dayabhaga and Mitakshara schools of Hindu law since they reveal the fixation of the orthodox tradition on the chastity of native women, a compulsory condition to preserve the hierarchical social order. In this process the crooked nature of the reform movements that had more to do with the reestablishment of high-caste authority than improving the abject condition of native women's life is also clear. Prior to 1937, under both the Dayabhaga and Mitakshara schools of Hindu law the widow only succeeded to her husband's estate in the absence of a son, son's son, or son's son's son of the deceased (Carroll 1989: 2-3), a legal model that indicated the unfeasibility of the high-caste widow's right over her husband's property as kulin polygamy was profusely practised in Bengal.[82] However, if the widow inherited her husband's estate she would hold that only for her lifetime; at her death it went [rather than to her own heirs] to the nearest living heir of her deceased husband and thereby maintained the priority of the male authority in the lineage system intact. According to the Dayabhaga law, the widow (in the absence of a son, son's son or son's son's son) succeeded to her husband's share whether or not he was a member of undivided coparcenaries. However, in Mitakshara school, she succeeded to his estate only if he were separate and had simply a right to maintenance if she was a joint coparcener, thereby limiting the chances of the widow's right on her deceased husband's property all the more (ibid: 3).

The concurrence of the practice of the Dayabhaga law and extensive widow immolations in Bengal during this period was thus no coincidence. More importantly, the maintenance of the preordained Hindu social order was ensured under Hindu law of both the schools by setting forth the condition that it was only a chaste wife who was entitled to succeed to her husband's estate, which meant her claims would be undermined if she were subsequently to violate chastity (T. Sarkar 2001: 556). So even after the prohibition of the Widow Immolation Act in 1829, which was observed as the first step towards violating the innermost and purest area of Hindu existence, the marital structure of the Hindu system, the hierarchical, and the orthodox nature of the Hindu society still continued to exist with the assistance of these patriarchal legal arrangements. However, it was a further ruling of the Anglo-Hindu law, as laid down by the Privy Council in 1880 regarding the case of *Maniram Kolita* versus *Keri Kolitani*, that once a widow has succeeded to her deceased husband's estate, she does not forfeit her right to the enjoyment of that property until her death even if she has led an unchaste life (*Maniram Kolita* v. *Keri Kolitani*, ILR 5 Cal. 776 [P.C.] as cited in Carroll 1989: 3), which signalled a complete collapse of the social order as the chastity of women was not recognized as a precondition for property rights anymore. This ruling had the potential of damaging the entire scheme of the Hindu social order since losing the right over women's wombs meant losing the threads of the lineage system and the succeeding stratificatory social order. Moreover, in the discourse of cultural nationalism, a Hindu woman's monogamy was the fixed condition for national distinctiveness and moral superiority, upon which the native claim to nationhood depended. The self-proclamation of the basis of nationhood is well exemplified by the following statement: 'we are but a half-civilised, poor, sorrowful, subjected, despised nation. We have but one jewel, our chaste women, and that is the treasure of seven realms, a priceless jewel . . . this so-called subjection of our women produces this sacred jewel of chastity which still glows radiantly throughout the civilised world, despite centuries of political subjection' (Rajnarayan Basu 1874, cited in T. Sarkar 2001: 555). Women's chastity thus became a political issue apart from having tremendous social worth. It was as if the lost nation and its social order remained alive only in their threatened, challenged and contested wombs, although the threat of the collapse of the social order existed as early as 1856, when the Hindu Widow's Remarriage Act was passed.

With the Prohibition of Widow Immolation Act of 1829 Indian society was faced with the problem of dealing with the sexuality of young widows, and upon this already shaky structure of marital irregularity fell the blow of the 1856 Act legalizing widow marriage. Here again the debate rested on the question of the proper control of the widow's body and the irresolution regarding women's sexual influence in the society. This ultimately had a significant impact on the inheritance law ensuing from the new legal changes, since the purity of the caste order could only be maintained through the proper reproductive activity of women and the proper handling of the material arrangements bestowed on the descendants born out of proper wedlock. With this dependence on female sexuality to preserve the hierarchical social order, Hindu cultural tradition always projected female sexuality as innately evil and uncontrollable. Even Vidyasagar's moralist argument in favour of widow remarriage was a reflection of a widely shared traditional fear of the sexual anarchy that could arise out of uncontrolled female sexuality.[83] With the Widow Remarriage Act of 1856 the unmanageable nature of female sexuality was raised yet again to frighten elderly and unappealing husbands within the threat that their dissatisfied wives might kill them since the choice of remarriage was easily accessible (T. Sarkar 2001: 556-59). The resistance waged against the Act denied women's authority on the ground that her body was her husband's property, an age-old native patriarchal belief that ultimately benefited the settled hierarchy (ibid: 552). Henceforth even after the death of a Hindu man, if his wife did not end her life on his pyre (since by that time widow immolation was legally prohibited), the indissolubility of Hindu marriage still existed in the form of the enforced ascetic celibacy of widows, simply because the bodies of the widows were still deemed the property of their deceased husbands without whose consent no one could fertilize the women. But with the legalization of widow remarriage in 1856 once again the indissolubility of Hindu conjugality was challenged and so was the entire social structure based on it.

Thus, on the one hand the menace of young widows in society made the stringent rule of female sexuality more vulnerable, more so, because the widows under the Dayabhaga law, now had the option of exercising their autonomy;[84] on the other hand the Widow Remarriage Act invited a crisis, concerning the purity of the wombs of native women. In many cases there was ample scope for confusion in relation to the changed lineage pattern after remarriage, which posed a threat against the distribution of property following the family tree pattern. In some cases the courts allowed only low-caste widows to inherit the property of their late husbands to avoid dissent amongst the upper classes (ibid: 546-51). But since the Act was drafted to change the status of the high-caste widows, as they were the official torchbearers of the social progress that the native society was trying to achieve, verdicts were passed where it was stated that the high-caste widows about to remarry had to denounce all claims to their deceased husbands' property (ibid).

Low-caste widows, as an effect of this arrangement, had to lose their rights to share their dead husbands' property too since that would have improved their social status and set an example for their high-caste sisters at the same time (ibid). To simplify the situation, some of the subsequent rulings aspired for maximum gains for both the groups: rights to remarry for the upper-caste widows and for the lower-caste widows the right to share their husbands' marital property. Subsequently, the high-caste widows were only allowed to remarry by abandoning all their previous associations with their deceased husbands' families, and as a result denouncing their property rights so that the material order of the upper strata remained intact. It is arguable that even under the Dayabhaga law widows who survived their husbands' demise could enjoy a usufruct on their husbands' property only on the condition that their chastity remained unscathed. More importantly, even after the banning of widow immolation the widow still remained the mere half-body of her husband so her entire existence was still determined by her deceased husband, and the relationship between private property and the chastity of the women, although no longer unbreakable, still largely enforced strict celibacy practiced by the young widows. Nonetheless, when the Widow Remarriage Act was passed factors like widow remarriage and non-chastity simply overrode Hindu property settlements and the lineage system, which subsequently threatened the lineage-based social chain of command.

In regards to matters, which involved the private aspects of native existence (marriage, inheritance, and property rights of women), there was only one area of undisputed acceptance amongst the interested parties, that is, imposing social norms in conformity with the tenets of orthodox and scriptural Hinduism, which were essentially brahmanical in nature. Change in any other direction required official intervention and authorization and that door could only be opened by legislation, such as the Prohibition of Widow Immolation Act of 1829, and Hindu Widow's Remarriage Act of 1856. Yet even these Acts in their application and interpretation, due to multiple socio-economic constraints, and moreover due to the constant fight between the colonial intervention and the colonized elites' pledge to protect their tradition, were transformed into an instrument for the propagation and imposition of brahmanical values and subsequent patriarchal preservation of the chastity of native women. The ultimate result was the continued supremacy of brahmanical values, which was to be ensured by shielding women's chastity.[85]

NOTES

1 The origin and nature of *baniya*-ship in early Calcutta is described by Bholanath Chunder thus: 'The mode in which business was then transacted, required advances to our workmen for buying the materials for the articles of their handiwork. The country possessed no manufactures or merchants on a large scale, capable of executing extensive orders, and delivering the goods contracted for on the appointed day. The articles had to be collected throughout the country by means of agents . . . there volunteered from among our ancestors, individuals willing to stand as securities, and occupy an intermediate position between the strangers and their countrymen. . . . Both the "dobhashi" [interpreters] and "Baniya" being secured, the English started their business in right earnest and reagular style.' For details of this business transaction and the subsequent social changes that it brought in the native life see Chunder 1978: 462-63.

2 Similar were the beginnings of many other wealthy Bengali families. Laksmikanta (Noku) Dhar, founder of the Posta Raj family in north Calcutta, was said to have saved the life of an Englishman in distress, and through him, found his way into the upper strata of the society. Pritiram Marh, who was born in a low-caste poor family and traded in bamboo logs, made his fortune when the price of bamboo went up in 1780, and set up his palatial mansion in Janbazar. For details see Pramathanath Mullick 1935: 27, 125.

3 A '*pirali* brahmin' is one who transgresses the traditional norms of the caste because of contamination by Muslims. The term 'pirali' historically carried a stigmatized and pejorative connotation. Its eponym is the vizier Mohammad Tahir Pir Ali, who served under the governor of Jessore. Pir Ali was a brahmin who converted to Islam; his actions resulted in the additional conversion of his two brahmin brothers. As a result, orthodox Hindu society shunned the brothers' Hindu relatives (who had not converted), and their descendants

became the pirali, among whom numbered the Tagores. This unorthodox background ultimately led the Tagores to dispense with many of the customs followed by orthodox brahmins, including taboos against meat consumption. But like most other successful brahmin families of Bengal the Tagores also claim their ancestry from those pure brahmins believed to have been invited by King Adishur from Kanauj, showing the ultimate value of pure Brahmanism. For details see Krishna Dutta and A. Robinson 1995. *Rabindranath Tagore: The Myriad-Minded Man* (New York: St Martin's Press): 17-18.

4 This story is beautifully narrated in Pramathanath Mullick 1935: 134-35 and also in Prankrishna Dutta 1981: 20.

5 The life of Nabakrishna portrayed here is taken from Pramathanath Mullick 1935: 4-5 and S. N. Mukherjee 1977: 20. See also Sumanta Banerjee 1989: 25-34.

6 The fact that Rammohan's reformist endeavour was also not free of brahmin influence is pointed out by Lata Mani 1998.

7 When Lord William Bentinck's government had finally abolished sati by a regulation in December 1829, Radhakanta Deb, along with his conservative Hindu friends, formed a society called Dharma Sabha and protested against this measure by presenting a petition to the Governor General on behalf of the orthodox section of the Hindu community. For a discussion of this see Swapan Basu 1978: 112-25.

8 The list compliled by Radhakanta Deb in 1822 was further revised in 1839 and is cited in Brajendranath Bandyopadhyay, ed, *Sambad Patre Sekaler Katha* 1994: 753-58. This list is also used in Rudrangshu Mukherjee's 'City with a Past', March 2006: 41.

9 Similarly, when the widow of one of the most well-known baniyas, Ramdulal Dey, died, his son Ashutosh Dey held a funeral ceremony for three to four days and one hundred thousand rupees were distributed among the poor who poured into the town from every corner of Bengal. At the death of the widow of Nilmani Mullick, a scion of the well-known merchant family of the Mullicks, there gathered a great number of poor people who were given one rupee each. See Pradip Sinha 1978 and Pramathanath Mullick 1935 for details.

10 For example, Fanny Parkes, a travel writer who lived in India between 1822-46 because her husband worked for the East India Co as a writer, mentioned a cup presented in the Calcutta races by Dwarakanath Tagore as a luminous example of extreme bad taste

such as only a babu could conceive of.

11 The description of the house goes like this: 'The house was approached on an entrance road, brilliantly illuminated at night, and entered through a marble hall. On the right of the foyer was an elegant staircase adorned with statues of Cornelia and the Gracchi, the Venus Baigneuse, and Psyche. At the top of the stairs was a central hall, of Terpischore, whose walls were hung with fine paintings and whose floor was adorned with statues of a reading nymph, and a recumbent Venus embowered in roses. On the left of the hall was a spacious veranda, decorated to resemble a Mongol tent, with leafy walls and garlands of flowers, in the centre of which was a throne of crimson velvet and gold embroidery, with pillars of solid silver chased and inlaid with gold . . . Outside was a spacious lawn surrounded by a meandering stream over which passed four rustic bridges. In the centre was a fountain, and beyond it a life-sized statue of the huntsman Meleager and his hound. In the distance a life-sized Venus could be seen rising from an artificial lake. On one side was a small island on which stood a Japanese temple, in the centre an Ionic temple containing copies of the celebrated group of Canova, and at the far end a Chinese pagoda covered with lights of every shape and colour and further illuminated by brilliant stars rising from the water's edge' (R. Mukherjee 2006: 12-23).

12 Unless indicated otherwise, English translations of Bengali quotations used are mine.

13 Nandakumar (1705-1775), as mentioned, was a supremely ambitious man of ambiguous social origins who became the collector of Burdwan in place of Warren Hastings (1732-1818) and it was due to his close connection with Hastings that he earned the coveted maharaja title. Later this friendship turned out to be one of the most infamous sagas of enmity.

14 By leading this kind of extravagant lifestyle Dwarakanath Tagore, grandfather of Rabindranath, was perceived as a threat against the orthodox brahmanical social order and created a rift between Dwarakanath and his devout Hindu wife, Digambari, who was so troubled with her husband's way of life that she refused to continue any physical relationship with Dwarakanath. However, as a true Hindu wife she performed all other wifely duties and after taking advice from learned pandits declared that it was not necessary to

entertain a physical association with one's husband in order to perform one's wifely dharma. Digambari valued her religious identity more than her existence as a wife and she maintained this stance until she died. See Deb 2004: 5-8.

15 The babus by this time had almost reached the end of their wealth due to severe changes in the trade and commerce scenario of colonial Bengal; see T. Bhattacharya 2005.

16 Until the 1820s, the bhadralok was socially identified with Hindu elite groups, without being adorned with any special term, because most zamindars and the educated elite were Hindus. For a detailed discussion of the emergence and social significance of the term 'bhadralok' see ibid.

17 Bhabanicharan Bandyopadhyay, *Kolikata Kamalalay* (1343 BS/ 1936), pp. 8-9.

18 *Foreign Miscellaneous Series*, National Archives of India (F.M.S), No 130, ff. 113-18.

19 L. N. Ghosh 1983: 155-57; I have used the Bengali translation of L. N. Ghosh's *The Native Aristocracy and Gentry of India* (1981), *Kalkatar Babu-Brittanto* 1983: 7-85.

20 For details of this marriage see Sengupta 1990.

21 These dals are mentioned in B. Bandyopadhyay, *Kolikata Komalalay*, 1936: 29.

22 For example, Radhakanta Deb probably had the largest dal in Calcutta and used to enjoy supreme authority in native society simply because the majority of the members of his were brahmins. The second largest numbers of were the Dakshin Rarhi kayastha families of Calcutta, who considered Deb as their social leader.

23 See *Samachar Chandrika* of 8 June 1843; 23 Nov 1843; 4 Feb 1844; 6 Oct 1845.

24 This is reported in Deb's *Samachar Chandrika* 24 September 1831.

25 For an analysis of the movement initiated by Derozio and his pupils see Sumit Sarkar 1985.

26 This incident is reported in *Samachar Darpan* 1830, quoted in Brajendranath Bandyopadhaya, vol II, 1994: 171. For a more detailed account of similar acts of defiance amongst the *Derozians* see Sivanath Sastri 1907.

27 For a discussion of the Brahmo movement against orthodox Hinduism see Khastagir 2006: 43-88.

28 I collected this information from the *Bengal Spectator*, I, September 1842, reprinted in Binoy Ghosh, vol. 6, 1963: 35.

29 It was through Calcutta that Lancashire textiles poured into the country and food grain and raw materials were pumped out, with a favourable balance of trade that paid for Britain's trade deficits with the rest of the world. For details see A. Bagchi 1972.

30 Muslims were preferred by Europeans as servants and cooks as presumably having less stringent pollution taboos, unlike the Hindus; see Sumit Sarkar 1997: 166.

31 As migration into Calcutta swelled with the opening of railways, the bulk of immigrants came in fact not only from villages of Bengal but also from poor adjacent areas like north Bihar, the eastern United Provinces, and Orissa. In fact, they constituted the major part of the workforce of the jute mills in Calcutta, and the mass of casual and menial labour as well. By the beginning of the twentieth century, 36.3 per cent of the population of Calcutta spoke some version of Hindustani. The Bengali speakers had no more than a bare majority, constituting 51.3 per cent of the inhabitants of the metropolis. For details see *Census of India* 1901, vol. 7, 4: 72 and Sumit Sarkar 1997: 166.

32 *Jajmani* is an institution of the pre-industrial subsistent village economy with. two connotations, one religious and the other economic: *(i)* a *jajman* is one who employs a brahmin for the performance of any religious ceremony, generally in a particular locality and his fee becomes customary, even hereditary; and payable even when the brahmin does not perform the ceremony. *(ii)* an institutional arrangement that makes the brahmin dependent for subsistence on the jajmans, his clients. Hence the institution passed from religious into social relations, of which payments played an important part.

33 This region was the worst affected by a famine followed by socio-political upheavals and decades of anarchy. The perilous nature of daily existence could best be illustrated by a story of Vidyasagar's grandfather who travelled with an iron staff, with which he once beat off and killed a bear just a few miles from Midnapore town. For the details of how weapons were carried by people for personal safety, see *Vidyasagar Charit* (autobiographical fragment, published posthumously in 1891, in Datta, *Vidyasagar Rachanabali* 1994: 409.

34 Act 12 of 1841 provided for the sale of the zamindari if the zamindar failed to pay arrears of revenue before the sunset of the

day previous to the day fixed for auction in the proclamation for auction sale.

35 The devastating spread of malaria was also one of the major causes. An early biography of Vidyasagar by Chandicharan Bandyopadhyay bears witness to the panic inspired by malaria, which first appeared in Jessore in 1825 and spread over Nadia, Barasat, and 24 Parganas, and then again struck Burdwan and Hooghly, in 1867-69; see Bandyopadhyay 1895 and 1969.

36 The opulence and power enjoyed by the Tagores in spite of their tainted *pirali* origin is a clear example of that phenomenon; for a detailed view see, S. Chowdhury-Sengupta 1993; T. Bhattacharya 2005.

37 The same matters regarding the Muslims were to be determined by the *Shariat;* see J. D. M. Derrett 1968: 233.

38 Vidyasagar's father, Thakurdas, gave up the family profession of teaching Sanskrit which was losing its significance and he was in financial straits. Vidyasagar turned down the offer of a Judge-Pandit's job in Tripura, even after he performed brilliantly in the *Smriti* and Law Committee examination, aged seventeen; see Datta, *Vidyasagar Charit*, p. 214.

39 Until around the 1830s, company administration needed the reproduction on a fairly extended scale of the Sanskrit (as well as Persian-knowing) literati, and the channelling of official patronage to the Sanskrit College and the Calcutta Madrasa made perfect administrative sense even apart from the classical interests for Oriental scholarship. Sanskrit College offered learned Indian scholars salaries that were fairly high for the time. For details of how Sanskrit pandits earned their fortunes see Sumit Sarkar 1997: 225.

40 See King 1999; Inden 1986; and Breckenridge and van der Veer 1993.

41 Here the term 'westernization' is used in the sense of the imposition of a western norm, in relation to which Indian religious thought, institutions and practices are seen as aberrations or distortions of the normative (i.e. western) pattern of behaviour.

42 By textualization of Indian religion, or for that matter any religion, we mean the hermeneutical method that is forcefully used to fit different aspects of a religious system in a literary structure. This tendency tends to forget that religious systems are not texts. For a detailed discussion on this see Lawson and McCauley 1993: 214.

43 Before the colonial era the use of these texts as the unchallenged source of Hindu existence was quite unheard of. The importance of local customs and traditions, although at times contrary to the text-based social norms, were very much the trend among different caste groups. The pan-Indian application of text-based norms and the gradual imposition of these norms as legal canons as an aftermath of colonial rule changed the scenario in favour of brahmanical way of life. See King 1999 for a detailed discussion of the towering influence of colonial rule on non-brahamanical native existence in this respect.

44 For a discussion of this transformatory phase of Hinduism see King 1991; S. Sugirtharajah 2003. *Imagining Hinduism: A Postcolonial Perspective* (London: Routledge); Marshall 1970; and Inden 1990.

45 For a comprehensive discussion of the difference between the majority of the Indian population and all those whom we have described as elite and the role that this difference played in Hindu identity formation see Ranajit Guha 1982. 'On Some Aspects of the Historiography of Colonial India', in Ranajit Guha, ed *Subaltern Studies*, vol 1. (New Delhi: Oxford Univesity Press): 1-8.

46 For example see the works of Ibbetson 1883; Nesfield 1885; Risley 1908, all British officials who contributed to the collection of Census data and studies of castes and tribes in British India during the late nineteenth and early twentieth centuries.

47 See T. Sarkar 2001 and Thapar 1993.

48 At this stage the excavation of Indus Valley civilization clearly had not taken place as yet.

49 Romila Thapar claims that the notion that caste society was essentially a system of racial segregation and grew from linguistic misapprehension. For a detailed discussion of this see Thapar 1993.

50 However, the British government which did not want to be embroiled in inter-caste politics responded in favour of the brahmins in adjudicating caste issues by following pre-colonial practices through consulting ancient scriptures, which they thought to be the only authentic basis for solving Indian social issues. For a discussion of colonial misinterpretations of caste practices and their extremely significant influence on post-colonial Indian social structures see U. Chakravarti 2003 and 1998; D. Gupta 2000; Srinivas 1968; Bandopadhyay 1992; Mani 1989; Caroll 1989; and Chowdhry 1994.

51 The move made by Deputy Census Commissioner Gait to exclude

castes not served by the brahmins in the Census report in 1910 is already mentioned. However, when his chief, the Census Commissioner Risley ordered that the classification of each caste was to be done by social precedence recognized by the native public opinion of the present day, Gait promptly ordered that any explanation and decision related to this issue must rest with enlightened public opinion, which indicated clearly that only the high-caste, elitist opinion should prevail. See T. Sarkar 2001 and U. Chakravarti 2003.

52 Rajendralal Mitra was born in a respectable kayastha family from an eastern suburb of Calcutta. Mitra later became famous as one of the most learned men of India and one who was famous for his mastery of the English language. With the completion of his early education he joined the Medical College in December 1837 but dropped out in 1841. He tried being a lawyer but his legal education was also not completed. He applied himself wholeheartedly to mastering different languages: Sanskrit, Persian, Urdu and Hindi, which helped him in his career in the Asiatic Society, Calcutta. He later became well conversant in French, Greek and Latin. In November 1846 Mitra was appointed Librarian and Assistant Secretary of the Asiatic Society, and he was elected in 1885 as its first native-born President. He had also been its Secretary in 1857 and 1865 and Vice-President from 1861 to 1865 and from 1870 to 1884. He was again its Vice-President between 1886 and 1891. Thus honours were heaped upon him, by an institution that was very much British at the time. Very fittingly it was he who wrote its centenary history, published in 1885. A non-brahmin who was highly influential was very pro-brahmin. See Bandyopadhyay 2004.

53 See Mani 1989 for the discussion on the dilemma involved in the Brahmanization of Hindu tradition by social reformers like Rammohan Roy.

54 See Bandyopadhyay's severe reaction against reformative social actions undermining the brahmanic influence in Swapan Basu 1978 126-31.

55 See Mani 1989 and Bandyopadhyay 2004 for a critical analysis of the traditionalist compromises of Rammohan and Vidyasagar.

56 See Bandopadhyay 1997: 1-99 and 2004: 11-77 for a discussion of this tendency.

57 Brahmanization or the process whereby non-brahmanical forms of

Indian religion are colonized and recreated by hegemonic brahmanical discourses and can be distinguished from the more general process of Sanskritization. The confutation of the two terms originates from the mistaken association of sanskritic culture exclusively with the brahmin castes. As Milton Singer has suggested, Sanskritization may follow the kshatriya, vaishya or even the shudra models. See Singer 1964: 84-119. Srinivas, in his account of of Sanskritization, has also pointed out that Sanadh brahmins of western Uttar Pradesh in India do not follow a culture that is sanskritic in nature. See M.N. Srinivas 1968: 20. Although Brahmanization in the widest sense of the term cannot be universally equated with Sanskritization we use 'Brahmanization' as a useful term for sanskritic Brahmanization to denote a particular and influential type of Brahmanization, but we do acknowledge the differences involved between Sanskritization and Brahmanization as in many cases the latter is the imposition of brahmanical culture whereas the former is the emulation of brahmanic forms by non-brahminic groups.

58 For a comprehensive discussion of the colonial roots of Indian nationalist consciousness, see P. Chatterjee 1986: 21-33, and King 1999: chapters 1 and 2.

59 See, for instance, Brian Hatcher 2001 for a discussion of how pandits from around Bengal and across the country were drawn into Calcutta in search of employment. Some were recruited by the early Orientalists, and pandits from as far as Gujarat and Benares found positions at the Sanskrit College. Others found work with the missionaries, assisting them in their quest to master India's many languages so as to propagate the Gospel. Some of them worked as court pandits for the city's indigenous nouveaux riches. The result was a coherent Brahmanization of not only Hindu religion, but also of native identity.

60 For example, early British administrators such as Warren Hastings and William Jones were Orientalist scholars who in their keen interest to know about India and its traditions embarked on a serious study and translation of Sanskrit texts with the belief that it would enable them to govern efficiently. Even a casual glance at the production of oriental literature under the governorship of Warren Hastings, such as Halhed's *A Code of Gentoo Laws* 1776, Charles Wilkins' translation of the Bhagavad Gita 1785, and Jones' recodification of Hindu Laws 1794, demonstrates the close link between colonial

power and the production of knowledge.

61 The Aryans, it was argued, were implicitly superior to the non-Aryans as they were the initial conquerors who had founded civilizations in Europe and Asia. The brahmins of ancient India, according to their traditional lore, were supposed to be the descendants of Aryan conquerors who migrated to India from the highlands of Central Asia, a tale that blended perfectly with beliefs among European occultists that white 'Caucasians' too had originated from the same Central Asian mountains. Subsequently, the concept of the Aryan race as the creator of ancient civilizations was born. See Leopold 1974: 21-36

62 See V.G. Hatalkar 1973 and Rajani Kanta Gupta 1896 where they provide sketches of the great historical figures of Hindu India, the Rajputs, Marathas, and Sikhs, in an effort to produce a national consciousness, self-respect, and a feeling of pride in one's country.

63 See Mani 1989.

64 See, for instance, U. Chakravarti 2003, and Leslie 1989 for an overview of how the lives of high-caste women were under scrutiny.

65 See Sumanta Banerjee 2000: 73, who has analysed the colonial-moral world view in the nineteenth century. Thus, in our view, the process of social reform in response to British clonialism in turn revitalised rigidity of the social hierarchy.

66 For a discussion of the reformist and revivalist trends of Hinduism, see Mani 1989; M. Sinha 1994. 'Reading *Mother India*', *Journal of Women's History* 6, 2: 6-44. Bandyopadhya 2004; and T. Sarkar 2001.

67 For a discussion of the importance of conjugality and the chaste Hindu female body, see T. Sarkar 2001: 191-225.

68 See S. N. Mukherjee 1970: 33-78, and P. Sinha 1978: 62-85.

69 Here, unlike Marxian historians who tend to explain the predicament of the bhadralok in terms of failure to transform themselves into a full blooded bourgeois modernity, the result of which was the production of a weak and distorted form of modern bourgeois liberal values, we refuse to confer on 'the productive principle' a propensity to transform all kinds of social relations. As Mani suggests, 'the theoretical difficulty with this position is that it appears to take as an article of faith the universal claims of capital regarding its capacities to create the world in its own image, to inexorably bring liberal European values in its wake. Empirical analyses represent individual baniyas, zamindars, and businessmen as adjusting to, negotiating,

and manipulating the changing economic and political context of the late eighteenth and nineteenth century, reconstituting their practices in accordance with the new regime. However, at the theoretical level they are still conceived, by the ideals of their European counterparts, as the bearers of an emergent and 'universal' bourgeois consciousness, Mani 1998: 45.

70 For a discussion of the transition to private property, see Ranjit Guha 1963. *A Rule of Property for Bengal: An Essay on the Idea of Permanent Settlement* (Paris: Mouton).

71 For a criticism of the Marxian standpoint in relation to social changes in colonial Bengal see Salahuddin Ahmed. 1965. *Social Ideas and Social Change in Bengal, 1818-1835* (Leiden: Brill): 26-51; Rajat K. Ray 1975. Introduction. In V. C. Joshi, ed, *Rammohan Roy and the Process of Modernisation in India* (New Delhi: Vikas): 16-17; T. Sarkar 1985: 18-36; and S. N. Mukherjee 1975: 67-69.

72 Rammohan's interest in sati is said to have been kindled by the death through immolation of his sister-in-law in 1812. For a discussion of Rammohan's personal experience of this, see Collet 1962: 106.

73 The unprecedented strictness of the rules and regulation of the Sabha became a source of fun and ridicule in Calcutta and the following report published in one journal illustrated the contempt that the pro-brahmin attitude of the Sabha received: (The repeated mentions of fire indicated the pro-sati stance of the Sabha since it was the funeral pyre of the deceased husband where the immolations took place, and the editor of the pro-*sati* newspaper, Bhabanicharan's fixation with high-caste social norms was ridiculed by renaming him as Kagalicharon or a man of no repute):

Rules of the Shubha [*sic*]:

.... That none to be allowed to become a member of this Shubha [*sic*] who cannot burn his finger in red hot fire, without giving any signs of uneasiness.

That every member on entering the hall, where the meeting is held, swear that he has sacredly observed the rites and ceremonies of fire worship. That he has everyday drink hot water only, that he has fed the God of fire before he has taken his dinner, that he has never made use of any cool water, nor even that of the Ganges, and that he has taken no meal that has been kept cooling for some time.

That if any member, be found not to have kept a fire in his house any day, he be no longer, considered one of our Shubha [*sic*].

That if found that any member has paid a cool regard to what Baboo [*sic*] Kagaleechurun, our secretary, says, he be expelled from the Association, and that no fire be ever allowed to be taken to his house . . . (Based on a report published in *Calcutta Monthly Journal* cited in Swapan Basu 1978: 134).

74 Rammohan even took a brahmin cook with him when he left for England in 1830 so that he did not lose his caste by eating any food of any questionable origin in an alien land. See Mani 1998: 46.

75 This phrase is borrowed from Mani 1998: 47.

76 Even the Brahmos who were referred as the 'female emancipationists' and the torch-bearers of liberalism had differences of opinions as to the degree of social freedom to be permitted to women. During the 1860s Brahmo women held their own prayer meetings, separate from men. By the 1870s, men and women started mixing freely, establishing the atmosphere of a large family wherein all members of the opposite sex were treated as siblings and hence such closeness was acceptable. However, in a public formal event such as the weekly prayer, women still sat behind a curtain, maintaining purdah. Staunch liberals like Anandamohan Charan Khastagir and Durga Mohan Das dared to sit with the women of their families in the general body of congregation and the conservative lobby of the Brahmo sect reacted sharply accusing the women involved of acting out of a 'love of ostentation'. See Borthwick 1984: 260-261.

77 Lord Macaulay was the author of the famous Minute on Education of 2 February 1835 where these qualities of trusted native allies are mentioned. For key passages, see W. M. Theodore de Bary 1966, vol. II: 49.

78 Arguing against widow immolation Rammohan Roy in his second pamphlet dismisses the charge that native women lacked in resolve. He said '. . . in a country where the name of death makes the male shudder, the female from her firmness of mind offers to burn herself with the corpse of her husband.' Here Rammohan is clearly suggesting that women who undertake sati are the real heroes and thereby inadvertently eulogises the whole process as exemplifying women's strength and character. See Mani 1998: 74.

79 This consequence is mentioned in *Nuton Panjika* 1870-1871: 1. See also T. Sarkar 2001.

80 Rammohan's argument that sati was related to women's property rights

under the Dayabhaga law has been accepted by a wide range of scholars. For example, see Nandy 1975: 172-73, and Rajat K. Ray 1988. 'Indian Society and the Establishment of British Supremacy, 1756-1818'. In P. J. Marshall, ed, *The Oxford History of the British Empire,* vol 2. (London: Oxford University Press): 39-40; 72-78.

81 See the detailed report in *Tattvabodhini Patrika* no. 140, Chaitra 1776 Shaka in Benoy Ghosh, vol IV, 1963: 158-62.

82 Since kulin polygamy was practised in Bengali society, a brahmin man with more than twenty marriages in his account rarely died without any progeny. For a detailed discussion of the kulin system see Inden 1976.

83 See Bandyopadhyay 2001: 40-77 and 127 for a detailed discussion of Vidyasagar's moralist position on widow remarriage and its consequences. Dipesh Chakrabarty shares a different view on this in claiming Vidyasagar's moralist argument was merely to kindle the bhadralok fear of individual scandals threatening their new sense of domestic responsibility. See Chakrabarty 2000. *Provincializing Europe: Post-Colonial Thought and Historical Difference* (Princeton: Princeton University Press): 127.

84 However, as Dipesh Chakrabarty has suggested, even after these laws were enacted the widows remained untouched by the economic rationalism of colonial modernity, and legal rights or economic dependence were never issues to them as the deprivation of all claims to their husband's family was more heartbreaking and socially isolating for them. See ibid: 131-33. However, that legal rights bestowed on the widows projected them as potential threats as independent authorities to the patriarchal social order cannot be denied.

85 See Carroll 1989: 3-26 for a discussion of the brahmanical nature of these reformative laws.

3

Preserving the Caste Hierarchy: The Duties of Domestic Goddesses

THE 'WOMAN QUESTION' AND THE NEW CONSTRUCTION OF PATRIARCHY

By the second half of the nineteenth century the need to respond to the colonial modernizing mission and to the unsatisfactory work conditions under colonial rule in British India had led Bengali male agents who gained a certain amount of social agency because of their very success in turning the new developments for personal gain, otherwise unthinkable to the other members of society surviving under colonial rule, to construct a definition of their own identities, responsibilities and, more importantly, their relationships with their women at home. Thus at the intersections of colonial modernity and these men's response and active participation in Hindu homes, families, and daily lives where every aspect had been a part of continuous debates and contests, the identity of the native male agents was coming into being. Furthermore, the domestic arena was the ground where the main ingredients of ideal womanhood, chastity, fidelity and patience were nurtured. The caste-driven nature of the ingredients crucial in formulating the newly constructed ideal of womanhood comes into focus. This not only introduced an entirely new approach to the varied features of a contemporary model of womanhood,[1] but also invigorated the traditional hierarchical social structure by effectively eulogizing the conventional norms prearranged for native women. As a result, locating the construction of the ideal of womanhood in a caste-based society becomes successful. This accordingly exemplifies that there is a correlation between the passionate maintenance of the native's inner domain and the safeguarding of caste principles—an association that deserves to be properly scrutinized in order to establish the fact that the 'woman question' in colonial Bengal did not lose its significance with the rise of nationalism. That the caste bias towards a native ideal of womanhood was steadily transferred to the 'native negotiators' of different aspiring, and ambiguous social groups could only be properly demonstrated if we focus on the intersections of the natives' inner domain and their social status, and how these minute domestic details adopted afterwards by the people of lower orders strengthened the claims of their social promotion.

Once again, the domestic principles mandatory in upholding the superiority of native traditions and the matching ideal of native womanhood take us back to the 'women fulcrum'. Here women swivel between the two extremes of tradition and modernity; native women positioned at the core of the vacillation of uncertain social situations on the one hand were of fundamental importance in maintaining the pious nature of native existence, and on the other they were employed as emissaries of indigenous obligation towards the western notions of unorthodoxy and rationality. This swing was principally supervised by caste principles. The elements that were considered to be instrumental in maintaining the inviolability of native domesticity and consequently retained the caste-based social structure via the tailored ideal of womanhood are examined later. The result of controlling native women's lives via the traditional path of native social order under the perilous threat of a foreign authority ultimately reproduced a hierarchical social order.

MEASURING PATRIARCHY IN THE DOMESTIC ARENA AND THE SUBSEQUENT IDEAL OF WOMANHOOD

> When you become a householder you have to look out for so many things . . . You have to try hard to protect your husband, yourself, your offspring and your home from evil.

> At every step of the way you have to look after your husband's happiness; you have to work very hard to keep your husband's love. Is all this an easy task? On top of that there are all these other things to consider—family relations, male and female servants, guests and beggars, the cow and her young, society, the government and dharma.
>
> Dhirendranath Pal, *Conversations with the Wife* [*Strir sahit kathapakathan* (henceforth *CWW.*) 1883: 81] cited in Walsh 2004: 51

Owing to colonial rule, European bourgeois domestic discourse was perceived as a naturalized and universal standard of family life to many native male agents through the interactions and complex exchanges of the nineteenth-century's colonial relationships. Under the guise of the benevolent task of bringing modernity to the natives, daily life, the intimacies of family relationships, in fact, all elementary forms of life were brought under the scrutinizing gaze of the colonial masters. As a result, the basis of universal civility became bourgeois domesticity and the life of the women, the core factor of that domestic existence (Comaroff and Comaroff 1992: 44). Moreover, since the colonial regime extended its dominion over all spheres of public life in British India, and native men had to work outside the home to earn their living under the supervision of their colonial masters, the only space that was left for leading an authentic Hindu way of life was confined to the domestic and family area.

At the same time, from the second half of the nineteenth century the requirement to act in response to the 'civilizing mission', the new circumstances of life and work in British India, and the subsequent discontent among the native agents, led Bengali men to redefine not just their individual identity but, more importantly, the identity, role, and relationship of the women residing in their home, the only area where Bengali men could still exert their authority (see also Chapter 1). As a result the entire domestic world, from household organizations, to matrimonial and parental relationships, became the site of social disputes. Although the native social agents advocated significant changes in the indigenous approaches associated with domestic life in order to meet the standards stipulated by the colonial regime, they were troubled by the social consequences of women's rejection of indigenous customs and had no alternative but to argue yet again on behalf of the supremacy of native traditions (Walsh 2004: 36-37), at best with some necessary alterations. Was the compulsive advocacy of indigenous traditions an outcome of the mounting pro-independence spirit among the natives? Was this the consequence of the increasing dissatisfaction of the western-educated Bengali elites against the continuous aggression and humiliation that they had to face in the public arena under colonial rule? Or was it an attempt, once again, to impose a patriarchal social structure? An affirmative to any of these questions without specifying the essential components of the deal between the advocates of superior indigenous traditions, which were predominantly brahmanical in nature, and the preservation of an unadulterated domestic life, would once again fail to account for the fundamental discriminatory nature of social arrangements. The latter were based on caste and endorsed throughout the belief in a 'golden past' of indigenous tradition.

Instead, Bengali women were the central focus in the domestic world comprised of family units that were both patrilineal and patrilocal. Women, in general considered as a category as inferior as the shudras, were still deemed important because of their unique reproductive power, and this power had the capacity to upset a social order based on caste hierarchy. The connection between women, reproduction and the preservation of caste arrangements (see Chapters 1 and 2) will, at this stage, facilitate an understanding therefore of the necessity of safeguarding the domestic arena, imposing on women the role of defending the purity of that domain, and indicate that the underlying motivation was the need to protect the hierarchical social system. Accordingly, growing dissatisfaction against the colonial regime followed by increasing nationalist sentiment amongst native agents gained focus and strength by means of emphasizing the superiority of native domestic life based on scriptural traditions in contrast to the British. The brahmanical social structure and the purity of women were presented and refurbished as the carriers of this glorious tradition this time to face the challenge posed by a foreign power.

Subsequently, in upholding the hierarchical social order the supremacy of the high-caste groups remained unaffected. The complexity of the discourse around domesticity, given that this discourse happened to be the benchmark of civilization for both the colonizers and the colonized (Comaroff and Comaroff 1992: 67) in a variety of material and ideological contexts, leads us to explore the constituents that generated a renovation of native women and their domestic life. This trend eventually became a model available to native agents of different social strata in order to achieve their respective social goals and it confirmed the caste-based nature of this entire discourse. Before analysing the factors that played a decisive role in developing the model household and the ideal woman, let us briefly examine the strategies master-minded by the native male agents who in reality were the chief negotiators of these social changes. Consequently, the contestations among and within the urban, elite native agents against the colonialist ideologies of rationalism, nationalism, and market economics came to define the domestic world of Bengal, and, more importantly, the life of its women. Simultaneously, the tradition-obsessed nature of the arrivistes from lower origins, in their endeavour to bolster their recently earned social status, initiated the process of renovating orthodox and hierarchical native tradition (Borthwick 1984: xi-5).

These anti-colonial contestations that led to the formulation of a new ideal of womanhood can be seen as simply the conservative influence of ancient scripture-based religious traditions that regained their ground by reviving ancient values. However, decoding the factors behind the unequivocal reliance on the scriptural basis what becomes detectable is that beyond this typical representation of the nineteenth-century domestic world is the assumption that an exclusively feminine sphere can be kept separate from the public sphere in which the supposed 'real' battle for indigenous validity was taking place. Whereas, the contestations of home, family and, most importantly, native woman as Walsh (2004: 10) has rightly pointed out, highlight the dynamics of native survival, as previously un-thought of habits and practices were forced into consciousness and contestation. Such commotion in the apparently undisturbed domestic front could not be kept separated from what was happening at the outer world as acknowledged by Partha Chatterjee (1999), Sumit Sarkar (1997), Tanika Sarkar (2001), and Walsh (2004). However, a further insightful look at the building blocks of the native domestic arena and the prearranged way of life of native women leads to an understanding of what really underlies these efforts: the vigilant preservation of a caste-based hierarchical social order. While, it could well be argued that the refurbishment of native domesticity with women at the centre was not always based on caste strategies, the ensuing establishment of caste supremacy was, on the contrary, the result of this entire reorganization of domestic order. No matter what approach one implements it leads towards the manifestation and consolidation of a hierarchical social order. Let us first take a brief look at the colonial contribution to the production of a nineteenth-century Bengali domestic discourse. It was because of the colonial influence that the Enlightenment themes of order, reason, and science became deeply imprinted on the native way of life and were subsequently considered as the essential components of daily domesticity as well (Borthwick: 1984; Walsh: 2004).[2] That this overt inclination towards rational values and their orderly administration ultimately paved the way for a meticulous caste establishment is significant here.

It has generally been agreed that domesticity was a discourse of the nineteenth-century European middle classes. With the growth of industrialization, capitalism, and new methods of mass production of the late eighteenth and early nineteenth centuries, ideas about the proper ordering of home and family relations became integral to bourgeois ideology (Luke 1989; Davidoff and Hall 1987; Comaroff and Comaroff 1992). Essential to this European domestic discourse was a conviction (fundamentally similar to the domestic ideology of the native subjects in colonial India) that the proper maintenance of human relations and social order required a patriarchal family system with a gendered division of labour with the husband as the head of the family unit (Davidoff and Hall 1987). Throughout the nineteenth century the European gendered spheres of activity were further demarcated, and subsequently 'home' came to be perceived as the husband's safe haven from the aggression and humiliation of work and employment in the outer world, and wives were adorned as the doyennes of the house. They were the proverbial 'angel of the house', viewed as the guardians of order and organization in the domestic world, a superior moral force in shaping the lives and characters of children and, most importantly, a constant source of support and comfort for their otherwise distressed husbands (Walsh 2004: 12).

To this extent, the European domestic tendency seems to be in tune with the domestic format followed in colonial Bengal. But the disparities between these two systems become obvious only if one takes a look at the inherent secular structure of nineteenth-century European bourgeois ideology. European domesticity was, as mentioned earlier, arguably a secular discourse stamped with Enlightenment themes of order, reason, and science. System, order, and efficiency were the most important components of daily domestic existence, a customary observance of which would ensure a methodical ordering of the domestic sphere (ibid). Concurrently, European bourgeois classes with their ambition to extend their hegemonic control led to a promotion of domesticity[3] as a natural and universal way of human existence, the proper maintenance of which would guarantee a civilised standard for human life.[4] Thus, although, nineteenth-century European domesticity was indebted for the strength of its conviction to earlier Christian, specifically Protestant, traditions, it still justified its ideological principles and sociological distinctions predominantly through principles of natural law.[5] In contrast, the domesticity of native colonial life in nineteenth-century India was wholly dharmik in nature, in which the word *dharma* entails not only a sacred, spiritual, and moral element, but also a secular, material and natural one.

To illustrate further structural differences between nineteenth-century European domesticity and the trend prevalent in Bengali domesticity it is necessary to point out that the Hindu way of social life based on caste stratification is theoretically constructed out of units primarily originated from blood and semen, entities that belong to the natural order and essentially beyond the control of anyone, alongside the monistic nature of Hindu dharma (Inden 1976: 11-27). As a result, in defining one's social location birth is the central symbolic act of kinship[6] in Bengal.[7] To illustrate briefly, a person receives his/her body and the subsequent social status from the parents, which is thought to be made up of the different but complimentary substances of the bodies of the father and the mother. Here, the father plants the seed, which is nourished and grown in the field of the mother. As is the case in agriculture, seed and field must be closely matched to one another; otherwise the resultant crop will be poor in quality. As a result, the qualities of seed and field, of the bodily substances of husband and wife, that match them to one another are not only 'natural' qualities, as the term 'nature' is thought of in western culture, but at the same time 'moral' qualities. Arguably, according to Hindu dharma the 'natural' and the 'moral' are coextensive and the universal code of action or dharma of every person is supported by right and orderly actions that are a perfect blend of the 'natural' and the 'moral'. Each person, each thing, and each genus of things has its own code for conduct (*svadharma*) (Nicholas 1995).

A wrongly planted seed, however, can never achieve its dharma, and similarly a human seed planted in an improper field produces improper fruit, that is, a child lacking the qualities and dharma of either parent and thereby polluting the entire social structure. Consequently, all the *sanskar*[8] or life-cycle rites are based upon the latent paradigm of marriage and consequent reproduction in the Bengali (Hindu) social structure (ibid).[9] Here again, marriage is arguably the most important sanskar through which the social order, the family, the lineage and, of course, the hierarchical social order is maintained. Thus the significance of the proper preservation of domestic life through which the marital status of the partners gets established on a firmer basis enhances in Hindu society. This perfect social situation can be achieved only when women, who are inherently imperfect in nature are properly trained to look after the welfare of their husbands and all that adheres to them, for example, household, reputation, kin, ancestors, descendents, deities, and so on (Harlan and Courtright 1995: 186). In other words, the wife needs to learn the imperatives of *patibratadharma*, which etymologically means moral action (dharma) that is rooted in vows *(brata)* undertaken for the protection and well-being of the husband or lord *(pati)* (ibid). These duties and the orientations that frame them are presented formally in classical treatises on morality (eg, *Dharmashastras*) and informally through patterns of behaviour and expectations regarding a married woman, which are passed through generations, encoded in rituals, and celebrated in mythology and folklore. The domestic world and family life were the core spheres of women's activity, particularly because this is the place where reproduction and childcare took place. It is also the context where women were the main agents for the proper functioning of these activities and the safeguarding of the home and consequently the outer world, and most significantly the continuance of a dharmik social order rested on caste stratifications for the welfare of all.

The anxieties regarding the proper maintenance of domestic life thus turned out to be anxieties about women going astray. The nineteenth-century domestic manuals, therefore, present the same concerns, and focus predominantly on wifely virtues and produce another series of advice on how to be a loving wife, how to look after a husband returning home from a hard day at work, how to maintain the cleanliness of the home, and so on. The most notable feature of the recommendations designed for nineteenth-century Bengali women was the profound European influence accrued from the colonial masters that ultimately gave rise to a newly devised ideology for women.

ADVICE TO THE IDEAL WIFE IN HIGH-CASTE WRITING

The traditional Hindu views of women's roles were based on ancient Sanskrit scriptures, which had their origin in everyday life motivated by material interests of different agents. It was this tendency that subsequently consolidated social hierarchy in India.[10] Orthodoxy urged male family members to protect their women from their wicked bent towards sexual promiscuity, which could corrupt the social order through illicit associations with men of lower strata, thereby offering the lower groups an opportunity to overthrow caste hierarchy. Subsequently the restriction of upper-caste women to the confines of a domestic inner space became mandatory, and accordingly all other avenues for a woman's personal development were blocked; for example, education for women was deemed to be the cause of a husband's death (Borthwick 1984: 61). The world of a woman had to revolve only around her husband and in-laws. Her husband was her god; her devotion to him was supreme, independent of her husband's character or behaviour to her as indicated by *Manabodharma-shastra*. It was advised that 'a virtuous wife should constantly serve her husband like a god, even if he behaves badly, freely indulges his lust and is devoid of any good qualities' (*Laws of Manu*, trans. by Doniger and Smith 1991: 115).

As each person, each thing, each genus of things, had its own code for conduct (*svadharma*), similarly in the wife's moral universe, the husband functions as the point of orientation for all her actions. Her devotion, therefore, was not necessarily borne out of romantic affection or even friendship with her husband. Indeed, in terms of the logic of patibratadharma his behaviour towards her was irrelevant to her commitments to her own required moral orientation; her actions were not derivative of his. For, as Manu insisted, a neglectful or even abusive husband may be constructed as a more demanding challenge for a wife's devotion (ibid). Therefore, the more abusive the husband, the more daunting the challenge was for the wife; if after going through a series of suffering she still emerged as a patibrata, then she was deemed to be ideal. Consequently, the constraints for women defined by orthodoxy, to maintain the sanctity of the family system and therefore the social order were effectively eulogized, since upholding one's familial and social obligations even over and against one's own needs and desires was seen as preserving one's particular dharma. Following this justification, similarly to women, men were also expected to submit their individual desires to the demands of family and society. Nonetheless, the responsibilities for women endowed with reproductive power were imposed much more to maintain the hierarchically based exactness of family and social structure. Furthermore, the alleged innate licentious nature of women was a threat to the social hierarchy and thus the daily life of women was placed under continual surveillance.

Attuned to the ancient scriptural advices, nineteenth-century Bengali manuals[11] must also be read within the context of the revitalization of women's responsibilities with the same overall preoccupation with system, order, and subservience. However, there was additional inclination towards economy and cleanliness that were found in the household manuals written for English, American or Anglo-Indian women in this period (Walsh 2004: 46). The immediate need to respond to both colonial ideology and the new conditions of the home and the outer world led Bengali men to construct new definitions of their new identities, roles and, most importantly, their relationships with their women at home. Owing to the imperative inclination towards education a wide range of books and magazines were published in the latter half of the nineteenth century on family relations in India. However, manuals were the most important genre in an enormous range of literature produced for women to advise them on home management, account keeping, child bearing, hygiene, and cooking. These manuals, unlike essays and novels that were gaining popularity among the Bengali intelligentsia,[12] were written in simple language for women of limited education with the exclusive objective of offering them advice on how to become the ideal woman.

In spite of the growing trend in women's education the native agents were worried about the suitability of education and the book-reading habits of their women (*Bangiya Mahila*, henceforth *BM*). Manuals were harmless readings for these women, since they were written in chaste language and were suitable for all housewives, in contrast to the language of plays and novels depicting romantic love and adultery.[13] Another important thing to note here is that most of these manuals were written by male authors of a specific background. As Walsh has pointed out, much of the period's domestic literature was written by the members of the religious reform society, the Brahmo Samaj.[14] More than any Hindu group Brahmos were identified with the social reform of women's conditions, but this concern for woman was in perfect tune with the traditional brahmanical way of living and is undeniably explicit in most of these manuals. The male-authored nature of the Bengali manuals owes this specific approach to the social scenario in which female writers were still a rarity, as female education itself was a rare phenomenon before the second half of the century. Our suggestion is that manuals principally offered advice on how to become a good wife and an ideal woman, as it was more acceptable to society that the advice came from male authors rather than females, whose status was yet to be established.[15]

Before entering into the world of Bengali domestic manuals let us first discuss their key features. Most obviously, all the manuals insisted on high moral standards for native women, who were undoubtedly representatives of high status. These manuals were mostly divided into two sections: the first part offered advice on virtues such as chastity, shame, respect, loyalty, love, hygiene, cleanliness, frugality, and so on, as prerequisites of a good wife, and the second part was devoted to channelling all these exceptional virtues into the qualities and responsibilities of a good mother. The core content of this advice literature was how a new bride ought to perform all her duties as a good wife, and how she had to learn a set of behavioural rules conducive to the groom, his family and to the social order. Only by internalizing all these rules would she be able to act upon her duties as a wife and subsequently become a successful mother. The texts in their main objective to structure a new model of domesticity upheld the virtues of traditional norms, and amended some to ensure the smooth running of the contemporary social order. The young woman who entered into wedlock became the chief vehicle of this process of social management on whose performance as a patibrata, a *grihalakshmi* (being like *Lakshmi*, the goddess of fortune of the home), and a *sugrihini* (a good housewife who takes meticulous care of domesticity) the success of the family and the society was dependent. The discussions in these advice manuals demonstrates how during the last decade of the nineteenth century with the growth in nationalism, these women became the emblems of nationalistic virtue as well. As a bride or a daughter-in-law a woman had to satisfy and look after the specific needs of every member of the husband's family; then as a mother she was expected to give birth to a son within the preordained social structure of reproduction and bring her son up so that he became the ideal member of his clan, society, and later nation.[16]

The journey to the world of these manuals starts with Dhirendranath Pal (nd), an advocate of Brahmo ideology. We have chosen to focus on Dhirendranath's work *Conversations with the Wife* (*CWW*) not only because of the ideal balance maintained by Dhirendranath between tradition and modernity in his manual, establishing the uniqueness of this customized model of womanhood, but also because of the social milieu from which he came from. Although very little is known about Dhirendranath Pal, from the long list of his English publications, it is clear that he belonged to the educated bhadralok, playing an exemplary role in reconstructing the ideal of womanhood. At the same time, his last name Pal indicates his non-brahmanic origin, and supports the claim that men of relatively lesser origins, who by some means made their mark in the social life of colonial Bengal, were in many cases more attentive to maintain the supremacy of ancient Hindu customs and traditions and, as discussed earlier, ultimately strengthening the brahmanical way of life.

In fact amongst all the nine manuals translated by Walsh in

her *How to Be the Goddess of Your Home: An Anthology of Bengali Domestic Manuals* only one author belongs to an authentic brahmin origin (Walsh 2005). Amongst Dhirendranath's twenty works were at least seven that focused exclusively on women and marriage (ibid: 43).[17] From the content of his writing it is evident that he was a Brahmo (ibid) with his clear preference for women's literacy and education, and for reformed exercises of health and hygiene.[18] Yet for all his reformist ideals Dhirendranath was a strong defender of an indigenous Hindu, rather than a high-caste way of life, delicately promoting bhadralok superiority by upholding the ancient Indian traditions in an attempt to fight back against colonial aggressions. Dhirendranath projected the hostile attitude of the colonials as reasonable in so far as they stressed the wretched conditions of native women, which in turn warranted the colonial intervention in indigenous life, as the abject condition of the entire native society needed the benevolent touch of a colonial magic wand. Dhirendranath and many other writers in nineteenth-century Bengal, in spite of their different approaches to the 'woman's question', thus never compromised on the issue of superiority of native customs over colonial domestic standards.[19] They argued for a reformed domestic order but within a model they identified as strictly Hindu. Nonetheless, while the new ideals of womanhood turned out to be an amalgamation of traditional native principles and modern European beliefs, brahmanical orthodoxy undeniably prevailed. The following speech by one of Dhirendranath Pal's imaginary wives exemplifies what the bhadralok wanted from their wives:

> I am not standing in front of you today to plead for 'women's independence'. I have not been sent here by your mothers to tell you, 'Give us the right that men have.' Let us go out in the carriage for an airing,' or 'Turn us into memsahibs'. Women do not want all this. Women do not consider any of this. (*CWW*, as cited in Walsh 2004: 55)

Dhirendranath urged social reforms for native women but within the parameters of Hindu customs, according to which the bond between the husband and wife was the most important and decisive component of family life where family was the central factor of human existence, and the relationship between the spouses is the most decisive element for the maintenance of caste purity and the resulting social status. Accordingly, Dhirendranath devoted an entire chapter to family relationships, where drawing heavily from the colonial concept of romantic love, he tended to reduce the importance of the larger family, a phenomenon largely dominant in scriptural recommendations for women (*CWW* 1883: 18). However, Dhirendranath skilfully subsumed the larger familial responsibilities for native women within the four relationships between a husband and a wife explicated in *CWW*.[20]

Husband and wife, says Dhirendranath, have four relationships: *(i)* the 'partnership' relationship; *(ii)* the 'wife' relationship; *(iii)* the 'confident' relationship; and *(iv)* the 'spiritual' relationship.[21] As partners, the first task of the spouses is to run the family unit smoothly (*CWW* 1883: 18). The prominence of the efficient management of a family unit in all these manuals, including Dhirendranath's, highlights the requirement of the control over women and her sexual inclinations by restricting her activities to normatively prescribed duties within the family circle where she, as a good wife, needs to take care of household responsibilities. This emphasis on efficient management of domestic duties results from the liaison between the hierarchical social structure and the role played by women in the conservation of such a society. Dhirendranath claims that almost everything a woman needs to know for the smooth running of a family life comes from the 'partnership' relationship and thereby incorporates the entire gamut of housework and family responsibilities under the banner of this relationship (ibid). But why are the responsibilities towards the larger family so important in the Indian context whereas European domesticity predominantly prioritised the importance of the romantic association between the couple? To describe the spousal relationship simply as Indian tradition was, perhaps, due to the fear that an inclination toward a romantic bonding between the spouses might weaken family stability.[22] The emphasis on tradition thus made romanticism a secondary aspect of Indian domesticity and conjugality. Consequently, Walsh discusses how in Dhirendranath's book compassionate marriage is envisaged with hesitations (Walsh 2004: 59) since romantic love is endowed with the potential for weakening family loyalties. However, like many other gender historians of nineteenth-century Bengal,[23] Walsh does not pay attention to the hidden hierarchical requirements of Bengali society which are deemed to safeguard family order. Neither does she offer an answer to the question why it was so significant to protect the family order as per the Bengali (Hindu) social model.

Similarly to Walsh, Partha Chatterjee (1993), Tanika Sarkar (2001), Sumit Sarkar (1994), and Mrinalini Sinha (2000b) discuss the importance of maintaining the domestic order by drawing inferences from what was happening in the public sphere. For these authors, the order of the home was dominated by changes in the public world, an approach undoubtedly necessary in order to demonstrate the multifaceted changes taking place in Bengali domesticity. It is certainly the case that changes in the public sphere affected native domesticity as well: the home became the battleground for the colonizers as well as the colonized. However, the preoccupation with the domestic sphere was not exclusively a colonial phenomenon. The hierarchical social order required proper maintenance of the home since this is where the hierarchical ideology originated.[24] The colonial period witnessed a more neatly structured version of this same tendency. The minute detail of whatever was taking place in the home was intrinsically related to the interrelationship between the caste order and domesticity: the importance of domesticity thus always remained a constant factor in the Hindu social order. The changes happening in the public sphere during the colonial period, although influential, did not place domesticity at the core of Hindu existence for the first time. A detailed look at the importance of the marriage rules and preordained mating formulas taking place within the domestic order in safeguarding the caste order long before the colonial rule took place would exemplify this point. Just like the age-old process of restraining women's existence to the boundaries of the domestic arena, the set of domestic laws advocated in the colonial era turned out to be nothing but a stylish and astute strategy to protect the caste structure. The influence of the colonial claim to superiority over and against native domestic life, which in many ways did provoke a more passionate safeguarding of the indigenous home, perhaps for the first time so vigorously, cannot be disregarded. But the aspiration that motivated the native agents almost remained the same: safeguarding a hierarchical social order masked in the name of tradition. Alternatively, it can also be said that maintenance of a caste-based social order was not always a matter of great concern to many natives; they were certainly worried about the disruptions caused by a colonial rule that were proving to be detrimental to the native traditions. Saving these traditions was thus an important task, and the result was a eulogized projection of a traditionally superior social structure that was hierarchical in nature. In this process, because any criticisms of the native social life made by the natives themselves could prove to be treacherous, the caste question not only remained unresolved, it was actually revived with full vigour.

In the four aspects of conjugal relationships mentioned by Dhirendranath Pal, the 'partnership' relationship absorbed almost all the aspects of household work and family relationships. Nearly everything that a woman needed to know in order to maintain good quality family life came under the 'partnership' relationship. Elucidating them one by one, Dhirendranath suggests that the husband advise the wife on various domestic duties as follows: *(a)* spending money according to a good policy; *(b)* behaving well with people; *(c)* keeping the house orderly and learning how to do the housework; *(d)* making one's husband happy; and *(e)* knowing about medicine (Walsh 2005: 51). All these aspects of domesticity are essential in keeping everyone in the household happy, healthy and, most significantly, the family order intact. And when family as the basic social unit remains unperturbed the prearranged social order also remains undamaged. Second, comes the 'wife' relationship. According to Dhirendranath this is the physical relationship between husband and wife. The physical aspects of conjugal relationships had previously been considered as an aspect not to be discussed in public but it was now candidly examined.

Because of this relationship the wife needs to learn four subjects (Dhirendranath's *CWW* 1883: 18-52): *(a)* menstruation; *(b)* midwifery; *(c)* child rearing; and *(d)* child education'. The husband accordingly advises his wife: 'People say this is a relation that should be kept very secret and hidden. But should we feel that way about something that results in our birth?' (ibid: 51). Native sexual activities, especially the unclean and unhygienic means of dealing with childbirth were under severe criticism by the colonial regime (Borthwick 1984: 152-64), and so modifications to approaches towards these activities became unavoidable. However, a cautious equilibrium was maintained by restoring older, indigenous representations of devotion-driven conjugal relationship rather than prioritizing the scientific and European version of conjugal relationship that speaks of the reproductive system candidly (Walsh 2004: 60). Nonetheless, knowing more about intimate reproductive processes was now promoted as valuable for native women as it might help them to give birth to healthy offspring, something their ancestors were not sufficiently expert in and consequently the native males were accused of having fragile bodies and an effeminate nature that could only reproduce weaker progeny.

The last two relationships mentioned by Dhirendranath, the 'confidante' and the 'spiritual' associations between the spouses, provided the ultimate framework to reiterate the superiority of native traditions obligatory for preserving the native social order under threat from the colonial adversary. In the 'confidante' relationship, as the name of the relationship suggests, the husband asserts that a wife is advised to familiarize herself with her husband's way of life, to become exactly like him (*CWW* 1883: 21). The alleged western-educated liberal husband demonstrating his modernity declares, 'When neither husband nor wife has any special selfish concerns of their own, they become friends very easily' (ibid). But ultimately returning back to the conventional standpoint the husband questions: 'Do you know how the husband and wife's friendship grows? By the wife's learning to be like the husband. If she tries to do this, there's no limit to what she can accomplish' (ibid). Once again the accomplishment of a woman is determined by her submission to her husband's way of life, and it is by her absolute submission only that a dharmik social order can be appropriately maintained.

It is important to note that from the second half of the nineteenth century the use of words like *patibrata* and *patibratya* (wifely duties prescribed for a woman) became frequent in Bengali literature (S. Chakrabarti 1995: 111), which, of course, does not mean that these words suddenly became important to Bengali society. Rather, while chastity and fidelity of a Hindu wife was always important in Bengali (Hindu) society, only during the second half of the nineteenth century when comparisons between British and native conjugality became a source of constant battle, words like 'romantic love', 'compatibility', and 'courtship' started dictating the bhadralok's idea of conjugal relationship.[25] Thus, the native social order had to incorporate the ideology of *patibratya* more and more into its vocabulary to assert the superiority of the native way of life.[26] By the end of the century the promotion of Bengali (Hindu) women's uniqueness went to the extent of eulogizing widow burning, asserting that no other women of any other culture would have shown the courage and valour that Hindu women possessed.[27] Long after the Hindu Widow Remarriage Act (1856) was passed an article published in the apparently progressive *Bamabodhini Patrika* (henceforth *BP*) proudly proclaimed that traditions like celibate widowhood made Hindu women so unique that even Americans were trying to emulate it.[28]

The same orthodox approach was further reinforced in the final form of the 'conjugal' relationship mentioned by Dhirendranath where he stated unhesitatingly that to develop a 'spiritual' relationship with her husband, the wife must make her husband 'her all' (ibid). A wife achieves the stature of a sati (here the word denotes the ideal woman, whose chastity and fidelity are beyond question, and not the widow who kills herself at her husband's pyre) only when her husband is everything to her. This relationship is a spiritual relationship and if this spirituality is not achieved in a marriage then it is no marriage at all in the eyes of religion (*CWW* 1883: 26).

The spiritual aspect of Hindu conjugality is of crucial importance here since it signifies that unlike the natural and scientific approach implemented in the European form of marriages, the indigenous form of conjugality claims a sacred basis for a proper family life. This enabled not only an assertion of the continuation of marriage after death but also the promotion of the superiority of the indigenous matrimonial bond to that of Europeans, limited as the latter was only to the present birth. The Hindu conjugal union was guarded by dharma and the *patibratadharma* (the duties of a wife) which continued even after the husband's death. Accordingly, Dhirendranath's imaginary husband elucidates the respective dharma of a husband and a wife: Dharma is the foundation of everything:

> If there is no dharma, fame, respect and wealth cannot be won; if there is no dharma, winning happiness is impossible . . . Consequently, both husband and wife need dharma and both must earn it. It is our work as men to earn wealth, fame and respect and we must learn whatever is needed to do that . . . It is your work as women to earn happiness and I will gradually instruct you in whatever you need to know for that. (*CWW* 1883: 26-36)

The decisive role of dharmik stipulation in the Hindu way of life becomes obvious in this remark. As a result, far from positing a dyadic romantic relationship between the husband and the wife the manual posits the conjugal relationship driven by religious conviction that includes all family relationships and responsibilities under the comprehensive blanket of the Hindu marriage system placed at the core of domestic life. An imaginary couple engaged in conversation on the actual worth of marital life in an article published in *Bamabodhini Patrika* claims: 'We should not be satisfied with ordinary love that everyone craves for; our goal should be to attain the divine love that only husband and wife, well aware of their destined duties, can obtain, and thus take refuge at the feet of the God Almighty' (*BP*, mid-Oct to mid-Nov 1874/ Kartik 1280 BS).

Another article published sixteen years after the previous one was more careful in emphasizing the spiritual aspect of Hindu marriages, and claimed, 'Dharma is the essence of Hindu Marriage. Physical relation is just an excuse here' (*BP*, mid-May to mid-June 1889/Jaishtha 1296 BS). At this juncture the significance of marriage for the Hindu way of life, once again becomes obvious, as does the motivation behind controlling the lives of native women in order to preserve a traditional social order at the birth of Indian nationalism. Here the perfect unity of the husband and the wife is figured as the unification of dharma with the family relations. This in turn manifests itself in the proper conservation of a larger dharmik social order in which every individual has her/his role to play according to her/his prescribed dharma and ultimately a dharmik social arrangement upholding a hierarchical society prevails. It is important to remember that in the renewed model of ideal women of the late nineteenth-century, the women for whom the domestic manuals and literature were written, belonged to a certain social rank with access to reformist activities. People of lower origins with lesser or no access to the educated and/or affluent circles of society had hardly any access to reformist agendas and neither did their women. This unjust social order began to change at least to an extent because of opportunities of social advancement under colonial rule as several social groups of ambiguous origins aspired to ameliorate their low status by setting new standards for their women (see also Chapters 1 and 2). This change, in many cases, was only superficial, giving rise to a different kind of hierarchy amongst the lower strata of society.

Returning to the discussion of the elitist world of the native agents, those who were marginalized in the public sphere had to shift focus to the domestic arena. Thus the women at home, as some historians have suggested,[29] had to function in the rising nationalist imagination as a repository of Hindu traditions and spirituality. This new ideal woman had to be different owing to the mounting attacks of the colonial masters and the escalating sense of self-esteem among elite natives powered by the weapons of Utilitarianism and humanitarianism (Raychaudhuri 1988: 32-54) through their exposure to western education. The ideal counterparts of these native male agents would be the ideal Hindu wife, as Judith Walsh has summarized:

> The new wife was to be . . . literate and educated, trained in domestic skills, she would through her hard work and efficiently make her household a paradise of 'good order' an abode of peace. The culture and traditions she would embody would be those newly recovered from the ancient Aryan past.
> (Walsh 2004: 81)

The new ideals recommended for women were, however, not without potential disadvantages as literacy and education for women were conceived as a threat to indigenous domestic order. This in turn could damage the Hindu social order. This threat was coupled with the aspirations of the low-caste groups hopeful of demolishing the hierarchical social order encouraged by the colonials. The panic of the native elite order found expression repeatedly in Indian domestic literature exemplified in the 1890 Burdwan press: 'Will the woman who has obtained the BA degree cook or scour plates?' (Borthwick 1984: 104). This clearly shows that no other area of reformist prescriptions for the new ideal woman aggravated more anxiety than the idea that once educated women might stop performing their domestic duties. The most dreadful future reformists could possibly imagine was a domestic world occupied by college-educated, novel-reading females who refused to contribute to the domestic sphere any longer (Walsh

2004: 81). A female writer in *Bamabodhini Patrika* echoing the same anxiety claimed: 'We have learnt by virtue of our education that we are in no way inferior from men. Subsequently we have started disrespecting our men. But sisters have a glance at our glorious society; I cannot see any other society in this entire universe where women have such control over their husbands' (*BP*, mid-Sept to mid-Oct 1895/Ashwin 1302 BS).[30] The writer then goes to claim that Hindu society had always worshipped women, and Hindus thus, she claimed, could boast of having women like Sita, Savitri, Damayanti, and Arundhati, unlike British society where King Henry VIII deserted his innocent wife and had Anne Boleyn executed (ibid). However, those great days were gone and the columnist writes, with a lot of sadness, 'these great female characters are proof of what we were and what we have turned out to be!' (ibid).

Predictably, to demonstrate the superiority of native life one Bengali manual even went to the extent of pointing out how the daughters of Queen Empress Victoria were skilled in domestic work like cooking and rather than being ashamed of this, as imagined by some western educated native elites and misleadingly projected by the colonials themselves, the queen's daughters felt proud of themselves for performing their duties primarily as women (*BM* 1887: 19). This manual and many others belonging to that period[31] illustrated the need to restore the glorious native past in order to challenge colonial modernization. Consequently, the vigilant safeguarding of domestic life and women became essential for native elites who had lost face in the public sphere by losing the battle against the colonizers in the outer world.

In view of the mounting requirement to protect native domesticity the Bengali manual by Giribala Mitra and Jayakrishna Mitra, *Ramanir Kartabya* or *The Duties of Women* (*DW* 1890), exclusively focused on the intimate details of home and domestic life and particularly on the skills of the housewives that were necessary to run native households. Earlier, many manuals had included a chapter or two on domesticity[32] but perhaps had not felt the need to explicate the details of domestic life to such an extent. As a result *The Duties of Women* is loaded with recipes, sewing and mending instructions, and all the possible details of maintaining a prosperous native domestic life (ibid) without disallowing the European influence altogether. For example, this book certainly demonstrated that the reconfiguration of the nineteenth-century domestic sphere was a global phenomenon.[33] Nevertheless, the incorporation of native traditions was done deliberately. For instance, the advice on how a woman should brush her teeth and keep her body clean were not just a result of a European notion of healthy living; these techniques although adopted were carefully melded in a Bengali and indigenous manner. The authors, Giribala Mitra and Jaykrishna Mitra (probably Giribala's husband or brother), predictably belonged to the influential bhadralok faction. Giribala most likely wrote the original instalments that were published in *Bamabodhini Patrika* between 1886 and 1888, in which she focused on the intricate details of native domestic practices (Walsh 2004: 132). Giribala's social standing is evident here from her easy access to an eminent magazine like *Bamabodhini Patrika*, which perhaps is indicative of her Brahmo connection as well.

Jaykrishna Mitra, on the other hand, probably edited Giribala's writings in Brahmo and subsequently high-caste Hindu fashion. Between 1888 and 1890 he also added materials to the original magazine articles and published the whole collection as a book (ibid). Ultimately, the book described the domestic sphere as the most authentic sphere of native identity, and the women as the 'rulers' of this consecrated region. As native women were endowed with paradigmatic virtues this area remained untouched by foreign aggression, and consequently native identity remained uncontaminated in the home. Thus the establishment of the uncontaminated superior nature of native domesticity gave back to the native agents what they lost in their battle outside. The book became quite successful and was eulogized by both the Brahmo and the Hindu leaders (Walsh 2004: 132) as the objective of the book was in harmony with the goals of both the groups, that is, the protection of the indigenous social order by incorporating certain changes in native domestic life that would neither become dominant enough to endanger the superiority of native traditions nor fall short of conforming to the methodical and scientific nature of colonial domestic guidance. Notably, the bhadralok of both these groups with their fresh exposure to European science and technology had a weakness for scientism and sought to apply scientific methods even in the native domestic arena (ibid), methods which were considered to be the marks of intellect.[34] This book not only fulfilled all these various requirements but also concentrated on the chaste and steadfast characters of native women, which was essential for restoring the superiority of native traditions.

The Duties of Women brought into focus the enduring association between the proper maintenance of a Hindu home and appropriate implementation of hygiene rules in order to prevent the contamination of the domestic world, as well as the greater social order caused by faulty execution of rules of cleanliness. The house should not be built in a malaria prone area, which was dangerous for the health of the members of the family; the house must not be near a pond either as children of the family might drown; the house must be constructed far away from quarrelsome neighbours in order to avoid their negative influence on the family (*DW* 1890: 5-29). Then again, the home had always to be clean, healthy, and attractive. The latrine should always be away from the bedrooms to avoid the spread of germs (ibid). All the rooms including the cowshed should be regularly and thoroughly cleaned, for cleanliness improved everyone's health (even the cow's who provided the family with milk) (ibid). To avoid illness, the air in all the rooms had to be 'pure', which meant it should be free from bad smells, which in this text and many other domestic manuals of the nineteenth century were assumed to be the main cause of disease (ibid).

The importance of purity of the household is worth noticing, as well as the paradigm of order to be maintained in the domestic arena. For instance, *The Duties of Women* claimed that, rice, dal, flour, and all other things should have separate containers decoratively arranged in rows with each item's name neatly written on the container (ibid 1890: 10). Also, the utensils in the kitchen had to be properly arranged according to their use; plants should be lined up in a row; seeds from the garden should be stored properly. Overall, everything must be organized in such a way that even a stranger walking into the house would face no problem in locating things (ibid). Highlighting the importance of purity and orderliness *Duties of Women* thus elaborately illustrated the importance of these two factors in native existence, factors which completely coincided with those required for the preservation of the hierarchical social order. Similarly, several articles in *Bamabodhini Patrika* offered detailed explanations for the significance of hygiene, purity, and orderliness. These articles devoted pages to discussing the following issues: how to deal with the problems of ants, insects, and unwanted entries of cats and dogs in the kitchen; how to purify water; how to get rid of germs in a scientific manner, and so on. The magazine, in fact, came up with several couplets written in simple colloquial Bengali on the issues of hygiene and cleanliness so that the less educated housewives who did not have access to advanced level books could memorise and apply them without anybody's help.[35] This emphasis on cleanliness and an organized maintenance of domesticity extended the importance of purity and orderliness in a larger social context. The internalization of these important virtues in the family life had helped to cement these values in a larger socio-political arena, encompassing the fundamental ingredients of the caste hierarchy that distinguished the essential dichotomy between purity and impurity, orderliness and disorderliness and, most importantly, the value-based disparity between the high and the low-caste groups.

With respect to *The Duties of Women*, the importance of adorning the home in an attractive manner is stressed, further consolidating the divide between the domestic and public spheres since home is the only refuge for the husband after all his dreadful experiences in the outer world. Moreover, the home must look beautiful so that the husband feels the urge to return home and does not deviate from his dharma as the ultimate authority in the domestic world. If the home is unhygienic, chaotic, and visually unappealing then the husband feels unenthusiastic to go back home, and might obtain similar contentment from the outer world and engage in undesirable associations. This would be an alarming move capable of violating the social order in which proper execution of respective dharma is essential to preserve the collective structure. Thus, *The Duties of Women* proclaims that food must be in containers, which ought to be the sleeping place for the cow, even the pattern in which potatoes were to be scattered across the sand in the corner of the storeroom, all must be 'beautiful to see' (*DW* 1890: 10-25). And, most importantly, the wife, the manager of the domesticity, must take care of every aspect of domesticity on her own, which suggests how with the introduction of education and other modernizing factors the patriarchal social order was always anxious in case women would no longer take any interest in domesticity. An article in *Bamabodhini Patrika* befittingly remarks,

> If Hindu women acquired the coveted BA, MA degree, and could recite on the one hand Vyas, Valmiki, Manu, Parashar . . . and on the other Homer, Shakespeare, Shelley, Milton; could solve the theorems of geometry in just one minute, if she became a Lilabati in her mathematical aptitude, and Khona in astrology; if she could defeat Bararuchi, Galileo, Newton in solving the most complicated scientific puzzles; if she sang sweeter than Devi Saraswati, but still could not run her home perfectly we would have no hesitation in declaring that her education was incomplete.
>
> (*BP*, mid-Oct to mid-Nov 1894/Kartik 1301 BS)

While the home had to be well organized, clean, and beautiful, so did the housewife who ran it, as she was the central force behind the domestic world. If the wife who was the supervisor of the household looked ragged and unattractive then the endeavour to maintain the domestic sphere in an appropriate manner would be meaningless. In a situation like this the husband would have no motivation to return to an unappealing wife after a long day at work. She had to be supremely organized, industrious, and at the same time remarkably gorgeous. Another article in *Bamabodhini Patrika* necessitating physical beauty for women thus declares:

> The thirst for beauty is inherent in the human race. Beauty has a quality that is invincible. Human beings always wanted to remain engaged in adoring beauty and women are the manifestation of humanity's eternal quest for beauty... Beauty is the abode of love, and the woman adorned with beauty, love and purity is endowed with the capacity to take us closer to the God.
>
> (*BP,* mid-April to mid-May 1899/Baishakh, 1296 BS)

In an 1881 essay contest on the topic 'model housewife', Parbati Basu, who won the competition, ascribed to the concept of model womanhood all the qualities essential to conform to the nineteenth-century colonial project of modernization along with the native aspirations of self-governance by means of projecting their womenfolk as a faultless creation. Thus, her ideal woman was splendidly gorgeous, well behaved and, most of all, virtuous, coupled with qualities like good education and well resourced with the knowledge of domestic science previously considered the forte only of her colonial superiors (Borthwick 1984: 196). As a result even if the most trifling domestic issue grabbed her attention, for example, 'Any shirt without a button, any torn clothing . . . any pillow without a cover, any dirty sheet, anything that hasn't been moved and need dusting, she attended to all these things with care' (ibid).

In the final chapter of *The Duties of Women* the mandatory assiduousness of the model woman is cited thus:

> She has so much work that at times she does not get to eat or rest. Every in afternoon she mends all the clothes, quilts, socks, shirts, and so forth, . . . Once a year she rids the entire house of dirt and cobwebs. The floors in every room of her

> house are so clean that they can be slept on without a mat. The things of the house are so tidy and are so pleasingly arranged that just seeing them is soothing to the eye.
> (*DW* 1890: 115)

It is her industriousness practised with conscientiousness, and her dedication towards her feminine, and certainly, wifely dharma that were imperative for maintaining the native family structure unharmed, which is emphasized persistently in the nineteenth-century domestic literature.

Before examining the wifely duties in terms of a wife's classified relationship to her husband, let us look at some other domestic responsibilities that were no less significant in the creation of an ideal feminine figure and, more importantly, an ideal social order. For example, financial skill was one of the prerequisites for this ideal, since a financially skilled wife would save considerable money and accelerate the prosperity of her husband. Borthwick has pointed out how unlike in the first half of the nineteenth-century the bhadralok were living in a way that placed less value on the ostentatious exhibition of wealth; in the latter half of the century they had to maintain a steady level of expenses due to the new stress on education and health (Borthwick 1984: 187). An urban bhadralok's monthly salary was 150 rupees a month during the 1890s of which he had to pay for the education of his male children, ranging from an average of 100 rupees a year to 1000 rupees for education in England, considered to be a mark of the highest social repute. Moreover, the cost for female education was even higher (ibid: 188). Food had become more elaborate, and the reformed and modernized women's dress including petticoat, chemise, and often shoes, was far more expensive than a simple sari (ibid: 188-89). Owing to direct colonial influence the house had more furniture: sofa, couch, easy chairs, basins, piano, and reading lamps. There was mandatory subscription to progressive causes like newspapers and journals. Apart from this extensive list people who had left the family home to earn more money in Calcutta had to pay rent, and send money to their families as in many cases they were the main bread earners (ibid). In a situation like this *Suruchir Kuteer* (1878, cited in Borthwick 1984) by Dwarakanath Ganguly, an archetypal moralistic novel for the bhadralok, focusing on the virtue of thrift, became quite popular.[36] In a review of this book a Brahmo writer summarized the problem thus:

> Western civilisation has created many domestic wants; we now aspire to a mode of living which is more costly than the one we were used to. . . . We always set before our eyes the residence of a well-to-do European without caring about our means, and we would often go to spend every pice that we earn to live according to our ideal. An Englishman would never exceed his means, but would try to save something out of his earnings and yet live better. . . . The secret of all this is the English wife. She is well versed in domestic economy. Thrift is a part of the education of an English wife. She knows how to make her husband and her children comfortable and yet save something.
>
> (*Surucheer Kuteer* or 'Thrift in Indian Homes' cited in Borthwick 1984: 190)

Accordingly, the ability to keep accounts and practise strategic frugality were qualities sought in the new housewife. To save the husband's money, *The Duties of Women* advises that a wife could make her own perfumed body oil instead of buying an expensive product, sew socks, and stitch buttons (*DW* 1890: 15, 82, and 89). She should buy the right amount of ingredients for cooking meals so that nothing is ever wasted. Moreover, by being an expert cook she could make scrumptious dishes out of ordinary ingredients (ibid: 11 and 42). She must also save money by learning rudimentary medicine, and the manual suggests this could spare the husband the expenditure of seeking advice from English doctors (ibid: 104). Although the woman had no earnings of her own, her role in the household economy was a contributing factor to the family's wealth, and hence could enhance the reputation and authority of the family in the society. This is where a simple woman in a Bengali domestic system became the grihalakshmi who by inculcating all the auspicious qualities that the goddess Lakshmi possessed could transform a bare home into an abode of fortune and peace. The reputation of the domestic unit thus became reliant on the careful observation of the wifely duties performed by the woman in the family. Even though all these activities required more work from the wife, it was to be taken in good grace since the wife was the servant of her husband, and his family, and her existence was determined by her unconditional obedience to her master.

Apart from some daily readings, which she had to carry out for educational purposes, and which were considered to be a primary feature of the ideal woman, she should not waste a single moment but engage herself in immense domestic duties (ibid). Let us now focus on the master-servant relationship between the husband and the wife since colonial criticisms against the allegedly degenerate relationships shared by Hindu couples based on an unjust form of marital association had to be countered. Spinning skilfully the understanding of native conjugality *The Duties of Women* claims native women were not the servants of their husbands in any familiar sense. It was a special union between the spouses in which the love, affection, admiration, and commitment of a wife for her husband transmuted all the work she did. This transforming power was the innate faculty of any patibrata woman that bestowed her with the ability of immense industriousness and eventually she could perform all her allocated duties analogous to her wifely dharma (*DW* 1890: 40).

A DISCOURSE OF DEVOTION AND CHASTITY: REWRITING CASTE HIERARCHY

The nineteenth-century Indian 'woman question' is suffused by biographical and autographical literature of native women testifying to the valour, vigour, strength, and determination of native female existence.[37] Powered by these virtues these women not only struggled to break free from indigenous customs such as purdah and the ban on female education, arguably the two most condemned areas of native living, but also by the virtue of their newly constructed image successfully effaced the indigenous existence from the disgrace of a decadent survival. In Bengal some women learned to read[38] with secret and occasionally straightforward assistance from their husbands and other male members in the family; moreover, they confronted conventional customs of dress and behaviour to step out of their imprisoned existence within the boundaries of the domestic world, an action necessary to be compatible with the emergent requirement of their male counterparts' yearning to prove their contemporariness to their colonial superiors. Some of them, taking one-step further travelled alone to study aboard and resisted family contempt and mockery to become proficient public speakers.[39] But the account of valour and vigour is only a partial representation of the nineteenth-century native woman's condition.

These changes were the fruit of social changes that were enjoyed by only a few women of advantageous position. However, even those fortunate few were placed within the refurbished orthodox social pattern in which the intrinsic worth of a woman's existence was exclusively determined by her devotion to her husband strictly following a brahmanical paradigm. Two examples support this claim. The first concerns a Bengali upper-class woman, Dayamayi Sen. She was committed to her daily practice of drinking the water in which her husband's feet had been washed. He left her with a constant supply in a metal pot whenever he went away. Many people warned Dayamayi that drinking this water was unrefined and her act was superstitious but she replied that to regard one's husband as one's all was the most important aspect of a Hindu woman's existence.[40] Another woman, Prabhabati Devi, once again belonging to a distinguished family, realized that whenever she performed the Savitri puja her husband's image kept replacing the icon of the goddess. Predictably, after a few attempts she abandoned the puja and started worshipping her husband instead (Borthwick 1984: 147). However, the performance of orthodox social practices by the high-caste native women in many cases resulted in drawing a negative inference from these women's non-heroic presence in the wider society with only a few women from upper-class background able to exemplify the models of valiant heroine.[41]

In this context, Partha Chatterjee has pointed out that the nationalist scheme of applying reform as a device for native women explains the enthusiasm with which late nineteenth-century women took it up. In this process these women did not hesitate to justify the importance of so-called feminine virtues such as housework, chastity, self-sacrifice, submission, devotion, kindness, patience, and the labours of love in order to achieve the benefits of reforms offered to them by their men (P. Chatterjee 1993: 130). Taking the argument one step further, Walsh asserts that it was not just a case of the simple reaffirmation of feminine values as claimed by Chatterjee, nor was it a case of false consciousness in women's lives struggling for a change. It was instead an exacting combination of devotion and iconoclasm in the lives of nineteenth-century Indian women that defined their transformed existence (Walsh 2004: 144). However, in spite all these arguments and counter arguments to grasp the real nature of the altered identity of nineteenth-century Indian feminine existence none of these scholars attempted to clarify why only a careful set of feminine virtues were persistently given importance by the male authorities to reaffirm the patriarchal codes. Further, it is important to note that some traits were consequently altered. For example, as discussed, all the domestic manuals consistently propagate the importance of serving one's husband as one's god and the role of woman's chastity and fidelity in maintaining the native social order intact, whereas considerable changes were allowed in the way of life of native women in terms of their educational pursuits or learning music and dance, qualities once totally forbidden to Hindu women.[42] These changes, in my view, were adopted only within a prearranged social model and accepted only because they ultimately did not pose any threat to the native social order. Thus, as long as native women adhered to the qualities of chastity and fidelity, trivial external reforms were tolerable.

The nature of the set of feminine virtues chosen by the 'new patriarchy' which registered a new model for native women require to be demonstrated to elucidate how these virtues again played a dominant role in protecting the hierarchical nature of the social order. The personal relationship shared by the couples consisting of the physical aspects of the marital association was undoubtedly the most significant area in Hindu marriage.

We begin exploring the intimate aspects of conjugality with a manual written by Purnachandra Gupta in 1885. A baidya by caste, he was an exponent of Vaishnav Hinduism (Walsh 2005: 78), and probably drawing influence from Vaishnav romanticism argued in favour of relaxation of customary restrictions on the married couple so that the couples could meet and speak more freely during the day (ibid). However, just like many of his contemporaries he believed in the crucial role of establishing the husband's authority over the wife, and argued against higher education of women. In *Banglar Bou* (The Bengali Wife, henceforth *BB*) the section on the proper age of marriage exemplifies the claim that restoration of particular traditional norms prescribed for women were not unintentional, moreover, even if they were, the effortless outcome of this triumphant renovation of traditionalism based on a set of brahmanical values ultimately headed for a continuation of inherited discrimination among different members of the native society, a propensity delightful for the upper-caste groups. In the section titled 'The Proper Age of Marriage' Purnachandra asserts:

> The human race was created to protect the Lord of the World's creation. Humans, by virtue of intellect and ability, hold the highest place among all living creatures. Their purpose is to protect the laws of the omnipotent Lord. . . . Then there is birth. This is created through the union of men and women. If a farmer is unskilled, the earth is not fertile and the crop is disappointing. If a sapling is

> planted but not properly tended, it will never bear delicious fruit. In exactly the same way, if a wife is not trained properly, there can be no hope of a well-behaved, honourable and conscientious successor.
>
> (*BB* 1885: 80)

This manual by Purnachandra, resembling many other manuals,[43] stipulates that the purpose of marriage is to produce commendable offspring. But 'well-behaved', 'honourable', and 'conscientious' descendants can only be obtained if the wife/mother is skilled in customary Hindu norms, which are chastity, faithfulness, resoluteness, subordination, domestic competence, and the like. Ensuring these qualities in a wife would guarantee a 'well-behaved' child, a characteristic that we might interpret as conducting oneself in ways sanctioned by traditional society. The honour embodies the proper implementation of reproductive laws laid down by the hierarchical social standards, and one that guarantees the continuance of a discriminatory pattern of social functioning. The third quality envisaged in a good child is his conscientiousness,[44] which is an indispensable trait in the maintenance of a caste-based society, as the inattention of a child (who later has to take forward the legacy of his ancestors[45]) to the often discreet imperative aspects of a hierarchical social structure might damage the social order. As a result, ensuring good progeny is imperative for maintaining the social order and thus an unblemished and righteous marriage is imperative. Thereby, a chaste, faithful, dedicated and subservient wife becomes one of the main conditions for ensuring an appropriate offspring and an intact social order. Further, for the mother, the production of well-behaved children is the most desirable objective of her life since motherhood is the most important function in the life of a Hindu woman.[46] The birth of children, especially sons, sanctified the marriage bond. It is only after the birth of a son the true purpose of a Hindu marriage is achieved, since a son born of a proper wedlock is the provider and inheritor of property. More importantly, he is the one who could perform oblations to ancestors. In other words, he is the preceptor of the lineage and the preserver of the social order, and it is only a chaste and faithful Hindu woman who could give birth to such a son. An article in *Bamabodhini Patrika* eulogizes the coveted status of Hindu motherhood thus, 'as the churning of the ocean gives forth nectar, so the churning of the ocean of language produces the sound 'maa'. The imagination of a poet holds no sweeter image than this.'[47] However, to ensure the birth of such a son who is conscientious, righteous, and faithful to the dharmik social order one must pay attention to a number of other aspects of social life that pave the way for a right marriage and the birth of right progeny.

Child marriage is obligatory for the proper management of society since only a very young wife married to a mature husband could receive and absorb the education necessary for her to develop into an ideal wife. Moreover, early marriage is also a way to establish a wife's love for her husband, since at an early age her mind remains unadulterated and unlike her relationships with her parents and siblings her relationship with her husband necessitates a lot of nurturing. Purnachandra validates child marriage thus: 'So it is understandable that the person with whom we have lived since childhood is the very one for whom we feel the greatest love. Hence, it is most possible for a girl to become devoted to her husband, to become, in fact, the one "for whom the husband is her life" when she, at a very young age, gives her hand in marriage to a man who is already mature' (Purnachandra Gupta 1885: 81). It is worth noticing that in his attempt to offer a romantic view of child marriage, Purnachandra does not acknowledge the fact that traditional Hindu custom did not foster any closeness between the newly wed couple. In addition, husbands and wives were prohibited from meeting or talking to each other during the day. The only time they could spend time with each other was a few hours at night, only after the wife had finished the day's tasks. Under such circumstances probably only one relationship could develop and that was the sexual relationship.[48]

However, Purnachandra adds, 'If girls are married between the ages of eight and ten, one need not fear them coming to any harm.

It is from about the age of eight that children start to understand the world around them, and if, from the same age, they also receive good counsel, there is no better way for them to become educated' (ibid). Here again Purnachandra strongly emphasizes the role of a patriarchal scheme for woman's education and raises the question 'Under whose authority can girls be best educated?' The answer that he offers is reasonably common:

> Girls can be truly well educated only if they remain under the authority of those with whom they will . . . voyage across the ocean of life until they die. And the person under whose authority a woman will spend her life is no one but her husband. Therefore she should be under the husband's authority for that whole period. In conclusion, those who want their daughters to voyage through life as the kind of woman for whom the husband is her 'life' must consider it as their duty to finalize their marriage between the ages of eight and ten.
>
> (*BB* 1885: 82)

Here the fundamental association between puberty, child marriage, reproduction, and a cautiously maintained social hierarchy is passed under the cover of a concern with the welfare of women. Accordingly, Purnachandra claims, if girls are married much later after they achieve puberty (usually around the age of ten) their marriages no longer falls within the category of child marriage and therefore it cannot be considered as ideal marriages. As a result, the unfortunate girls fail to achieve the coveted status of ideal wives. Purnachandra also elucidates the harms of late marriage in a Hindu family structure, which deliberately or not strongly associates early marriage, the need of safeguarding the womb of a woman, and upholding the caste structure by reproductive edicts. Struggling against the reformist agenda of (moderately) late marriage for the benefit of the native girls Purnachandra declares,

> People say that girls should not be married until a thorough education has followed them to understand the world

> around them and until they have become able to clearly understand what the purpose of marriage is and what a husband is. We are not in a favour of such marriages. If girls wait so long for marriage, no one knows, perhaps no one even wants to know, how much evil this might do'
>
> (ibid: 82)

The evils according to Purnachandra are as follows:

> *(a)* If a girl gets married only after she completes her education then the lack of a firm bond of harmony between the couples is often noticeable. The reason being the guidance that the girl receives through her education; if she had received this guidance under her husband's supervision after marriage then such differences would have never arisen. *Therefore to ensure a blissful married life early marriage is desirable, as only through a peaceful conjugal relationship a systematic social order could be developed.*
>
> (ibid: 84; my emphasis)

> *(b)* There are diverse kinds of tastes and inclinations among human beings and the ability to distinguish between good and bad appears as soon as one approaches maturity and as a result each person uses his or her own judgment to decide their preferences. Accordingly, the more a girl approaches the age of maturity the more decisive she becomes about her own choices and as a result even if her parents chose a well-educated, handsome husband of reputed origin for her she might desire for something else. In a situation like this, once again, the holiness of the marriage system is threatened, since the fidelity of the wife owing to her unstable nature is not to be relied on. *As a result the transparency of the reproductive scheme is in danger, and so is the prearranged social structure determined by the stringent reproductive law.*
>
> (ibid: 85; my emphasis)

After establishing the requirement of child marriage Purnachandra goes on to detail the uniqueness of the Hindu marriage structure, which, according to him is unequalled in nature. A manual written by Girijaprasanna Raychaudhuri (1862-1899), who in his *Grihalakshmi* or the Lakshmi of the Home (1888) echoes Purnachandra and asserts the importance of the bond between the husband and the wife and how uniquely it is related to the preservation of family dharma. A brief background to the family of Girijaprasanna Raychaudhuri illustrates my claim that arguably more than brahmins it was people from other castes who advocated strict adherence to the orthodox Hindu practices in order to maintain social order. Born in 1862 Raychaudhuri was from a baidya family who became a lawyer and practised at the Calcutta High Court, a fact indicative of his social success. He took keen interest in writing and published several books. Three of these books were critical works on Bankimchandra Chatterjee's work and the rest were advice manuals. In Chapter 1 of his manual *Grihalakshmi*, Girijaprasanna Raychaudhuri highlights the exceptionality, the superiority of Hindu marriage, a divine union between two people that rises above the banality of ordinary marriages that occur in other religio-cultural systems. He explicates his point as follows:

> No other race on earth has imagined such a union, such a union of husband and wife. In the Hindu marriage the differences between man and woman are lost and they become one, woman and man are combined with each other. At the commencement of a marriage we see two individuals; at its conclusion only one. . . . Their union is such that two were two no longer, they have become one. The Self-Born One has divided his own body into two parts and made those into woman and man. When those two parts assemble and unite, that Self-Born One is created again. In the Hindu religion, whoever becomes the Self-Born One, attains release from reincarnation. This release is also the purpose of Hindu marriage.
>
> (Girijaprasanna 1888: Chapter 1, p 2)

Girijaprasanna's clarification of the exclusivity of Hindu marriage, therefore, takes the objective of Hindu conjugality to a different altitude. The Hindu marriage is just not about a romantic bonding swamped by carnal desires, it is not just a medium of procreation either; the foremost aim of Hindu matrimony is to attain liberation from the pains of rebirth. Rebirth can only be avoided when the dharmik order is properly maintained by the Hindus in their personal and social spheres and the proper maintenance of the order of the dharma is deep-rooted in the caste structure propagated by the Hindu social order. As the family is the most fundamental and atomic ingredient of the social order, the proper preservation of family dharma sustained by both the spouses is of crucial importance here and the implication of conjugality is all the more emphasized in the Hindu system by incorporating the notion of *ardhangini*, which signifies the true worth of a Hindu wife. The word *ardhangini* literally means 'she who is half the husband's body', and according to this concept because the husband and wife are one soul and one body, they mutually share each other's sins and virtues. However, while the husband and the wife are supposed to share each other's misdeeds and merits it is principally the wife's responsibility to appropriate her husband's actions without question as a true patibrata. It is my view that the strategy that functions behind the patibrata ideal, however, is that of control of reproduction, which in turns guarantees the maintenance of the social order, which sanctions caste discrimination and the assertion of the superiority of some lineages over others.

The imaginary husband in Girijaprasanna's manual highlights the significance of household dharma and claims that proper observation of householders' dharma is the best means to end the suffering of rebirth, since through nurturing the householder dharma people accumulate virtue and thereby use up their sins (ibid: 3-24). Girijaprasanna transfers the duty of maintaining household dharma to the women, stating that domesticity is an exclusive site where proper maintenance of the home and paying attention to the diverse needs of the family members, and all those who are part of the family including the servants, are of primal importance (ibid: 1-112). The husband, busy in fighting against the odds at the outer world, could not become a part of the household struggle, neither is he expected to do so, since the battle against the foreign suppressor is lot trickier than routine domestic actions (ibid). Furthermore, it is essentially the wife's duty to provide her husband with contentment and tranquillity when he comes back home after a long day of humiliation and disregard inflicted on him by his colonial superiors. Nonetheless, since the husband takes care of his part of household responsibilities by means of performing financial duties in the course of accepting abominable and demeaning jobs in the outer world, the reasonably easier job of managing the household is to be taken care of by his wife.

Women's magazines were full of instructions of how to do so. One woman advised her readers:

> When your husband returns home from his official work or business, don't burden him with anything, but whole-heartedly try to drive away the cares of his labour. At that time no bitter or unloving words should be said, and he should not be pestered for better ornaments or good clothes. Speak sweetly to him. Look, as God has placed the burden of caring for the wife on the shoulder of her husband, the Supreme Father has likewise given women the responsibility of driving away their husbands' cares.
>
> (Umasundari Dasi's *Naricharit Kabya*, cited in Borthwick 1984: 119)

Accordingly, all the domestic duties, all the household functions and several other tasks like, helping out every member of the family and others, taking care of family members, and so on, are therefore appropriated by the wife, since these are parts of her wifely dharma. Only by performing her wifely dharma could she contribute to the overall preservation of the social dharma, and consequently accomplish a place for herself in society. In fact, by performing her dharma unfalteringly she could attain the venerated status of Sita, Savitri and Damayanti, who are remembered and revered by all the Hindus even today, a motivation alluring enough to initiate women into the domestic world. As one female manual writer proclaims, 'For as long as the sun and the moon endure, their sacred names will keep India bright' (Nagendrabala Dasi 1904: 8).

Thus, the different socio-religious, economic, and political requirements of a particular period formulated a new ideal of womanhood in Bengal, meeting the diverse demands of different agents coming from varied backgrounds with contradictory socio-political, and economic interests, all tied to a closely neat social structure going through a massive change. This new ideal re-emerged as a grihalakshmi, and a patibrata, or what we prefer to call her, *nabya adarsha nari*, literally the new ideal woman who also possessed some new qualities essential to comply with the demand of European modernity. This ideal woman is a wife who would bring happiness and prosperity through her righteous conduct. As Lakshmi, she is the goddess of fortune to her husband and also by staying within the boundaries of the inner world of domestic regulation her potentially dangerous sexual impulses could be controlled. Thus the term *grihalakshmi* encompasses the entirety of family obligations, relationships, and household duties that would ultimately guarantee the restricted existence of the woman. Nonetheless, the patibrata ideal still remained crucial since not only by performing household duties could a woman perform her wifely dharma but also unconditional obedience of a wife still remained arguably the most important factor obligatory for preserving the social order adorned by dharmik injunctions. The new model woman reflects how colonial rule brought in certain changes that forced the bhadralok to refurbish the ancient model of perfect womanhood and also gave this image a novel look by incorporating qualities earlier unthinkable, all still within the parameters of traditional brahmanical norms.

NOTES

1 The new ideal woman had to be reinvented as the embodiment of the reform-based new virtues that the native elites compulsorily went through. For example, literacy was the most important virtue among them. For an examination of the newly adorned virtues of native women see, eg, Jaykrishna Mitra 1890.

2 The actual nature of the overwhelming impact both of domestic discourse in the nineteenth century was, however, a complex process of collaboration, both subtle or obvious in nature, between the colonizers and the colonized. As the Comaroffs have shown, the same domestic discourse and discursive behaviours that stood for civilization in the colony were returned 'home' again to the metropole. Colonialism, they write, 'played a vital part in the formation of modern domesticity *both* in Britain and overseas . . . Historians have underplayed the encounter with non-Europeans in the development of western ideas of modernity in general, and of "home" in particular . . . . Scenes of distant battles with savagery . . . became the cautionary currency of an urgent moral offensive in the urban "jungles" of Victorian Britain, where the poor were seen to be as uncivilized as the most beastly blacks in the bush. Here lay the basis of a dialectic domesticity, a simultaneous, mutually sustaining process of cultural reconstruction at home and abroad' (Comaroff and Comaroff 1992: 45).

3 I emphasize that European bourgeois domestic discourse was able to capture the central stage in the global arena through the interactions and complex exchanges with the colonies in the nineteenth century. There were multiple ways in which the colonies and the metropole influenced each other. As Cooper and Stoler insist, 'Europe's colonies were never empty spaces to be made over in Europe's image or fashioned in its interests; nor, indeed, were European states self-contained entities that at one point projected themselves overseas. Europe was made by its imperial projects, as much as colonial encounters were shaped by conflicts within Europe itself.' See Cooper and Stoler 1997: 15.

4 The Comaroffs have pointed out that the term 'domesticity' can properly be applied to the unique historical form of home and family relations. They insist that far from being a normal or natural standard of human family life, nineteenth-century European,

middle-class domesticity is a discourse used by certain groups of European elites at a particular historical moment to establish their own claims to cultural hegemony. See Comaroff and Comaroff 1992: 39.

5 Although many early nineteenth-century European manuals saw good orders as God's will and men and women's family lives divinely ordained (Davidoff and Hall 1987: 176), the careful structuring of family life, marriage, reproduction, and social ordering claimed to be originated from and based on the sacred declarations that we see in Indian domestic life is definitely a scarcity in European structure.

6 By 'symbolic act kinship' we mean the value-added marital structure of Bengali society that plays a determinant role in the maintenance of the stratificatory social order and the act of preordained procreation created out of it. The manipulative marriage system and the calculative reproductive activity that accomplishes it are ensured through the symbolic actions of marital exchanges and reproductive accomplishments, which in turn safeguard the caste-based kinship system.

7 As well as in the wider context of Indian culture in general in which the origin of a person is the primary determinant of his or her social status, notwithstanding other influential socio-economic ingredients like money or education. Even then, the caste factor is hardly absent in any of these areas.

8 A *sanskar* is an act that completes a person by moving that person bodily toward the most organized and self-controlled position he or she is capable of achieving. See Nicholas (1995) and Inden (1976).

9 But there are, of course, limits on the maximum state of organization and self-control that any human being can attain at birth, eg, a person born as a female is always considered to have more limited capacity for refinement than a male. Similarly, a person born as a shudra remains intrinsically limited by the natural and moral qualities inherited in birth by his or her body. As a result, women and shudra both are expected to live their lives under the control of upper-caste males. Moreover, what any of the sanskar life-cycle rites can achieve in the purification, refinement, and completion of a body possessing chaotic qualities is severely restricted by the inherent limited capacity of a female with a low-caste body. Further ritual work is thus, at best, wasted and, at worst, productive of results opposite of what were sought because of its

inherent inappropriateness. For further details see Inden (1976).

10 See, eg, Leslie 1989.

11 During 1870-96, the *Catalogue of Printed Books* showed fifty-nine domestic manuals of all types in publication, with 55,900 printed copies of these books in circulation. Forty-two of these books were manuals written specially for women (Bengal Library 1879-96). For the years 1800-1930, the National Library's Bengali language catalogue listed approximately 40 domestic manuals, depending somewhat on how the category was defined (Bengal Library 1867-1914; National Library 1959, 1963), All these figures are collected from the Indian government's *Catalogue of Printed Books* and the *Catalogues of the National Library* and the *Bangiya Sahitya Parishad.* The census figures and all other figures are verified from Borthwick 1984:108, and Walsh 2005: 10-11.

12 Along with the growing literacy rate among women (almost exclusively from the upper strata of society) there developed an appetite for novels and dramas among these new readers. See, eg, Deb 2004 who offers details of the habit of reading of novels and dramas by women in the prestigious Tagore family.

13 Bankimchandra Chatterjee, one of the pioneers of modern Bengali literature, wrote several famous romantic novels. Bankim successfully combined the old sanskritic style of Kalidasa with Shakespearean melodrama. Bankim's novels became a source of sustenance for upper-caste Bengali women, for whom these literary works were the only windows to the world of romance and adventure, although deeply embedded in the traditional brahmanical structure. Satyajit Ray's masterpiece celluloid creation, *Charulata,* based on Tagore's short story *Nashtanir* (The Broken Nest), demonstrated how the heroine, who fell for her brother-in-law out of sheer loneliness used to spend her time devouring Bankim's novels, a dangerous tendency the orthodoxy always despised.

14 Founded in 1828 the Brahmo Samaj was opposed to idolatry and many other orthodox Hindu social and religious practices. As a result, Brahmos were often expelled from their own caste communities and disinherited by their families. During the late nineteenth century the Brahmos operated almost as a separate caste within the Bengali society: practising their own religious beliefs, rituals; their children's marriages were arranged only within the Brahmo community (Walsh 2005: 11).

15 However, there were female manual writers like Nagendrabala Dasi (1878-1906) who although had no formal education wrote the manual *Woman's Dharma* (*Nari Dharma*) in which she reaffirmed the older patriarchal traditions. To her 'husband is a woman's only god'. To this end she decried the reforming tendencies of modern Indian society that had led women away from the heroic goddess-like character of ancient Hindu women and she filled her manual with traditional quotations and references eulogizing characters like Sita and Damayanti. It is probably Nagendrabala's otherwise unsatisfactory life that claimed her allegiance to an older patriarchal order that at least enabled women to attain the status of goddesses.

16 For a discussion of the 'new family', see Borthwick 1984.

17 The titles of Dhirendranath's books suggest how passionately he was engaged with women-related issues of that period. Dhirendranath's published work includes *Conversation with the Wife* (*Strir Sahit Kathapokathan*), *The Female Companion* (*Sangini*), *Women's Physiology* (*Naridehatattwa*), *Mother* (*Janani*), *The Hindu Wife* (in English), *The Hindu Science of Marriage* (also in English), and *Husband and Wife* (*Swami-Stri*).

18 The Brahmo fascination for a healthy and clean life-style and reformative approach towards women following a western paradigm is illustrated in Borthwick 1984.

19 For a similar trend see *Ma o Chhele* (1887); *Bangiya Mahila* (1887); *Nari Dharma* (1900).

20 The same trend is observable in Chandicharan Bandyopadhyay's *Ma o Chhele* (Mother and Son) (1887), Taraknath Biswas's *Bangiya Mahila* (Bengali Women) (1887), Nabinkali Dasi's *Kumari Shiksha* (Education for Girls) (1883), Jaykrishna Mitra's *Ramanir Kartabya* (The Duties of Women) (1890).

21 For Dhirendranath these are *angshi* (partner), *stri* (wife), *sakha* (confidant), and *adhyatmik* (spiritual) relationships respectively (*CWW*: 11).

22 For more on how the romantic bonding between a couple was viewed as a menace to societal good see Borthwick 1984: 114-40.

23 For instance, see the work of Partha Chatterjee (1993) who does not probe enough the caste-dominated nature of Hindu domesticity and thus announces the disappearance of the 'women question' by the time nationalism had taken centre stage. It is Chatterjee's denial

of the multi-layered nature of the social structure that builds up his conviction in this regard and leads to his failure to probe the emergence of the same issues at amongst the low-caste groups, which is essentially equivocal. Additionally, it is this tendency of Chatterjee that leads him to stress a monolithic inner core of native domesticity that is only brahmanical.

24 Leslie's work (1989) offers a clear example here. Medieval Bengal witnessed a similar trend in safeguarding domesticity against different kinds of social threats. See K. Chakrabarti 2001.

25 Even a superficial scrutiny of the manuals confirms this claim.

26 According to Nirad C. Chaudhuri, before colonization Bengali society never felt either proud or happy with concepts like *satitwa* or *patibratya*. During the first half of the nineteenth century Bengali society with its direct exposure to the British tried to accommodate the high qualities of their masters and at the same time in order to prove its worth to the masters, emphasized the high qualities of indigenous culture as well. The western thesis of romantic love, courtship and so on gave rise to the native's antithesis of patibratya and satitwa. See Nirad C. Chaudhuri 1389 BS/1981: 148-49.

27 On the Dharma Sabha, which took up the task of defending the traditional Hindu women and Hindu practices from the onslaught of various quarters, see C. Bayly, ed, 1996.

28 This article published in *Bamabodhini Patrika* (mid-Nov to mid-Dec 1885/Aghrayan 1292 BS) did not name any author and claimed one American missionary Jeremy Taylor using the examples of Hindu women to ask American women to be like them. The article, however, did not offer any details about Taylor or his writings from where the materials of the article were collected.

29 See, eg, I. Chatterjee 1990; T. Sarkar 2001 and M. Sinha 2000a.

30 Basic education for native women had to be accepted in order to fight against the accusations that Bengali (Hindu) women were inferior. For an overview of dilemmas facing the bhadralok regarding women's education see Borthwick 1984: 104-06; see also Chapter 2.

31 All the nine manuals that Walsh 2004 has mentioned as 'the most frequently used' Bengali domestic manuals despite acknowledging the need for European modernization eulogized indigenous tradition.

See, eg, the Bengali manuals *Ma o Chhele* (1887); *Bangiya Mahila* (1887); and *Dasi* (1900).

32 For example, Dhirendranath's *Strir Sahit Kathapokathan* (1887) and Tarakanath Biswas' *Bangiya Mahila* (1887) do not focus exclusively on domesticity.

33 A reading of this book will clearly reveals its hybrid nature, it indigenised foreign discourse of domesticity whose various components: food, ingredients, clothing, furniture, and other household materials are not always traditional, but certainly local and indigenous and, more importantly, a maintainer of native superiority, a clearly nationalistic trend influential in the last decade of the nineteenth century.

34 See Raychaudhiri 1988 for a discussion regarding the bhadralok attitude towards European scientific didactics.

35 See *Bamabodhini Patrika* (mid-Sept to mid-Oct 1881/Ashwin 1288 BS) and *Bamabodhini Patrika* (mid-Nov to mid-Dec 1894/Agrahayan 1301 BS).

36 *Suruchir Kuteer* was a Brahmo publication, mid-Oct to mid-Nov 1881/first published in 1878, and went into a second edition of 1000 copies by 1881. See *Bengal Library Catalogue* (1881), I.

37 See, eg, the autobiography of Rasasundari Devi, 1809-1900, *Amar Jibon* and Tanika Sarkar's interpretation of it (1999).

38 Brahmamayi Das, Agharkamini Roy, Kailashbashini Devi, Sharadasundari Devi were tutored by their husbands. Shanta Nag learnt to read upside down, secretively following her brother's lesson from the other side of the reading table. Rasasundari learnt to read letters from a copy sheet stolen from her son. For more on these fascinating women see Borthwick 1984; U. Chakraborty 1963, Karlekar 1993, and T. Sarkar 2001.

39 See Amrita Basu 1999: chapters 3 and 4; Kosambi 1986.

40 See Saratchandra Datta, *Dayamayi Sener Sanksipta Jibancharit* 1890: 25-26.

41 Judging by the nationalist standards of consciousness of the late nineteenth and early twentieth centuries, scholars tend to focus on native women's heroic voices and neglect the large number of women who professed a subordinate and devotional demeanour. For example, the editors of an excellent anthology, *Women Writing in India* posed this question as the 'major principle' of selecting women's work for their anthology: 'what modes of resistance did

they fashion?' (Tharu and Lalita 1991: 36). An alternative concept of women's voice can be found in Julia Leslie's work on the practice of widow burning in India. See Leslie 1992.

42 A Gujarati journal *Stribodh* founded in 1857 even suggested that a good wife should learn how to play a musical instrument or sing melodious songs so that she could entertain her husband once he returned home after a long day at work (Shukla and Ahmed 1991: 65). In Bengal, liberal Brahmo families encouraged their daughters to take lessons in piano and singing as most Brahmo men exposed to western culture wanted their women to be culturally refined just like their western counterparts; a trend unthinkable even in the last half of the previous century. See also Deb 2004, and Borthwick 1984.

43 Here again I am taking into account the most frequently used Bengali manuals of the late nineteenth century, which are *Ma o Chhele* (1887); *Bangiya Mahila* (1887); *Dasi* (1900); *Bangali Bou* (1885); and *Ramanir Kartabya* (1890).

44 All these manuals refer to male children when they are illustrating the importance of having 'well-behaved', 'honourable', and 'conscientious' progeny.

45 As the male seed is more important than the female soil, the role of the male partner in rightfully maintaining the legacy of the family is superior, and hence the lineage is continued in his name. See Inden 1976, and L. Dube 1988 for discussions of the importance of the seed and soil analogy.

46 For an example of the how important motherhood was to Bengali women in this era see the work of Girindrabala Dasi (1897/1304 BS). In *Ramanir Kartabya* (Mitra 1888) Girindrabala, a moderately educated woman poet of the late nineteenth century, explains why motherhood is still considered to be the most important aspect of a woman's life. See especially p 305.

47 *Bamabodhini Patrika* cited in Borthwick (1984) p 151.

48 The wife of Keshab Chandra Sen would never speak to him in public, since her Hindu conditioning was very strong. One Jagamaya Goswami, even in the free atmosphere of the *Bharat Ashram*, spoke to her husband twice in four years. See Borthwick 1984: 112-13.

4

Gender and the Social Aspirations of Low-Caste Groups

In pre-colonial India, restrictions on women, as discussed earlier, were more of a problem for those who were high caste, privileged and subject to brahmanical gender codes, rather than for the lower-caste groups and untouchables.[1] Nonetheless, the subservient nature of upper-caste women's existence became a norm for women of almost all levels during the colonial period, cutting across caste and class lines. Furthermore, regarding the woman question, the woes of the upper-caste women were a fact of life for Bengali womanhood in general.[2]

The efforts undertaken by native reformists, as discussed earlier, were ultimately attempts to reclaim the superiority of brahmanical patriarchal control. However, to ignore the contribution of the marginal low-caste groups in this process as a failure of mobilization against high-caste dominance or as a manifestation of their passivity would be a flawed understanding of this important social phenomenon. Against the backdrop of the nineteenth century's unprecedented socio-economic and political changes, these marginal social groups developed their own social identities, which were in many cases distinct from, sometimes even opposed to, the upper castes' monolithic hegemonic identity. Their structurization of a new collective self and efforts at self-verification revealed their own perceptions of power relations in colonial society and, most importantly, their own positions within it. Some of these groups invented their own traditions, created their own myths and heroes, and used various symbols, both verbal and non-verbal, to give a concrete shape to their identity.[3] Attempts at self-affirmation by these minor social groups engaged them in conflicts, both violent and non-violent, with those who enjoyed social authority and high status.[4] To pay sole attention to these heroic attempts, however, would prevent analysis of the more mundane accommodation and integration of lower-caste consciousness, ambitions, and grievances within an apparently static and monolithic caste structure.

In a social milieu legitimated by an official discourse that drew its index of social status from upper-caste brahmanical models, arguably the most important referent point for social respectability and mobility was predominantly brahmanical.[5] Moreover, in order to comprehend the subjected society in a comprehensive manner colonial administrators were pushed into ethnographic action. These ethnographic studies aimed at codifying knowledge of the actual Indian situation based on empirical research.[6] But they were unable to escape from the scriptural stereotypes of the Orientalist period that had been so influential in the preceding century. As a result colonial administrators attempted to fit in all the castes and sub-castes into a racial model of the Aryan/non-Aryan dichotomy.[7] While secular factors and economic constraints were occasionally taken into consideration; the basic approach nonetheless remained the same. In other words, brahmanical principles were still considered to be the driving force as well as the central organizing factor of the Hindu caste system. On the other hand, when the colonial justice system started applying brahmanical codes in all private matters, such as marriage, adoption and inheritance, conformity to the brahmanical injunctions was made mandatory (Derrett 1968: 239-40). In the course of time, the colonial focus on Brahmanism began to affect the marginal caste groups as well. Because drawing administrative support from the 'newly educated Bengali intelligentsia' proved to be counterproductive in many cases, the colonial state sought to bring a myriad of social groups into its network, and consequently greater diffusion of wealth and education across caste lines occurred (see also Chapter 1).

When some of the low-caste groups began to acquire property or subinfeudatory rights to land,[8] they too felt compelled to abandon their previous family structures, social arrangements and practices, and to follow the brahmanical codes of marriage and patriarchal social order, the only recognized and reputable social structure under the colonial legal system (Bandyopadhyay 2004: 145). In other words, as *Sambad Prabhakar* (a Bengali newspaper created by Iswar Chandra Gupta in 1831) stated in an issue published on 30 June 1887: 'The Brahmin caste occupies the highest position and all laws and ordinances have been formed with special reference to that. All the other castes conduct themselves after the fashion of the brahmanical castes' (cited in T. Sarkar 2001: 209).[9]

This resulted in drastic changes to the lives of the women of the lower strata. The low-caste males in their new roles as the owners of property felt obligated to legalize their lineage system and this gave rise to the need to control female sexuality and reproductive power which had previously been mainly the concern of landed social agents who were, as mentioned earlier, people with agency to negotiate changes, mainly the brahmins and the other upper castes. Since the 'ethnographic state'[10] reinforced the privileged status of the brahmins, the upper-caste model of womanhood and imperative brahmanical ritualistic behaviours, authenticated their superior status, which subsequently became significant to many others, especially to those aspiring for an improvement in their social status.

Moreover, the decennial Censuses of 1881, 1891, 1901, and 1911 legitimized caste hierarchy and its associated brahmanical normative conduct based on ethnographic surveys (Dirks 2001: 198-227). Besides, in spite of the realization of all the difficulties in the enumeration of caste categories, the comparatively better scheme that the empire decided to depend on for this enumerative listing was the categorization based on the varna system, coinciding with the empire's elitist propensities and the vested interests of upper-caste native administrators in contributing to the design of this scheme (ibid). The result ultimately strengthened the elitist positions of brahmanical Hindu society and left the lower castes with the understanding that the 'object of the Census is not to show the number of persons belonging to each caste, but to fix the relative status of different castes and to deal with questions of superiority' (L.S.S. O'Malley 1913, Part I, cited in Dirks 2001: 223). This in turn resulted in groups claiming a higher place in the order of social priority, and emphasizing affiliation to one of the three twice-born varnas. Moreover, this trend also left marginal groups with greater incentives to embrace universalizing gender norms, indisputably brahmanical in nature. In other words, there was now an increased tendency amongst the lower-caste groups to emulate and reproduce brahmanical gender codes within their communities in order to benefit from the social mobility these codes offered within the colonial regime (Bandyopadhyay 1990: 31-100). As a result, women in this stratum of the society began to lose their autonomy as their communities, or at least sections of them who sought the benefits of social mobility, felt pressured to reinvent their identity within the ideological and normative structures of the brahmanical social model.

The urge to emulate the orthodox brahmanical gender codes was more keenly felt by the middle order of society and trading groups of these marginal sections, for example, the subarnabanik, gandhabanik, tili and mahishya, many of whom had already tasted the fruits of prosperity in the late nineteenth century and had almost achieved a position where they could remodel their identity under the bhadralok influence.[11] The lower ranked groups of the caste hierarchy, nonetheless, remained as marginal as ever.[12] Secondly, changing gender norms was the easiest way to achieve a place within the brahmanical social model, since other symbols of orthodox Hindu identity, such as wearing the sacred thread or observing particular rites were carefully monopolized by the upper-caste groups.[13] Interestingly, relatively upper-caste groups like the kayastha and the baidya also suffered at the hands of the brahmanical hierarchy insofar as brahmins were able monopolize the symbolic forms which enabled the acquisition and maintenance of power. The journal of the kayastha community *Kayastha Koustubh* was first published as early as 1844, in spite of the comparative respectable standing of their caste in the Bengali social order, in order to improve the social standing of this caste group against the hegemonization of the brahmanical order. The journal consistently argued in favour of the wearing of the sacred thread by the kayasthas or organizing ritual ceremonies to bestow kshatriya status on this group, thus contesting the myth regarding the shudra status of all the castes in Bengal other than the brahmins (*Kayastha Koustubh* 1282 BS/ 1875; cited in T. Bhattacharya 2005: 209).[14] Naturally the brahmins did not welcome these efforts of their social subordinates and tended to ridicule their attempts to improve their social status (ibid: 209).

Due to the contested nature of the various attempts to emulate the ritualistic pattern of brahmanical supremacy, areas related to prescribed notions of behaviours for women at the top order were rather easier to imitate and subsequently implement in the life of the women of the low castes. Moreover, as tradition and women always impinge upon each other, social authority that could have rather easily been achieved by changing the ways of life of women of a specific caste group was almost impossible to accomplish in emulating other socio-religious customs vigilantly protected by high-caste groups.

Controlling and restricting the lives of the marginal women was the most unproblematic and effective tool for improving male social status. In other words, this was the only area of their social existence where changing existential patterns did not warrant the approval of the superior social agents. Women were thus viewed as the property of a particular social group who could be used as the apparatus of social advancement. It must also be mentioned that although in the symbolic world of Hindu society the social codes that controlled the position of women were diverse in nature in each stratum of the social hierarchy, almost in every situation the burden of maintaining the honour of a social group rested on women. Thus the relative freedom of low-caste women began to be curbed in emulation of the cultural hegemony of high-caste brahmanical patriarchy in order to secure an improvement in the status of these groups. In an attempt to expand their newly received social authority all these upwardly mobile caste groups started their own exclusive caste associations in the early twentieth century and published their own journals, which became the medium of distribution for their ideas about various social reforms and their subsequent aspirations for upward social mobilization.[15]

The major social reform agenda for these groups comprising the subarnabanik, gandhabanik, mahishya, tili, teli and sadgope was to create a model structure for their women in terms of preferred norms of marriage, domesticity and education. We have already demonstrated that starting from the early nineteenth century, socio-religious rules sanctioned by textual authority were stringently observed by the bhadralok, many from non-brahmin origins and most of these standards were exclusively manufactured for women, as they were the benchmark for the social reputation of their male partners. Similarly, the upwardly mobile lower castes in search of social status also followed in the footsteps of the bhadralok and standardized their way of living, especially the life styles of their women, for example, addressing the lineage pattern, preventing marriage within the same *gotra,* that is, a lineage within a caste that prohibits intermarriage because members are descended from a common mythical ancestor, and also prohibits divorce (*Census of India*, 1931, vol. 5, part 1: 425).

Interestingly, as Ramkrishna Mukherjee's study of late nineteenth-century Bengal shows (1957: 120), 63 per cent of the caste Hindus and 31 per cent of the lower castes of Bengal practised child marriage during this period. On the other hand, in case of running the risk of widow remarriage, the educated and privileged upper-caste groups were gradually abandoning the practice of child marriage. Nonetheless, these ambitious lower-caste groups began to adopt it at the turn of the century. The reason for this was that privileged social groups had little to lose in abandoning previous social practices; on the contrary, the chaste model of Hindu widowhood fashioned on the brahmanical model of ideal womanhood was proving to be beneficial for them under colonial patronage.

At the turn of the century, socially upward, ambitious lower-caste groups had the burden of adopting the social practices previously only applicable to the bhadralok to gain social authority in terms of European modernism, already a well-endorsed form of social mobility among the upper strata of society that permanently altered the lives of their women. Consequently, by the second decade of the twentieth century these upward low-caste groups started to disapprove of their own practices of divorce and widow marriage as anti-Hindu and against the ideal of the eternal bond between husband and wife that exemplified the uniqueness of Hindu social order and accordingly adjudicated the caste status (*Mahishya Samaj*, mid-Aug to mid-Sept 1922/Bhadra 1329 BS).

Women of the low castes were now projected as the procreators and protectors of the lineage system who would act as guarantors of honour and integrity in any disputes related to inheritance. In this new social structure the male agents of these caste groups had no burden. Just like their social superiors, fidelity, although normative, was never a mandatory rule for the male members of the society. In this fascinating game of gaining social supremacy brahmins remained interested referees to monitor the complicated caste manoeuvres and the status re-organizing of some of these lesser categories. If some low castes could be promoted to a somewhat cleaner rank, then many more categories of brahmins could become their authoritative superiors to direct the humbler groups towards their much desired social superiority, without losing their own supremacy, of course. As Tanika Sarkar (2011: 337-51) points out, 'It was the internecine configurations among shudras that emerged as the constitutive site for caste formation, not a brahman-non-brahman mantle of social responsibility. Kayasthas and baidyas were classified as shudras by many orthodox brahmins well into the twentieth century'.

Thus the woman question was not the prerogative of only the

bhadralok, and neither did it lose its significance as soon as upper-caste male agents became involved with the more pressing issues of nationalism. Partha Chatterjee claims that as the nationalist movement gained momentum women's issues were relegated to the private domain, and men instead became preoccupied with more important issues of self-governance, since they had nothing more to gain from the 'woman question' (P. Chatterjee 1993: 117). Chatterjee, however, fails to address the multi-layered nature of the public sphere: where an issue becomes superseded at one level of society it may well take a dominant role at another level. I show, by revisiting a particular genre of low-caste vernacular literature that flourished among the aspiring low-caste groups as a vehicle for upward mobility and social authority, how women's issues still dominated their struggle for existence whereas for the upper-caste bhadralok, who became preoccupied with the discourse of nationalism, these issues lost significance.

The equation among tradition, social authority and the status of women was beneficial for the modernizing bhadralok in fighting against the colonial administration and in seeking eventually to obtain better treatment in the project of independence. This equation dominated the discourse of the nationalist movement as well. However, while the ideal woman was emblematic of the nation's suffering and subordination, her freedom and prosperity were not equivalent to the liberation of the nation (T. Sarkar 2001: Chapter 1). The same preoccupations with, and anxieties around the ambivalent nature of women's existence were once again reproduced in the vernacular literature and journals of the aspirant groups of the lower castes in late nineteenth- and early twentieth-centuries Bengal.

THE SOCIAL ASPIRATIONS OF THE LOW-CASTE GROUPS AS REFLECTED IN THEIR JOURNALS

Matching the intense demand of self-governance of this period, all the low-caste journals adopted a nationalist agenda, a tactful strategy that not only brought them to the mainstream nationalist table, but also ensured that they were heard immediately. However, given that their main agenda was to elevate their own social status by breaking the barriers of caste discrimination, the abject condition of their women, the most common and acceptable yardstick for measuring the success and/or failure of a social group, was a prominent theme. The journal of the subarnabaniks, goldsmiths, declaring the sameness of all the caste groups thus argues as follows:

> Many centuries ago when our Aryan ancestor settled down in this geographical region, for social benefit they created four distinct social groups based on their own choices. One group due to its keen interest in learning and other admirable quests became the most respected group in the society. Another group on the basis of its unique physical competence became the defenders of society. There was another group, which took a profound interest in mercantile activities and thus supplied the resources that organized the society. The remaining group became engaged in farming and weaving and served society with its various valuable contributions. If we look at the social structure thus constructed we would understand no group is inferior to another; in fact they are all essential pillars of society. Without one group the others would be worthless. We simply do not understand why, then, certain groups look down upon others.
>
> (*Subarnabanik Samachar*, mid-Aug to mid-Sept 1917/Bhadra 1324 BS)

In a similar manner, the voice of the mahishya community, the *Mahishya Samaj*, focussing on the positive aspects of this social division argued, 'Every social group has to contribute differently to the construction of the society. The different qualities of these different social groups will be properly manifested only when these diverse groups respect others and create a network of brotherhood among them' (*Mahishya Samaj*, mid-July to mid-Aug 1922/

Shraban 1329 BS). Here one must notice that these low-caste groups are not opposed to the social classificatory system in the form of the caste structure, but rather that they are against the discrimination that was consequent upon the stratification. Taking great pride in their vaishya way of life, for example, in the second issue of the *Sadgope* journal (the sadgopes were an agricultural caste), it was stated:

> Education and commerce are the two pillars of society. Education undoubtedly clears the evil doubts of the human mind, makes people better human beings. Similarly, commerce gives us the money that has the power to take care of the poor, eradicate the menace of poverty and diseases. Without wealth the prosperity of a nation is unfeasible. . . . nations which have taken care of the expansion of trade and commerce have achieved great prosperity.
>
> (*Sadgope Patrika*, mid-Aug to mid-Sept 1928/Bhadra 1335 BS)

Another article of the same journal criticized the upper-caste bhadralok tendency to evaluate their social status in terms of their educational qualifications and declared, 'If we are to present ourselves as an advanced society before humankind then we have to educate ourselves properly . . . education that does not discredit the value of agriculture and commerce in building a nation' (*Sadgope Patrika*, mid-Oct to mid-Nov 1928/Kartik 1335 BS).

Many of these marginal groups, however, articulated a clear concern with their social status in relation to their caste ranking by a constant identification with the vaishyas and not with the lowest of them all, the shudras. The mahishyas, sadgopes,and subarnabaniks repeatedly published articles reasserting their vaishya status,[16] and indeed in many cases they even tried to uplift their position by equating themselves with the kshatriyas (*Sadgope Patrika*, mid-Aug to mid-Sept 1929/Bhadra 1336 BS), indicating an intense push for social mobility. Some groups, on the other hand, realizing the necessity of maintaining an affable relationship with their caste superiors printed articles admiring the benevolent nature of the brahmins. They even advised their associates not to engage in attacks against the upper castes, as this would make their entry into the consecrated circle of the bhadralok more difficult (*Tili Bandhab*, mid-Oct to mid-Nov 1919/Kartik 1326 BS). The tili group's journal, *Tili Bandhab,* also appealed to its caste associates to aspire for social mobility in terms of their group identity, since there had been tendencies among some members of these caste groups to abandon their caste affiliation once they achieved social status in terms of wealth or education. They also criticized the attempts of these people to emulate brahmanical norms in order to achieve social authority and the journal pronounced that those who were going out of their way to spend money by emulating brahmanical rites in order to achieve advancement in this stratificatory social system did not realize that the power that they were going to gain out of these gestures was merely temporary. Unless these affluent marginal people took proper care of their fellow caste members, ensuring the advancement of the entire community their own prosperity would only earn contempt from their social superiors (*Tili Bandhab*, mid-Aug to mid-Sept 1919/Bhadra 1326 BS).[17]

Here, the claims made by historians like Dipesh Chakrabarty and Rajat Ray that the marginal (subalterns) only resisted modernity and lived with their own culture uncontaminated by western concerns with modernization and rationality demand critical analysis.[18] Contrary to these claims, western modernity was both embraced and resisted at the lower levels of the Hindu society just as it was among the higher castes of the society. According to Dipesh Chakrabarty (2000: 10-72; 1994: 21-33) the story of the relocation of western post-Enlightenment modernity to India was not one of 'transition' but of 'translation'; in this process, he emphasizes the untranslatability of certain aspects of Indian culture which refused to accept modernization and continued to survive as 'difference'. However, Chakrabarty comes to this conclusion by focussing on the literature of the high-caste Bengali Hindus (ibid). For him some aspects of the bhadralok idea of domesticity and womanhood stood as signifiers of 'difference' that consciously defied bourgeois modernity. With respect to subaltern groups, Chakrabarty assumes that they resisted modernity all together and protected their culture from western rationalizing endeavours (ibid).

Similarly, Rajat Ray in his work on gender relations and emotions, which is reconstructed once again from high-caste Bengali literature, comes to the conclusion that a renaissance in colonial Bengal occurred during the last decade of the nineteenth century, and exposed only a small group of Indians to the modernizing effects of westernization. Ray (1999: 121-299) consequently assumes, from his readings of high-caste literature, that the untouchables of society remained unaffected by the contradictions and dilemmas of modernity due to their inability to adopt and acclimatize to the changes that western modernity bought. Whilst the adverse reaction against western modernity or brahmanical traditions was perhaps partially true for some marginal groups like the hari, studied by Partha Chatterjee (1993: 187-94),[19] this was hardly the case amongst all the untouchables, as illustrated by Bandyopadhyay (2004) in his analysis of the encounters between high brahmanical tradition and the more egalitarian 'popular' religious cults of other lower castes.

Bandyopadhyay's study (1997: 1-111) shows that the middle-order trading and peasant castes of the subaltern groups embraced colonial modernity and were thus exposed to its epistemological contradictions. Subsequently, the bhadralok preoccupation with the 'woman question', insofar as it negotiated the demands of modernity and those of brahmanical patriarchy, was mirrored by the lower-caste focus on idealized womanhood in order to achieve social mobility. In the upward movement of these low-caste groups education too was an effective tool in enabling social advancement in way similar to that of the bhadralok. Low-caste agents chose to use their educational endeavours as a means of changing the external circumstances determining their social destiny.

THE RECURRENCE OF THE PROBLEM OF EDUCATION AND SOCIAL STATUS

The most important aspect of modernization in colonial Bengal was the spread of education (T. Bhattacharya 2005: 1-69). The growth of literacy among the low-caste groups resulted in a notable growth in vernacular literature which became the medium for conveying messages to both their caste superiors and the colonial regime. Importantly, this emphasis on education appeared to be an effective way of challenging the monopolisation of bhadralok culture by a privileged few. Table 4.1 (see p 182) shows that among the middle-ranked trading castes, such as the subarnabaniks and gandhabaniks, education arrived in the form of vernacular literacy, and not in English, as was the trend for their social superiors. In spite of the social resistance faced by these marginal groups as far as entering into the consecrated circle of education was concerned, peasant castes like the sadgopes and mahishyas were not far behind, and even some of the untouchable groups like the pods and poundrakshatriyas made significant progress in their educational endeavours (Bandyopadhyay 2004: 163-65).

Subsequently, in many cases, education became the most effective yardstick of social status among different marginal groups striving for upward mobility. Thus there appears to have been a push for English education among the comparatively educated subarnabaniks. The journal of this caste, *Subarnabanik Samachar*, published an article in which one observes a clear longing for social status that could only be achieved by higher English education. Accordingly, this article claims that the expertise of subarnabaniks in the fields of trade and commerce is unparalleled but in order to avoid complacency they need to improve their skills so that they could resist strong competition from other non-Bengali business communities who were immigrating to Bengal. Developing a competitive edge could only be accomplished by higher English education (*Subarnabanik Samachar*, mid-July to mid-Aug 1918/Shraban 1325 BS). The article states: 'If 15-20 subarnabanik youths went to get degrees from Cambridge and Oxford universities and then were to employ their high knowledge to the advancement of the business skills of their community... only then will the subarnabaniks thrive in prosperity' (ibid). The journal of the mahishyas, *Mahishya Samaj*, similarly warns members of the caste not to be satisfied with the basic education that they are getting at schools, since this education only prepares students for menial jobs and limits their aspirations (mid-Aug to mid-Sept 1922/Bhadra 1329 BS). Clearly the mahishyas were advising their people to compete with their caste superiors who by virtue of higher English degrees occupied senior posts in the colonial administration and in many other fields of the social order that generated more authority for them. The same journal in a different article declared that lack of education was the origin of their social degradation (*Mahishya Samaj*, mid-Jan to mid-Feb 1922/Magh 1329 BS). The sadgopes provided a statistical report showing the fairly complacent attitude towards education amongst caste members and warned them that if this trend continued they would never achieve the social status enjoyed by the brahmins, baidyas, and kayasthas (*Sadgope Patrika*, mid-Sept to mid-Oct 1928/Ashwin 1335 BS). The editorial of the same issue of the journal, acknowledging the necessity of education in order to compete with the upper-castes, however, warned readers that:

> The number of educated Brahmins, Baidyas, and Kayasthas is increasing in such an alarming rate that the jobs left are not enough for them. Then how can we, the less educated, aspire to achieve the same status as them? But that must not make us feel discouraged. Our skills in agriculture are not to be disrespected. Agriculture is the main strength of our society. We must feel proud to be a part of the great agricultural tradition of this country. But at the same time we must not forget that we need to be more educated to sharpen the skill we already have. We need to comprehend without proper education our existence would turn out to be worthless in this

competitive environment where every other social group is striving to prove its worth.

(*Sadgope Patrika*, Editorial, mid-Sept to mid-Oct 1928/Ashwin 1335 BS)

Table 4.1 Literacy amongst selected castes.

	Percentage of Literacy	Percentage of Literacy	Percentage of Literacy in English	Percentage of of Literacy in English
Castes	1901	1911	1901	1911
baidya	45.60	53.20	15.85	20.88
brahmin	35.80	39.90	8.90	10.90
subarnabanik	32.30	45.10	15.14	21.87
gandhabanik	31.80	31.40	10.18	5.86
kayastha	30.90	34.70	7.59	9.80
shuri or saha	20.80	14.90	1.07	1.84
sadgope	13.90	14.00	1.65	1.86
mahishya	13.00	10.90	0.52	0.72
barui	12.90	15.30	1.26	1.80
jogi	10.40	13.00	0.26	0.51
kalu	10.30	10.70	0.31	0.31
napit	9.80	11.00	0.61	0.87
pod	9.40	14.10	0.15	0.31
goala	6.30	7.70	0.39	0.65
jalia kaibarta	4.30	4.40	0.08	0.21
namashudra	3.30	4.90	0.04	0.22

Table 4.1 shows the percentage of literacy and the percentage of English education amongst different castes. It demonstrates how the agents of almost all the low castes were actively participating in a pedagogic effort to improve their social standing. In some cases these low-caste attempts were even more vigorous and sincere than those of the representatives of the upper castes. For example, the brahmins took second place in terms of their

educational accomplishments both in 1901 and 1911. The rate of growth for them was merely 4.1 per cent in those ten years, whereas for the subarnabaniks the growth was a massive 12.8 per cent. The gandhabaniks also succeeded in achieving a higher position than the kayasthas. Other than these two merchant communities, the subarnabanik and the gandhabanik, who were already relatively prosperous, other prosperous low-caste groups, the saha, sadgope, and mahishya, attempted to achieve improved social status also by means of education. However, the overall social setting still favoured the upper castes, and/or the bhadralok since the low castes' participation in English education was almost negligible except for the merchant communities who could afford it. Accordingly, the subarnabanik and the gandhabanik's accomplishments in English education were more impressive than those of the brahmin and the kayastha. However, although the mahishya or the sadgope communities succeeded in accomplishing basic-level education, they were far from achieving the elevated social status associated with English degrees. The anxiety revealed in the article published in the *Sadgope Patrika* just mentioned was thus not unjustified, since obtaining any job in the colonial administration required training in English, and was further exacerbated by the fact that by the end of the nineteenth century the job market for the native agents was almost exhausted.

Many of these marginal aspiring groups, perhaps, in order to assert their closeness to brahmanical tradition, emphasized the importance of religious education. The editorial of the sadgope journal in its very first edition emphasized the inclusion of religious education in the curriculum of schools and colleges in Bengal and declared that:

> In England the school and the chapel are as inseparable as husband and wife. In engineering colleges there are prayer rooms for British students, in the Aligarh Muslim College there is a mosque for the Muslim students. It is only Hindus who run away from their religion. There are more than eight

> hundred schools and fifty colleges under Calcutta University. Moreover, in Bengal there are hundreds of other primary schools. But we do not have any provision for practising religion in any of these schools and colleges. There is no Hindu temple in any of these educational institutions, no scope for offering puja or doing meditation. . . . Without religion, without proper knowledge of our great religious tradition, without reading our great texts we can only become a defeated nation.
>
> (*Sadgope Patrika*, mid-July to mid-Aug 1928/Shraban 1335 BS)

The gandhabanik with a similar tone accused modern English education of generating materialist propensities among different social groups. The journal argued that

> Western education has taught us nothing; we have only learnt to emulate the hollowness of foreign culture. And eventually we have forgotten our great traditions of religion, morality, and commitment. In this worldly competition of achieving degree-based education we have disregarded our great tradition of fraternal love . . . we need to understand that without the knowledge of the Supreme Being all our knowledge is insignificant.
>
> (*Gandhabanik Samachar*, mid-June to mid-July 1924/Ashar 1331 BS)

For all these lower-caste groups the most challenging issue was the issue of female education, which came, as we have seen, to the forefront in the nineteenth century. Many important personalities belonging to different elitist groups of nineteenth-century Bengal such as Radhakanta Deb, Iswarchandra Vidyasagar and Keshab Chandra Sen and an institution like the Brahmo Samaj became involved in this campaign (T. Bhattacharya 2005: 15-63). By the beginning of the twentieth century the lower and middle-ranked caste groups, the subarnabanik, gandhabanik, mahishya, tili as well as the kayasthas and baidyas also began to emulate the same trend (as mentioned in Bandyopadhyay 2004: 173) for practical purposes. Unsurprisingly, among them the more urbanized and more resourceful trading castes like the subarnabanik, because of their relative social authority among the marginal groups, could afford to take major steps in this direction. Wealthy members of this community donated money to run free schools for women, following in the footsteps of the influential nineteenth-century upper-caste individuals to assert social authority.[20]

In December 1925 they organized a women's conference to discuss, under the guidance of some eminent male personalities of their community, different ways of educating their women (*Subarnabanik Samachar*, mid-Oct to mid-Nov 1917/Kartik 1324 BS). The gandhabaniks also passed a resolution favouring the education of their women in their first *Mahasammiloni* or annual general meeting in December 1923. Both these merchant caste groups continued to publish articles on the problem of illiteracy among their women (*Gandhabanik Samachar,* mid-Jan to mid-Feb 1923/Magh 1330 BS). Even a peasant caste like the mahishyas, the most prominent amongst other peasant castes, took a great interest in female education and started urging the spread of literacy among women of their community through their journals. Again, it was the mahishyas who first brought out a female magazine following in the footsteps of *Bamabodhini Patrika*, the mouthpiece of educated Brahmo women of the nineteenth century.[21] The example was followed by other peasant castes like the sadgopes, who decided to publish special 'women issues' and promoted female writers (*Sadgope Samachar*, mid-Nov to mid-Dec 1935/Agrahayan 1342 BS). The success of these marginal caste groups in the much contested field of female education was certainly less spectacular but not unnoticeable. In 1938 a leading Calcutta daily reported that three namashudra girls had passed the Matriculation examination.[22]

Similarly to their social superiors, female education, however, remained a debatable area for lower-caste groups and subsequently created an impasse. On the one hand, it became almost mandatory for the aspiring caste groups to be a part of the reformist movement and to embrace modernity. On the other hand, this reformist trend had the potential to threaten the patriarchal harmony of the household, which, once again, remained the only area of autonomy where low-caste masculinity could exist untroubled.[23] These dilemmas and anxieties associated with the influence of European modernity and the nationalistic revivalism of the nineteenth century reverberated in the low-caste literature of the early twentieth century (Bandyopadhyay 2004: 174), similarly to that of bhadralok literature. These dilemmas and anxieties were ultimately to shape the model of low-caste womanhood following the high-caste brahmanical pattern.

REFORMS, DILEMMAS AND THE CHANGING IDEAL OF WOMANHOOD

The journals of the mahishya groups, *Mahishya Samaj,* for instance, indeed focussed on the concern for the nation, which however was intermingled with a concern for the pitiable condition of native women. In 1922 it published an address delivered by one Santosh Kumar Das, who spoke movingly about the wretched condition of native women and how this affected the condition of the nation in general: 'In the past we have not treated women as human beings; we have treated them as women. And now by confining them to the home and compelling them to spin *charka* [spinning wheel] we are aspiring for *swaraj* [self-rule]; even if we succeed in achieving it will not last long' (*Mahishya Samaj*, mid-Sept to mid-Oct 1922/Ashwin 1329 BS). Santosh Kumar's main intention was to draw attention to the abject condition of native women and he held male members of the society responsible. He then drew almost a parallel analogy between the wretched conditions of native women and the despicable conditions of the lower-caste groups in the society and resolutely claimed that any demand for swaraj would be meaningless without improving the situation of these deprived groups of Indian society and the status of their women.

The parallels between women and the hapless condition of the lower-caste groups were strategically addressed in another article of *Mahishya Samaj* published in 1916. The article claimed that the progress of caste groups was impossible without the progress of their women (*Mahishya Samaj*, mid-March to mid-April 1916/ Chaitra 1323 BS). Such pronouncements, was strongly influenced by the westernised attitudes of the bhadralok (T. Sarkar 2001: Chapter 1). The enlightened tone regarding the status of women is even more evident in an article in *Tili Bandhab* which argued that 'if we look at the history of any nation that has achieved greatness . . . we will find the vigorous contribution of their women.'[24] The principle that the progress of a nation, and the progress of a community depended on the welfare of its women led to most of these journals approaching the question of women's development with a good deal of seriousness. Subsequently, uncomfortable issues related to child marriage, widow remarriage, and female education that preoccupied higher-caste groups became issues of debate for the lower castes as well.

As the Hindu nationalist opposition to the Age of Consent Bill of 1891 gradually lost its dynamism, the custom of child marriage began to lose its sensitivity among the bhadralok section of the society. The reasons for this were the effects of education among the upper strata of society and its subsequent impact on the practice of dowry (Bandyopadhyay 2004: 166).[25] Moreover, at this stage of nationalist sentiment the nationalist leaders, unable to contest legislative action against the socially backward practice of child marriage, found it convenient to channel their efforts towards addressing the demographic decline of Hindus engaged in the practice of child marriage among them (ibid). The lower-caste aspirants, although initially enthusiastic practitioners of child marriage, gradually embraced the same argument following in the footsteps of the upper castes (ibid). Moreover, their inclination towards child marriage was by then represented as a mark of their backwardness. As a result, by the early second half of the twentieth century, the mahishya did not have any option but to launch a campaign against it (*Mahishya Samaj*, mid-May to mid-June 1912/Jaishtha 1319 BS). The gandhabaniks also sought to discourage the practice (*Gandhabanik Samachar*, mid-Nov to mid-Dec 1923/Agrahayan 1330 BS). Although among the subarnabaniks the rate of child marriage was already low, they still passed a resolution condemning the evil nature of the practice, showing their overall commitment to the prosperity of society (*Subarnabanik Samachar*, mid-Jan to mid-Feb 1927/Magh 1334 BS). The namashudras even went to the extent of declaring that any namashudra marrying his son under twenty and daughter under ten would be excommunicated (Bandyopadhyay 2004: 167).[26]

Here, once again, the critique against child marriage was not generated by an anxiety over the well-being of the child brides and the distress and pain they might undergo in the consummation of marriage.[27] Rather, the main focus of concern was the proper utilization of the reproductive power of the bride in the interests of the community and its lineage system, a concern that was inherited from their upper-caste superiors. Accordingly, aspiring caste groups related the issue of previously endorsed child marriage with the problem of producing weaker and effeminate progeny, an outcome of the Hindu eugenic scheme of the early twentieth-century.[28] The mahishya positioned the demographic decline of the Bengali Hindus and their own community in particular as the effect of this custom (*Mahishya Samaj,* mid-May to mid-June 1912/Jaishtha 1319 BS).

Many other caste groups, drawing a parallel between the benefits of female education and the reproduction of healthy descendants, claimed that because only an educated mother knew how to take good care of her children, and to make them truthful and proper citizens, educating women was necessary for the betterment of society. However, little girls were to be given education of a special kind, one that would make them better wives, and better mothers. If their education were to remain incomplete because of early marriage, their community would remain underdeveloped. Therefore, marriage, although the ultimate goal for a girl, had to come at an age when the girl had successfully learnt all the lessons of becoming a good wife and mother, since without these a child bride would only bring disorder to the family and the greater community as well to the budding nation (*Sadgope Samachar*, mid-Nov to mid-Jan 1928/Agrahayan-Poush, 1335 BS). As a result, *Tili Bandhab* declared that 'Rearing children should be the only goal of a woman's life, but unfortunately most of our women fail to understand the proper meaning of child rearing . . . This happens due to the lack of education among these women' (*Tili Bandhab*, mid-April to mid-May 1919/Baishakh 1326 BS). In other words, reform of women's condition was approached entirely from the perspective of welfare and progress of the family and the community.

Aside these reformist moves, there were still many people within the low-caste communities who did not agree with modernist reform efforts and remained loyal to the sanskritic model, even though this model disallowed them social mobility. Unsurprisingly, once again two different sources of social change become prominent here. One is the modernist, westernized version of social reform and the other the revivalist tendency inclined towards the brahmanical mode of social existence. The same conflict between modernity and tradition that had occurred amongst the bhadralok in their fight against colonial dominion to secure their social status resonated amongst the lower-caste aspirants of early twentieth-century Bengal. Both these trends, however, had the same goal: the (re)creation of an ideal of womanhood echoing the brahmanical ideals.

For the educated, modernist males of some of the lower castes the Victorian ideal of womanhood education and its model of female education became a natural choice. By way of example an article in *Sadgope Patrika* stated that:

> Today's women do not want to remain as the servant of their husbands, they want to be true life-partners of their spouses. But this pledge would remain just lip service since in the present circumstance there is a huge difference between the

> education and the subsequent thought processes of husband and wife. Unless this disparity is eradicated through proper education of women we can never create a new society devoid of social malice.
>
> (mid-March to mid-April 1928/Chaitra 1335 BS)

Another article written by a female writer, Asha Ghosh, encouraged women to become the true life-partners of their husbands in every possible manner, and thus they had to be properly educated (*Sadgope Patrika*, mid-June to mid-July 1931/ Ashar 1338 BS). Such constructions were no doubt influenced by the discourse of western modernity, which was already embraced by the upper castes for their socio-economic benefit, and therefore already established as expedient. Resonating with the upper-caste arguments in favour of educating their women, the low-caste literature thus declared female education to be the pre-condition for the progress of the community, as women were the protectors and nurturers of the clan's lineage, honour, and respect.[29] However, similarly to the upper castes this educational endeavour for women was not meant for their benefit alone. Women were to remain the maidservants of their husbands; education was viewed as nothing but a modern way of ensuring women were better able to fulfil their domestic, spiritual, marital, and maternal responsibilities. In other words, education was to make them perfect women in order to confirm the claims to social legitimacy made by the male aspirants of the marginal groups.[30]

Of all these roles, the most privileged one was motherhood, as a woman's most important responsibility was to carry forward the lineage effectively, and this was strongly emphasized in almost all the journals. For example, many of these journals claimed that the mental development of sons depended on the level of education of their mothers (*Tili Bandhab*, mid-April to mid-May 1919/ Baishakh, 1326 BS).[31] Further, the proper nurturing of sons also depended on the mother so that they flourished to become healthy young men (*Sadgope Patrika*, mid-Oct to mid-Nov 1929/Kartik, 1336 BS). Moreover, their moral progress was a reflection of their mother's education as was their sense of morality, commitment, and responsibility (*Sadgope Patrika*, mid-Aug to mid-Sept 1929/ Bhadra 1336 BS and *Tili Bandhab*, mid-April to mid-May 1919/Baishakh 1326 BS). This emphasis on motherhood and its association with the progress of the community, and nation was an important requirement of that period under the growing nationalist sentiment (T. Sarkar 2001: 5-65). In the *Subarnabanik Samachar* in 1924, an author mentions an English proverb which says that a son's education starts thirty years prior to his birth (*Subarnabanik Samachar*, mid-Aug to mid-Sept 1924/Bhadra 1331 BS), that is, with the beginning of his mother's education. *Mahishya Mahila* also argued that an educated mother's significance is more than a hundred teachers and that without female education no caste, community or society could ever prosper (*Mahishya Mahila*, mid-May to mid-July 1912/Jaishtha-Ashar 1319 BS).

Nonetheless, this encouraging discourse of social progress could not cover up the male anxiety of losing control over women and thus incited a lot of opposition against the reform programme. One Abanikanta Ghosh expressing his concern on the pages of *Sadgope Patrika* wrote, 'If after receiving education women start claiming equal rights with men then we will deviate from our gracious ideals' (mid-April to mid-May 1930/Baishakh 1337 BS). He argued that education for women which only instigated them to demand authority and power would lead to social calamity; as such an education would incite these women to disregard their great tradition, and to disrespect their husbands. He preferred, instead, that women should receive some ethical and moral guidance that would make them aware of their responsibilities to live up to the examples set by ancient women (ibid.).[32]

Many of the journals agreed that while women had been previously happy in their ordained roles within the family, and had performed these duties without thinking about their own happiness, the newly developed notion of women's liberation that they received from their exposure to western education meant that they had begun to ignore their familial responsibilities (*Mahishya Samaj*, mid-Feb to mid-March 1916/Phalgun 1323

BS; *Sadgope Patrika*, mid-April to mid-May 1930/Baishakh 1337 BS; and mid-Aug to mid-Sept 1930/Bhadra 1337 BS). The *Subarnabanik Samachar* echoing the same anxiety wrote that 'We do not want our women to develop themselves on a western model through college education . . . we do not want our women to give up domestic duties and become vivacious [the English word was used in the original] . . . We want that female education which has traditionally respected wifehood as well as motherhood' (*Subarna-banik Samachar*, mid-Nov to mid- Dec 1925/Agrahayan 1332 BS; cited in Bandyopadhyay 2004: 177). However, in spite of these anxieties, accepting that female education was an unavoidable reality, the low-caste male agents following the bhadralok example channelled the goal of higher education for women towards creating ideal wives and mothers. Unsurprisingly, this strategy worked in favour of both the patriarchy and the revivalist nationalist tendency of that period. The low-caste journals were thus full of examples of the ideal wife, who used her higher education solely for the benefit of the household, protecting the family from health hazards through her progressive western learning, providing appropriate basic education for the children, and so on. She managed the finance of the household efficiently, thus contributing to the family prosperity. Most importantly, she could take part in significant conversations with her husband regarding his work and other important issues instead of annoying him with the trivial issues of domesticity. Nevertheless, she would never fail to remember her responsibilities as a chaste, dutiful, trustworthy, and tolerant wife whose only function was to look after her husband and male progeny in the service of her husband's lineage.[33]

In contrast to this ideal image of womanhood the low-caste journals produced a caricature of educated, modern women as slothful, inactive and novel reading;[34] a reproduction of the high-caste mockery of educated elite women also found in high-caste journals and domestic manuals published in the late nineteenth century. *Mahishya Mahila,* showing utter contempt for these women, urged its readers to follow the path of grief and hardship, because only then would they learn to value the fruits of true femininity. The journal published an imaginary dialogue between two women, one of whom is the victim of modernization in the inner core of her domestic world and has subsequently forgotten the virtuous way of life prescribed for a pious Hindu woman. The other is endowed with righteous thoughts in spite of being educated and exposed to modernity. In a friendly chat the virtuous one warns her inferior friend that by entertaining her luxurious standards of living and indulging in laziness she was only bringing unhappiness to her family and thereby disrespecting the boons of grief and anguish that Lord Krishna endowed all virtuous women so that they would never become complacent and would remain at the feet of their husbands. Every woman was to crave an arduous life since despair and difficulty would remind her of her duties in life.[35]

Mahishya Mahila went on to list the domestic duties that any pious Hindu woman must perform in order to avoid complacency, laziness, and the disregarding of her duties as a patibrata, as she was the custodian of the honour of the family and the lineage (ibid.).[36] The journal describes a regimented day for a woman: how she is to wake up in the morning before anyone else in the family, how to fold clothes, how to wash utensils, how to cut vegetables, how to cook, how to clean the house, how to comb her hair, how to take a bath, how to feed everyone in the family and then only to eat her own meal; the list is endless.

All this advice was given with the brahmanical model of womanhood in mind. Taken altogether, the prescriptions for women stressed the importance of a woman's body as the upholder of the ethical standard of that particular society (ibid). In order to achieve social mobility, the lower-caste male agents not only adopted a brahmanical model for their women, in so doing they remodelled their entire domestic life which had previously been more lenient for women. They remodelled the most basic and important unit of their social existence, the life of their women along upper-caste, brahmanical lines and thus stabilized unwittingly the difference between the high-caste nature of collective existence with the low-caste one.

The superior and desirable qualities of womanhood could blossom only within the boundaries of the home as it was the abode of the family, the most basic and important unit of societal life. An article in *Mahishya Samaj* compared the family with the universe, which is protected by God, and the family is guarded by the *karta* (the patriarch) of the family (*Mahishya Samaj*, mid-July to mid-Aug 1922/Shraban 1329 BS). The duty of the women in the family was thus to keep the god of domesticity satisfied as all the miseries in the family are caused by not obeying his rule (ibid.). A woman's beauty, softness, and loyalty enhanced the power of the karta whose relationship to her is one of a master to a devotee, since women are innately weak both mentally and physically and lack self-defence and self-control (*Mahishya Samaj*, mid-Feb to mid-March 1916/Phalgun 1323 BS) and thus needed to be protected by their masters. Women were thus simultaneously disempowered and put on a pedestal as the *Gharer Lakshmi* (*Subarnabanik Samachar*, mid-Jan to mid-Feb 1920/Magh 1327 BS) or the goddess of the home who brings in happiness and prosperity not only to the family but also to the entire society and the nation. This was indeed a traditional brahmanical model of womanhood which was now emulated by the peasants and trading castes in conformity with the brahmanical universal ideal.

While cautiously following the brahmanical ideal of womanhood these low-caste groups were also aware of the modernist influences on the Hindu patriarchal social structure. Bengali novels written in the late nineteenth and and early twentieth centuries represented this trend by reconceptualizing the ideal womanhood in terms of romantic love and passionate encounters (R. Ray, ed, 1999: 90-94). According to this new trend, women were considered to be individuals with minds of their own, and premarital courtship and extramarital love were not perceived as an absurdity. However, the possibility of self-choice for women was rarely achievable within the boundaries of brahmanical marital structure, which was austerely patriarchal and caste based.[37] As a result, in spite of such daring romantic experiments there was a greater acceptance of an ideational relation between a man and a woman, and, as Ray shows, from the early twentieth century this influence started infiltrating village societies and low-caste communities (ibid: 135-41) owing to the spread of vernacular education among these so far neglected social groups. Subsequently, the low-caste literature explicitly disapproved of the reading of these novels as they could encourage wrong and dissident ideas in the minds of susceptible women (*Mahishya Mahila*, mid-March to mid-May 1915/Chaitra-Baishakh 1321-1322 BS). Emulating the bhadralok anxiety about higher education for women, the low-caste males' reaction became alarmingly fanatic and a biological argument against the continuance of this modernist trend started to be presented. Reflecting the bhadralok dilemma, the editorial in *Mahishya Mahila* took the argument to such an extent that questions were posed regarding the reproductive capability of educated women. It warned that

> After receiving education like men, women are forgetting their skills of doing domestic duties, cooking, child rearing, and other domestic skills . . . Excessive reading, thinking, and hard work have resulted in the flattening of their big bosoms, hardening of their hearts and lessening of their childbearing capacity.
>
> (*Mahishya Mahila*, mid-May to mid-July 1925/Jaishtha-Ashar 1332 BS)[38]

These questions figured in the western debate on women's education too in the nineteenth century.[39] It would be inaccurate, however, to suggest that there was full consensus on the issue of female education among the low-caste groups.[40] Some articles even argued in favour of educated women doing jobs and rejecting marriage proposals (*Sadgope Patrika*, mid-June to mid-July 1932/Ashar 1339 BS). Nonetheless that the effect of these articles was fairly limited compared to those eulogizing the brahmanical model of womanhood was due to the fact that it was that model which appeared to guarantee an elevated social status for the entire community. This being said it is important to note that debates of these kinds were less perceptible in the dalit literature for the simple reason that female education had either made no or very little progress amongst them and thereby posed no threat to domestic regulation and patriarchy (Bandyopadhyay 2004: 180).

Most of the peasant and trading castes welcomed a new model of womanhood for their women, placed at the crossroads between western modernity and revivalist brahmanical patriarchy and against the backdrop of colonialism and the escalating demands of nationalism. We have illustrated how from the second half of the nineteenth century the Bengali Hindu bhadralok had constructed the image of a faithful and devoted wife—the patibrata nari. For Dipesh Chakrabarty (2000: 82-87), it is the image of *grihalakshmi* that symbolised the bhadralok's attempt to celebrate the difference of Indian identity, resisting the dominance of colonial modernity, a claim, as we have pointed out, which is problematic.[41] For Chakrabarty, this attempt signified the highest form of personhood, one constituted by the idea of self-sacrifice, as contrasted with the bourgeois individualism advocated by European discourses of liberation and modernity. Whilst his observation is true in a limited sense, to accept it as universally the case would be to deny the ways in which European modernity was embraced by many native agents of almost all strata and employed to construct a utilitarian model of ideal womanhood. Chakrabarty, however, does not disregard the violence concealed in this patriarchal reconstruction of Indian womanhood.

Tanika Sarkar also sees in this teleological reconstruction the colonized male's attempt to rewrite the power relations within the family (2000: Chapter 1), one that in my view resulted in the imposition or adoption of the brahmanical ideal of womanhood in all social strata. According to Partha Chatterjee, this construction was the inevitable result of the need to reinvent the domestic sphere as the only remaining sovereign space where the otherwise dominated native males could exercise power and control, instigate reforms, and manoeuvre the results to ensure their own advantage (Chatterjee 1993: 116-34). From the discussion above it is clear, however, that all the debates that took place in Bengali public life in the late nineteenth and early twentieth centuries amongst the bhadralok, occupied the middle- and lower-caste aspirants' existence as well. The concerns with the ideal nature of womanhood was clearly reflected in their journals in the early twentieth century as they began to undergo the same process of contesting the dominance of both their colonial masters and their caste superiors, and attempted to ameliorate their low-status following the same brahmanical injunctions with respect to appropriate female conduct.[42]

Notably, during this period, without remaining solely confined within the debate related to their caste status, the low-caste aspirants attempted to be a part of the modus operandi of the nationalistic movement, the most significant social-political movement of the era, predominantly controlled by the upper-caste bhadralok.[43] The eventual outcome of all these efforts, however, was a total renovation of status of marginal women along brahmanical lines, which was arguably the most useful and convincing route for claiming social equality.

The re-imagining of low-caste womanhood took place within a framework where the ideological pillars of the bhadralok's modernist aspiration and the Hindu revivalist nationalist ambition were both indebted to a brahmanical ideal. First of all, the concept of the ideal women as historically located in the ancient Vedic period, could lay claim to exemplary female characters such as Sita, Savitri, Damayanti (*Mahishya Mahila*, mid-Sept to mid-Nov 1914/Ashwin-Kartik 1321 BS) who were viewed as the ideal models to be revered by the women. Locating the respected, elite, and ideal model of womanhood in the Vedic age ignored the existence of the servile *dasis* (female servants) of the same period, reflecting the similar attitude adopted by the nationalist movement, that principally disregarded the nature and fact of low-caste existence, and more so of their women, an aspect to which Uma Chakravarty draws attention (1999: 27-87).

This trend was exemplified in a variety of low-caste literature where the women of the marginal groups were summoned to challenge the low-caste action by their caste superiors by introducing their last names as *Devi*. Up until this point the devi appellation had been an upper-caste phenomenon where women were equated with the devi (goddesses) suggesting perhaps an attempt to inculcate the goddesses' standards of morality, righteousness, incorruptibility, and fidelity.[44] Following the same trend the gandhabaniks urged their women to stop introducing themselves as dasi (literally, 'maidservant') since this not only demonstrated the contempt they were nurturing among themselves, but also degraded them to the status of the shudra who were the actual *das/dasi* (the servants).[45] The journal thus argued that

> Our great custom teaches us to respect our elders. If we call ourselves as *das* and *dasi* then what tribute are we paying to our great Aryan tradition . . . For the last couple of hundred years *Subarnabanik* and *Gandhabanik* have been forcibly degraded to the status of the *shudras*. Without any fault they have lost their *vaishya* status and treated despicably. If these groups do not retaliate and renounce this servile status they will never recuperate their lost glory.
>
> (*Gandhabanik Samachar*, mid-Oct to mid-Nov 1923/Kartik 1330 BS).

Interestingly, while acknowledging the fact that the caste system was a pet project of the Vedic civilization of the alleged Aryan era, these social aspirants in an attempt to identify with the glory of Aryan civilization, which was an area almost monopolized by the upper castes, never condemned this social classification. Although low-caste literature occasionally offered cautions against criticizing the brahmins (*Tili Bandhab*, mid-April to mid-May 1919/Baishakh 1326 BS),[46] anything Vedic was infallible and beyond criticism.[47] It was, perhaps, not just coincidental that a similar revivalist trend in favour of caste-based native society was dominating the upper-caste nationalist movement at the same time. Likewise, most low-caste literature eulogized the caste-based social arrangement, claiming it to be a unique system through which every social group could flourish and cultivate their individual interests and thereby contribute to the prosperity of the society (*Gandhabanik Samachar*, mid-Aug to mid-Sept 1917/Bhadra 1324 BS; and *Mahishya Samaj*, mid-July to mid-Aug 1922/Shraban 1329 BS). The argument was that social decadence had been introduced into the social order due to the ascendancy of Islam (*Subarnabanik Samachar*, mid-April to mid-May 1922/Baishakh 1329 BS). Consequently, it was claimed by these low-caste journals that it was only during the Muslim era that Hindu women began to lose their freedom. The only female journal of the low-caste groups of this period declared that before the Muslim invasion women of all strata had access to academic pursuits, which were later suppressed by Muslim rulers and all these women were then confined to home, a claim which conveniently disregarded the difference of status between high- and low-caste women long before Muslim rulers came into power (*Mahishya Mahila*, mid-March to mid-May 1914/Chaitra-Baishakh 1321 BS).

Additionally, the leap from the medieval decline under the Muslims to the modern revival of model womanhood was argued by the lower castes to be mediated by colonial modernity through which the idea was ultimately established that educated women were the foundation of the construction of a successful nation (*Sadgope Patrika*, mid-Sept to mid-Nov 1929/Ashwin 1335 BS and mid-Aug to mid-Sept 1929/Bhadra 1336 BS). Here, one must recall that the ethnographic efforts of the colonial administration resulted in the Census survey suggesting the elevation (in some cases degradation of) the caste status of some groups on a permanent basis. Here, in spite of some minor discontent with the accuracy of the survey the lower-caste groups were generally appreciative of their colonial masters.[48] Nonetheless, during this period the escalating nationalist movement was impossible to ignore; lower-caste literature spent a good deal of time arguing that the primary condition for achieving the victory of the nation was the elimination of social inequities exemplified by caste discrimination (*Mahishya Samaj*, mid-Sept to mid-Oct 1922/ Ashwin 1329 BS). As a result the Census survey was considered to be the most effective tool for achieving that objective.

At this stage of the struggle the lower-caste groups, while accepting the value of western modernity for eradicating medieval Islamic influence on society and for building camaraderie with their high-caste superiors, were never willing to remodel their own women after their western sisters (*Mahishya Mahila*, mid-March to mid-May 1914/Chaitra-Baishakh 1321 BS). The need to incorporate certain modernist trends such as education was acknowledged but even that was to be modified to comply with brahmanic tradition. The effect was a deliberate cultivation of brahmanic feminine qualities among low-caste women, such as compassion, fidelity, trustworthiness, toleration, simplicity, beauty, and unconditional sacrifice, which were the key attributes of the brahmanical ideal woman (*Subarnabanik Samachar*, mid-Aug to mid-Sept 1924/Bhadra 1331 BS; and *Mahishya Mahila*, mid-March to mid-May 1913-1914/Chaitra-Baishakh 1320-1321 BS).

One must notice, however, that much of the literature was not entirely uncritical of some of the brahmanical ideal female characters. For example, the tilis questioned the revered status of epic female models such as Ahalya, Draupadi, and Kunti on the ground of their purported promiscuity. That these women are among the five *kanyas* of the epics, that is, that they were among the five most respected women of the brahmanical tradition, was scorned by the tili journal. It asked

> Have we ever tried to think why these women, who all were adulterous, were given such importance? If we tried to explore the real reason behind it we would understand that no women were urged to be like them. That all these women had a disgraceful sexual life, which no good woman should ever follow, has been emphasized by grouping them together.
>
> (*Tilir Gaurab*, mid-May to mid-June 1919/Jaishtha 1326 BS/1919)

But these apparent criticisms of some of the ancient female characters, frequently eulogized by brahmanical tradition, should not lead one to assume that the low-caste aspirants disapproved of the brahmanical norms altogether. On the contrary, in behaving in a more brahmanical manner than the original brahmanical approach towards womanhood, they were attaching great importance to the sexual purity of women, such that even epic characters like Draupadi and Kunti were not spared criticism. There is another interesting point to be brought to attention here: some of the lower-caste groups showed an inclination towards projecting the characters of their very own mythical figures as ideal characters. For example, the gandhabaniks were enthralled with the character of Behula, who was presented as their answer to brahmanical ideal of womanhood and a journal of this caste group went on describing her as, 'the *Sati* of all *satis*'; even Sita, Savitri, and Damayanti appear to pale in comparison (*Gandhabanik Samachar*, mid-Dec to mid-Jan 1924/Poush 1331 BS).[49]

This description, once again, could be viewed as a lower-caste attempt to defy brahmanical supremacy, but a careful look at the structurization of the character of Behula reveals the brahmanical influence on this lower-caste group's own attempt to create an ideal for their women. For example, Behula is considered to be the most ideal of all women because she is pious, chaste, trustworthy, tolerant, in other words a storehouse of all the attributes that are characteristically brahmanical in nature. The journal proudly claims that 'No other woman could take the journey the way she did with the decomposed, fetid corpse of her beloved husband against all odds' (ibid). Here the tremendous *patibratya* (the dharma of a patibrata) is what makes Behula the winner, and as one who undergoes the hardship that a woman has to face in order to prove her patibratadharma, the better patibrata she turns out to be (Harlan and Courtright 1995). Within this paradigm the low-caste heroine Behula emerges as a winner for the non-brahmin gandhabaniks, one, that is, however, unquestionably brahmanical in her nature and practice.

During the same period brahmanical gender norms became familiar to the people of the lowest stratum of the society, the dalits. On the eve of Partition in 1947 the dalits in Bengal, demonstrating a remarkable shift in their political allegiance, became a part of the larger Hinduization process of the early twentieth-century.[50] The Hinduization project of the upper castes on the eve of Partition accordingly brought the dalits into the larger fold of a community which had so far only condemned them as impure and untouchable. The religio-nationalist politics of early twentieth century thus replaced caste politics, at least initially.[51] On the other hand, the upper-caste groups also showed an interest in including marginal groups in mainstream politics since the major feature of revivalist Hinduism in early twentieth-century Bengal was the fear of losing out to the Muslims (Bandyopadhyay 1997: Chapter 1). The fear was related to the conversion of the dalits to Islam in order to escape their low status and this was one of the main reasons that the Hindu bhadralok began to pay attention to the dalits (ibid). Moreover, at the same time the physical strength of the dalits and the adivasis was an important tool for a Bengali Hindu society ridiculed for their effeminate ill-health by their colonial masters (Chowdhury-Sengupta 1998: 290). As a result, a number of Hindu religious organizations embarked upon a project of mobilizing these thus far undesirable groups under the banner of a homogeneous Hindu identity.[52] The Hinduization of dalits groups therefore became one of the most important phases in the history of early twentieth-century Bengal that arguably achieved its ideological goal when Jithu Sanyal, a santhal leader in Malda, a district in Bengal, attacked the Adina mosque in 1932, demonstrating the low castes' anti-Muslim sentiments (Sumit Sarkar 1985: 157).[53]

Here, the changes in the political stance of the dalits led to the teleological construction of a brahmanical model of womanhood for their women as well, revealing again, as I have argued, that resistance to colonial domination, social mobility and reformist tendencies relied on the refurbishment of the brahmanical ideal of woman to achieve their aims. For instance, different songs of the matua sect of the namashudra reveal that the value of chastity and fidelity were gradually embraced by the members of this marginal group. Judging by these songs, the ideal woman was one who worshipped the feet of her husband, and for her no other form of worship was necessary to attain salvation (Bandyopadhyay 2004: 186). During the same period the rajbangshis' Sanskritizing claim for their kshatriya origin fitted perfectly well with the Hinduization project since the demand of the rajbangshis brought them closer to the pan-Indian kshatriya movement led by the maharaja of Alwar (*Kshatriya*, mid-Nov to mid-Dec 1924/Agrahayan, 1331 BS). The proclaimed kshatriya status of the rajbangshis involved the duty to protect the weak and vulnerable of the society and its women were made the symbols of weakness and vulnerability (ibid), unambiguously a sign of brahmanical patriarchy, an essential ingredient of caste hierarchy.

However, the process of the hegemonization of gender ideology among the lower-caste groups was never absolute and unchallenged since there were always contesting voices against Brahmanization and the eradication of lower-caste autonomy (Gupta 2000: 1-42). More importantly, if the literature that we have discussed in this chapter offers evidence of assent or disapproval, then the silence amongst different sections of diverse caste groups was even more eloquent. The average circulation of these journals varied from 1000 to 1200 only (Bandyopadhyay 1990: Appendix 1). What this chapter highlights, however, is the tendency towards an inverse relationship between social mobility and status of women, as evidenced in the deteriorating social conditions of women belonging both to the high-and low-caste groups and the abundant debate regarding women's liberation in the caste literature indicates once again the tendency to connect women, social honour, and social authority or mobility.

That none of these efforts was free from ambiguity or contestation is indisputable. The only consistent feature that can be singled out of the processes of contestation and emulation is the central place of women of almost all strata, albeit varying widely in degree. All these women were faced with the difficulties of maintaining chastity, and fidelity and the fact that their way of life was subjected to fiercer scrutiny than ever before. But the suffering of the low-caste women was undoubtedly more than that of their upper-caste sisters as they not only lost their relative freedom but also they had for the first time the burden of protecting the honour of their entire community following the path of their privileged upper-caste sisters.

NOTES

1 See Uma Chakravarty 2003: Chapter 5. However, the patriarchal tendencies were not totally absent among the low-caste groups either, in fact in many cases, marginal caste groups were as patriarchal as their social superiors.

2 See Bandyopadhyay's discussion (1997: 34) of how in 1872 namashudra women lost their independence over a debate of status between the male agents of the namashudra community and the high-caste participants of a village called Amgram in Bakarganj (Faridpur, presently in Bangladesh).

3 See Bandyopadhyay 1997 and 2004, Srinivas 1971 and 1994 and D. Gupta 1997 and 2000 on the struggle of the lower-caste groups against the upper-caste hegemony during this period.

4 For a discussion of the low-caste protest and struggle against brahmanical hegemony and encroachment of the marginal space see Bandyopadhyay 1997 and 2004.

5 For a discussion of this trend see Dirks 2001: 61-66, and Bandyopadhyay 1990: 22-24.

6 See Risley 1891: vols 1-2; and J. H. Hutton 1963.

7 See T. R. Trautmann 2005. *The Aryan Debate* (Delhi: Oxford University Press); E. F. Bryant and L. L. Patton, eds. 2005. *The Indo-Aryan Controversy: Evidence and Inference in Indian History* (London: Routledge) for an understanding of the racial model of Aryan/non-Aryan dichotomy.

8 This term is borrowed from Bandyopadhyay 2004 to indicate the feudal nature of the tenancy rights given to the peasants.

9 For a discussion of Brahmanization of the colonial legal system see ibid: Chapter 1, and King 1999). For a more detailed understanding of colonial laws and their impact on the life of the masses see Caroll 1989.

10 I have borrowed this term from Dirks 2001.

11 For a discussion on the social mobility of low-caste groups aspiring to social mobility see Swaraj Basu 2003; see also Bandyopadhyay 1997.

12 For example, the kahars were an extremely marginal group, both socially and economically, and therefore could hardly afford to emulate bhadralok behaviour. But the situation was entirely different for other dalit groups who had been socially mobile in the nineteenth-century, gaining from the socio-economic changes under colonial rule. For example, the rajbangshis took advantage of the forest land reclamation in north Bengal and gained social authority, whereas the namashudras became the pioneer cultivators in the eastern districts of Bengal reclaiming marshlands. See Bandyopadhyay 1997.

13 The low-caste journals are full of grievances against the high-caste monopolization of the observance of these rituals that played a dominant role in asserting social authority. For example, the gandhabaniks started campaigning in favour of wearing the sacred thread to ascertain their vaishya status but the fear that this endeavour would be ridiculed by the upper castes was explicitly expressed in their journal. Similarly, they started their battle against the observation of 30 days of *asouch* or impurity prescribed for the lower castes. See *Gandhabanik*, mid-Feb to mid-March 1925/Phalgun 1332 BS. For a discussion of the debate around these brahmanical gestures as a mark of social mobility see also T. Bhattacharya 2005.

14 In fact, *Kayastha Koustubh* was the first caste journal of its kind that was published to strengthen the social standing of a particular caste group. See ibid: 209-30.

15 For a discussion of social mobility and the role of different low-caste associations in expediting the upward social mobility of aspiring social groups see Bandyopadhyay 1990: Chapter 3.

16 See *Mahishya Samaj* (mid-Nov to mid-Dec 1922/Agrahayan 1329 BS); *Sadgope Patrika* (mid-Aug to mid-Sept 1928/Bhadra 1335 BS; and mid-Nov to mid-Jan 1928/Agrahayan-Poush 1335 BS); *Subarna-banik Samachar* (mid-Oct to mid-Nov 1923/Kartik 1330 BS).

17 The same journal in a different issue accused its readers of

depreciating their own society which it contrasts to the brahmin and other upper castes who respected their caste companions (*Tili Bandhab*, mid-July to mid-Aug 1919/Shraban 1326 BS).

18 See Dipesh Chakrabarty 2000. *Provincializing Europe: Postcolonial Thought and Historical Difference* (Princeton: Princeton University Press). Notably, Chakrabarty's work, which is considered to be a major intervention in the debate on Indian modernity, does not address the caste question at all. See particularly D. Chakrabarty 1994: 54-87.

19 However, Partha Chatterjee (1993) points to the absence of any self-conscious effort to construct an alternative social order by the hari, popularly known as balaramis, named after the founder of this hari sect Balaram (1780-?). Rather, by raising the hari to the position of the purest of the pure, the self-determining originator of the universe, and by reducing the brahmins to a particularly impure and degenerate lineage, they actually subverted the very claim of the dominant ideology of dharma, that is, the actual social relations of the caste structure were in perfect conformity with its universal ideality. For a detailed discussion of the impact of brahmanical hegemony on subaltern or marginal identity see P. Chatterjee 1993 and Bandyopadhyay 2004.

20 In 1917 Kanailal Dhar, a wealthy subarnabanik businessman from Ahiritala in Kolkata, donated a huge sum of money to run a local girls' school where about 150 girls started receiving free education. Later on it was restructured on the model of the Mahakali Pathshala, the nationalist model for female education and moral training centre. The subarnabanik school eventually came to be known as Kanailal Dhar Abitanik Hindu Balika Vidyalay (Kanailal Dhar Free Hindu Girls' School), and continued to be financed by his son. The *Subarnabanik Samachar* urged others to follow this example. See *Subarnabanik Samachar*, mid-Aug to mid-Oct 1917/ Bhadra-Ashwin, 1324 BS, and mid-Nov to mid-Dec 1923/ Agrahayan 1330 BS.

21 A mahishya woman, Krishnabhabini Biswas, edited it and most of its contributors were women and most of its readers were mahishya or other women. It was started in 1911 and three years later an editorial in the anniversary issue argued that the purpose of the journal had been to save Indian womanhood from their present

state of degradation and reinstate them to their past glory, when they all were respected for their chastity, love, and devotion. It also proclaimed that *Mahishya Mahila* would take on the role of imparting those long lost qualities to women by giving them correct education. See *Mahishya Mahila*, mid-July to mid-Sept 1914/Shraban-Bhadra 1321 BS.

22 *The Hindustan Standard*, 12 June 1938, cited in Bandyopadhyay 2004: 174.

23 For more on this discourse see Tanika Sarkar, 2001.

24 Cited in M. Sinha 1981. 'Mother India: Feminism and Nationalism in Late Colonial India', *Feminist Studies* 26, 3: 623-44.

25 During the nineteenth century, the increase in the educational opportunities for the aspirant bhadralok ensured that these men were more able to secure respectable employment which in turn improved their value in the marriage market insofar as a western education elevated the social standing of the bridegroom and his family. See Bandyopadhyay 2001.

26 The *Sadgope Patrika* quoting eminent personalities like Rabindranath Tagore and Mahatma Gandhi advised their fellow people to stop this evil practice as it would only degenerate the potential of the entire race (*Sadgope Patrika*, mid-May to mid-June 1933/Baisakh-Jaishtha 1340 BS).

27 See M. Sinha 1994. 'Reading *Mother India*', *Journal of Women's History* 6, 2: 6-44; on the masculine psychology of a colonised nation in the context of nineteenth-century Bengal.

28 See *Mahishya Mahila* (mid-Sept to mid-Nov 1914/AshwinKartik 1321 BS; mid-Jan to mid-March 1915/Magh-Phalgun 1321 BS); also M. N. Srinivas 1998.

29 See *Subarnabanik Samachar* (mid-Aug to mid-Sept 1919/Bhadra 1331 BS), *Sadgope Patrika* (mid-June to mid-July 1931/Ashar 1338 BS), *Tili Bandhab* (mid-April to mid-May1919/Baishakh 1326 BS).

30 For example, as *Tili Bandhab* noted, an educated wife meant a happier marital life, better domesticity, and a superior social life: an overall improved community and a prosperous nation (*Tili Bandhab*, mid-April to mid-May 1919/Baishakh 1326 BS).

31 See also *Gandhabanik Samachar*, mid-Feb to mid-March 1925/ *Phalgun* 1332 BS; *Tilir Gaurab*, mid-Feb to mid-March 1919/ *Phalgun* 1326 BS).

32 In this context some opposition against western modernist education is also noticeable; was considered to be unfit for Indian women always trained in superior ideals. See, eg, *Gandhabanik Samachar* (Phalgun 1332 BS/mid-Feb to mid-March 1925), *Tilir Gaurab* (Phalgun 1326 BS/mid-Feb to mid-March 1919).

33 See *Mahishya Mahila* (Ashwin-Kartik 1321 BS/1914); *Mahishya Mahila* (mid-Feb to mid-March 1914/Magh-Phalgun 1321 BS, and mid-July to mid-Sept 1915/Shraban-Bhadra 1322 BS); *Sadgope Patrika* (mid-Oct to mid-Nov 1926/Kartik 1336 BS; and mid-Jan to mid-Feb 1928/Magh 1335 BS).

34 See *Subarnabanik Samachar* (mid-Nov to mid-Dec 1925/Agrahayan 1332 BS; mid-Jan to mid-Feb 1924/Magh 1331 BS); *Mahishya Mahila* (mid-May to mid-July 1925/Jaishtha-Ashar 1332 BS).

35 Moreover, as a woman the more she accepted her hardships, the more opportunity she would get to prove her worth as a true patibrata by serving her actual lord, her husband (*Mahishya Mahila*, mid-Sept to mid-Nov 1914/Ashwin-Kartik 1321 BS).

36 For a similar set of advice see *Sadgope Patrik*a (mid-Oct to mid-Nov 1929/Kartik 1336 BS).

37 Rajat Ray has shown how Vaishnavism defined the Bengali concepts of love in the second half of the nineteenth century. The western influence of romantic love, although acknowledged in Indian society, was never accepted in its original form. The older, characteristically Indian concepts of love, found in Vaishnavism were instead reasserted in attitudes towards gender relationships at the onset of nationalism. This tendency was evident in the literary creations of the period, for example *Rajani* (1877) by Bankimchandra Chatterjee, *Chokher Bali* (1903) by Rabindranath Tagore, and *Palli Samaj* (1916) by Saratchandra Chatterjee. In all of these the loss of the couples was sublimated by the parted couple's silent recognition of their mutual love. The hero and the heroine of the novels resolve not to unite in this world out of a deep regard for each other as members of a collective social organization in which caste ideology and subsequent pre-ordained behaviours for women and men played a decisive role. The heroine, although allowed to engage in romantic encounters, remains loyal to social restrictions in the end and to a greater extent than the hero; it was presented as her responsibility to lead the hero back to the path of dharma; in Tagore's *Chokher Bali*, the widow, Binodini, does not accept Bihari's courageous offer of

marriage, because she does not want him to be degraded in the community. See R. Ray, ed, 1999.

38 The same breast-flattening example of upper-caste women achieving higher education is found in Borthwick (1988). Borthwick has also shown how women's education has been singled out as the cause of the deteriorating reproductive capacity of native women. See Borthwick 1984: Chapter 3.

39 Sara Delamont 1978. 'The Contraditions in Ladies' Education', in *The Nineteenth-Century Woman: Her Cultural and Physical World*, Sara Delamont and Lorna Diffin, eds (London: Routledge): 134-63.

40 There were, of course, nonconformist voices, as there were articles published in *Mahishya Samaj* that prescribed western modern education for women's mental and spiritual development on par with their male counterparts. The articles even welcomed the prospect of talented women leaving their homes to pursue further higher education in notable educational institutions in the city. See *Mahishya Samaj*, mid-Oct to mid-Nov 1918/Kartik 1325 BS; and mid-Aug to mid-Sept 1922/Bhadra 1329 BS.

41 See note 18.

42 See *Sadgope Patrika* (mid-Oct to mid-Nov 1929/Kartik 1336 BS); *Gandhabanik Samachar* (mid-Aug to mid-Sept 1917/Bhadra 1324 BS); *Mahishya Samaj* (mid-May to mid-June 1922/Jaishtha 1329 BS).

43 See *Subarnabanik Samachar* (mid-Aug to mid-Sept 1917/Bhadra 1324 BS); *Sadgope Patrika* (mid-Aug to mid-Sept 1928/*Bhadra* 1335 BS). In these articles the authors argue in favour of the improvement of the social status of low-caste people since without taking them into consideration the overall development of the nation is impossible. The improvement of their caste status is thus synonymous with the prosperity of the nation, which was, however, impossible to achieve without the improvement of the status of their women. Interestingly, the same argument was used in the Hinduization process on the eve of the Partition in order to gain low-caste support against the Muslims. See Bandyopadhyay 1990 and 1997; Sushobhan Sarkar 1999; Sumit Sarkar 1985.

44 For example, most of the female contributors in *Bamabodhini Patrika* are identified as, for example, Charumati Devi (*BP*, mid-Oct to mid-Nov 1915/Kartik 1322 BS), and/or Ushaprabha Debi (*BP*, mid-Jan to mid-Feb 1912/Magh 1319 BS). Other eminent women of the

late nineteenth century such as the women from the renowned Tagore family were known as Swarnakumari Devi, and Jnanadanandini Devi, not using their actual last name. The trend of not using last names was entirely absent among the male elites of society perhaps because it was the male members who carried forward the lineage and thus their last name, indicative of their caste status, was important. However, since the women's participation in public was still not acceptable, the use of the word *Devi*, perhaps sanctified their pure status.

45 The trend of disowning shudra status was widespread among many of these marginal groups. For example, the sadgopes and tili efforts at upward mobility elaborated in detail their vaishya origin and the saga of being ill treated as shudras. The sadgopes and mahisyas even claimed to be kshatriyas and urged their fellow aspirants not to remain satisfied with their vaishya status. See *Sadgope Patrika* (mid-July to mid-Aug 1929/Shraban 1336 BS); and *Mahishya Samaj* (mid-July to mid-Aug 1922/Shraban 1329 BS). See also *Tili Bandhab* (mid-Feb to mid-March 1918/Phalgun 1325 BS). The gandhabaniks argued that in ancient times they were on amicable terms with the brahmins and to prove the authenticity of this declaration, they went on claiming that old texts like the *Padmapuran* has examples of this harmonious coexistence between these two social groups, which would have never been possible had the gandhabaniks been not as powerful as the brahmins. On the other hand, this argument also tried to invalidate the degradation of the gandhabanik to the status of the lowest of all castes, the shudras. See *Gandhabanik Samachar* (mid-Nov to mid-Dec 1923/Agrahayan 1330 BS). Importantly, all these attempts to validate these claims by reference to scriptures once again illustrated the brahmanical influence among these low-caste groups.

46 However, the same journal unhesitantly praised the educated and dignified style of living of the brahmins, perhaps, illustrating their anxiety not to speak against the powerful brahmins. See *Tili Bandhab* (mid-Nov to mid-Dec 1919/Agrahayan 1326 BS).

47 See *Gandhabanik Samachar* (mid-Aug to mid-Sept 1917/Bhadra 1324 BS); *Mahishya Samaj* (mid-May to mid-June 1922/Jaishtha 1329 BS).

48 The *Tili* journal published an article stating support for the British Empire in 1917 at a time when the nationalist movement was ruling

every aspect of native existence. See *Tilir Gaurab* (mid-Nov to mid-Dec 1917/Magh 1324 BS). The same journal published a eulogy for King George V in 1919, praising the charitableness of colonial rule *Tilir Gaurab* (mid-Aug to mid-Sept 1919/Bhadra 1326 BS). However, the tilis were dissatisfied with the Census report of 1911, which equated them with the telis, an oil-producing community with a position considered to be demeaning by the tilis. Tilis are cultivators. The distinction between telis and tilis is a critical one. According to my research, the telis are decidedly inferior to the large agricultural castes but the distinction between tili and teli, as observed in Bengal, is unknown in other parts of the country, although there are divisions, of which the Rathod teli is the higher (in Maharashtra), within the caste itself. In Bengal, however, telis are more influential, in terms of their money-power, which of course cemented their social status, something the tilis could hardly achieve. They claimed to be vaishya, a business community of comparatively upper-class status whereas the telis, according to them, were shudras. See *Tilir Gaurab* (mid-Feb to mid-March 1918/Phalgun 1325 BS). The sadgopes faulted the Census survey by claiming two lower-caste groups had introduced themselves as sadgope in order to elevate their social status. See *Sadgope Patrika* (mid-Sept to mid-Oct 1918/Ashwin 1335 BS).

49 Behula is the heroine of the Bengali epic *Manasamangal*, composed between the thirteenth and eighteenth centuries CE. Although the purpose of this epic was to glorify the significance of goddess Manasa, it is more famous for depicting the love story between Behula and her husband, Lakhindar. Manasa is a goddess of disreputable origin worshipped mainly in Bengal where the epic based on her life tells how she gained recognition for herself as a potent member of the Hindu pantheon, a struggle which resembled the low caste's fight for recognition. Manasa is said to be the daughter of Kashyap, a famous sage, and Kadru, the sister of the serpent-king Sesh. Unlike her uncle, Manasa is still actively worshipped as a goddess who protects and saves humans from snake bites.

There is also another legend behind Manasa, in which she is considered to be the daughter (out of wedlock) of Lord Shiva. Manasa requested Shiva to include her in the pantheon so that she would be worshipped by humans. Shiva responded by saying that if the merchant Chand (of Anga kingdom) agreed to worship her, she would be included amongst the goddesses. When Manasa approached Chand, he refused to worship her because of her disreputable origin. This infuriated Manasa, and she killed all his sons. After this event, Chand's wife Sanika gave birth to their seventh son, Lakhindar. Manasa's wrath had not been pacified even by the time Lakhindar's marriage to Behula was arranged. She vowed to kill him on the *phoolshajya* (the night after the wedding, when bride and groom sleep together for the first time). To counter the threat, Chand planned to construct an iron room for Lakhindor's phoolshajya. However, Manasa threatened the blacksmith, and asked him to keep a small pinhole in the room. As nobody noticed this hole, in the night, Manasa sent a very thin snake to enter the room through the pinhole. Once inside the room, this snake turned into a cobra and bit Lakhindar, killing him instantaneously. Behula overcame her grief and built a boat to go to heaven to present this injustice to the gods. Lakhindar was then revived by the gods. After she returned from heaven, Behula managed to persuade Chand to worship Manasa. However, Chand grudgingly agreed to worship her only with his left hand. To this day, Manasa is the only Hindu goddess worshipped by the left hand.

Behula's non-brahmin origin and her unyielding struggle resemble the low-caste's fight for social justice and thus Behula becomes the ideal woman to the low-caste people. Interestingly, the *Manasa-mangal*'s characters (for instance, the three main characters, Manasa, Chand and Behula, were constantly fighting against destiny and the same trend is reflected in the low-caste groups' struggle against ill fate) are deprived of their dues and engaged in relentless struggle to regain their status. For a detailed view of Behula's life and her archetypal image as an ideal wife see Mandakranta Bose 2000.

50 It is to be noted that the dalits of Bengal became particularly involved in the Partition movement because they were to be directly affected by the proposed new international territorial boundaries, which entailed the loss of their homeland in East Bengal (Bandyopadhyay 1997). There was, therefore, every reason for them to be involved in the Partition agitation.

51 For a detailed overview of the shifting loyalties of the dalits in Bengal see Bandyopadhyay 1994: 349-91. Also see Bandyopadhyay 1990: Chapter 4; and Bandyopadhyay 1997.

52 For example, from Dec-Jan 1934-35, Swami Pranabananda of

Bharat Sebasharm Sangha started working among the namashudras, poundrakshatriyas and other dalits in the four districts of East Bengal. From 1938 he intensified his efforts to organize the Hindu community of East Bengal and embarked in mobilizing the untouchables and the other lower castes so that instead of defecting from the Hindu community they enhanced its power. See Swami Vedananda (1991: 355-86). Again, the Hindu Mahasabha from the beginning of its establishment in Bengal in 1923 also targeted the lower-caste groups for political mobilization as a part of its campaign for organizing Hindus against the Muslims.

53 From the late 1920s the leaders of the Hindu Mahasabha started claiming that the Hindus were the natural birth community of India: whoever followed a religion born in India was a Hindu. By definition, all the tribal groups of Bengal were Hindus and there was an organized campaign to mobilize them in the defence of the Hindu community. The consequence of this trend was an implicit communal passion that resulted in anti-Muslim sentiment. Jitu Santal was famous for such communal mobilization among the santal community in Malda.

Conclusion

> Caste attaches to the body, not to the soul.
>
> (Partha Chatterjee 1993: 194).

The idealization of the role of women in colonial Bengal played a pivotal role in maintaining the structural solidarity and ideological superiority of the caste system. The structure was able both to incorporate and suppress challenges made by lower orders, whether of the bhadralok or the low castes. The marginal low-caste groups, in spite of their resistance to brahmanical norms, negotiated with their social superiors in terms of addressing, assessing, and adjusting the rules and norms governing the freedom of women belonging to their castes. Most importantly, I have attempted to explain the efforts of the bhadralok from non-brahmin origins, who became almost 'more brahmin than brahmin', placed between the high- and low-caste groups, to socialize their women in the same style adopted by the privileged upper castes. Indeed, all the groups adhering to a brahmanical scheme projected an ideal for women in order to reaffirm, reinforce and/or achieve social status and legitimacy. To establish the brahmanical nature of the low-caste groups' socio-economic and political objective I have also highlighted the high-caste texts, which projected the character of the native women in an ideal manner, only reinforcing a brahmanical patriarchy that portrayed the superiority of the native male agents. The similarity between the contents of the high- and low-caste texts and journals illustrates the continuous struggle of the high-caste agents to maintain their social authority and the low-caste aspirants' efforts to accomplish social advancement in a transformed social atmosphere under colonial rule. Henceforth, this ideal was conferred with a monolithic status which became almost unavoidable for any agents aspiring for social mobility. These social agents coming from different caste and class backgrounds were aiming for the same goal; social respectability seemed to have been attracted by the high-caste model in such a way that they began to emulate and thus legitimize the ideologies of hierarchy and domination. Here the high-caste model of the socio-political and religious existence was certainly not always explicitly outlined in such a way that these diverse group of agents could readily follow. In most of the cases, however, the lower- and middle-caste groups took an ambivalent attitude towards social mobility in emulating high-caste doctrines. But amidst this ambivalence, suspicion, and discontentment regarding the effectiveness of the adoption of high-caste models for achieving social respectability, one formula that seemed to be relatively efficacious and adaptable to almost all the social groups was the prescription related to the control of female sexuality and its auxiliary agendas.

For the low-caste groups the brahmanical ideal of womanhood symbolised a token of resistance, struggle, and absorption at different times, at different levels of awareness, encouraged by a diverse set of goals and also varying in the nature of the action taken. Yet all these can be summarized into one objective: social prosperity or respectability. Thus while I have found the people of the lower order to have been concerned with their exploitation by the upper castes, the relatively advanced sections of the same marginal groups in terms of financial prosperity were more preoccupied with achieving comparative social acceptability, and were more interested in being a part of brahmanical ritualistic symbolisation. The relationship between these two elements was perhaps symbiotic, since both felt the same need to destabilize the hegemonic brahmanical order and to turn it to their favour. However, in reality their resistance very often accentuated the overpowering influence of the same brahmanic religious system and its ideologies. It is this ambiguous tendency of conflict and disassociation with brahmanical hegemony, which remained as a reality for low-caste identity. To recognize this ambiguity is nonetheless neither to underplay nor overlook the relentless struggle of marginal groups against an unjust social system. Neither do I underestimate the role of the upper castes in shaping the unique history of colonial Bengal through their own complex approaches and aspirations. To summarize these processes of social construction and reconstruction I have attempted to encapsulate the ambiguous, ambitious, and mystifying tendencies of the native agents of almost all strata during one of the most vibrant periods of Bengal's history where the framework of an ideal of woman-hood, brahmanical in nature, was mobilized in the service of a diverse range of political and social projects.

It has also been illustrated how the widely publicised education policy for native women turned out to be a modern variant of the upper-caste efforts at renovating traditional gender codes in order to challenge the superiority of the colonial rulers. Education was the privilege of a certain group of upper-caste people who nominated their wives and daughters to become a part of this hallowed circle of education only to reinforce or produce their own social glory. I thus focussed on the social implications of education in order to reveal that the role of education was rarely unrelated to social authority, an authority which in turn was determined by caste origins. Accordingly, it revealed how social control over education combined with the economic authority of the upper-caste groups to devise a caste-motivated educational policy and how the low-caste aspirants desired to achieve social mobility by following the same procedures. Further, as education became one of the most important means of ensuring social authoritativeness it once again turned out to be the prerogative of high castes.

The bhadralok need, however, to respond to the colonial modernizing mission, and humiliating experiences in the public sphere led Bengali men to construct a new standard to redefine their identities and, most importantly, their relationships with women at home. At the intersections of colonial modernity and the native agents' responses to and active participation in Hindu homes, families, and daily lives, every little ingredient became an aspect of continuous debates and contests, all of which were directed at reaffirming and remodelling the identity of Bengali men. Furthermore, the domestic arena was the primary ground where the main ingredients of an ideal womanhood, chastity, fidelity and patience were nurtured. The caste-driven nature of the ingredients crucial in cultivating the ideal of womanhood, not only introduced a new approach to a contemporary model of Bengali womanhood,[1] but also invigorated the caste-based social structure by eulogizing the norms prescribed for native women. This in turn revealed that there was a correlation between the determined maintenance of the native's inner domain and the safeguarding of caste ideology. The superiority of native traditions and the centrality of the ideal of native womanhood in preserving that authority were vitally important considerations. Bengali women as a 'social fulcrum' oscillated between the extremes of tradition and modernity and were placed at the core of this vacillatory process against the backdrop of a continuous struggle between orthodoxy and modernity. The constricting control over native women's lives ultimately re-emphasized brahmanical hegemony as an unavoidable reality here.

Brahmanical hegemony is not just a matter of opinion, or ideological manoeuvring, but it is something truly total in nature insofar as it constitutes the substance and limit of common sense for most people under its influence. Brahmanical material and ideological hegemony in nineteenth-century Bengal (and perhaps thereafter as well) set the boundaries for both the upper-caste and the lower-castes' limit of existence and aspirations to a large extent. And in this process, as brahmanical hegemony was structurally organized on the basis of oppressive social norms designed for women, the ideal of brahmanical womanhood emerged as the yardstick for an enduring model of womanhood, and indeed for Indian-ness in general. Here, once again it was not just a structuralist position that has been taken to emphasize the unconditional dominance of hierarchical principles in the caste structure and the ensuing ideal of womanhood, resulting in a complete acceptance of the inequalities, without any acknowledgement of exceptions to the general rule. Rather, it was contestation, renewal, and reconstruction that gave the ideal of brahmanical womanhood innovative shades as selective and creative appropriation or unscathed emulation by the marginal groups sustained the fundamental structure of this ideal.

Accordingly, if the hierarchical ideology had a clear run in asserting its supremacy, this blend of conflicting interests and aspirations would never have been possible. At this point, it is important to assert that structuralism that does not go beyond 'the structure of the mind' is indeed idealist, and this book has constantly been concerned to link ideology and materiality. Therefore, it has sought to unveil the form of ideological masking, 'the way in which an ideology makes the historical reproduction of a social formation appear to be a necessity grounded in an "objective" ahistorical reality' (Östör, Fruzzetti and Barnett 1982: 643-44). Consequently, the contestation between the ideological and the politico-economic interests in the caste structure has been the central ground of this book. Examining ideological forms is not to approve them, or to reject history. Rather, it has been sought to demonstrate that the recognition of the operations of ideological forms is a necessary step in almost all social inquiry. A Marxist understanding of social relations, however, would suggest that caste ideology is merely a dominant trope or a smoke screen that potentially conceals class struggle. Thus we have wanted to show that lower castes and untouchables could see through the ideological functions and structure of the caste hierarchy but were unable to dismantle it.

Additionally, I have resisted the tendency to view the brahmanical ideal of womanhood, which was adopted by people of different caste status with different aspirations, as one invented by the colonials. Instead, I wanted to demonstrate that under British domination the caste system became a single system designating and, above all, *including* India's diverse forms of social identity and authority. This journey through the path of the colonial history of Bengal has demonstrated how this homogenization served the idealization of womanhood that functioned as a tool for social mobility for all social groups whether they were reaffirming their social status or aspiring for it. By no means have I intended to claim that for any of these various groups, caste was either seamlessly embraced or disowned. Adjustment and coexistence, if not friendly incorporation, were neither unprecedented nor unusual at different levels of the caste structure and in different ways. In the process of absorption, alteration, and amendment, caste identity was often fragmented along class lines, thus making it more ambiguously transfigured. It is the difference between class as a system of production and caste as a system of reproduction ascertaining hierarchy on a hereditary basis that differentiates the Indian system of stratification from other stratificatory social arrangements as I have argued implicitly, and at times explicitly, in this book. I have thus explained how caste as a system of discrete units within a larger system of production makes endogamy a crucial element of the caste structure and this in turn makes caste groupings a gendered system of social hierarchy. The caste system cannot be maintained without the tool of endogamy, and this is why the subordination of women was made mandatory. Moreover, any specific caste in the caste order has an identity only in terms of its distinctiveness to other castes maintained through endogamy.

Once again, it is endogamy that enables the dispersal of certain kinds of production relations and also provides the caste structure with the flexibility of being able to include disparate groups whilst maintaining the cultural discreteness of the each new participant group that becomes a part of the system. For all these reasons, endogamous marriage and, most importantly, women play a crucial role in the maintenance of this hierarchical structure and as a result the caste system ritualized female sexuality as means of maintaining separation between each social group. It is the ritualized and henceforth idealized pattern of female sexuality that uniquely composes the caste order, a structure which is overtly patriarchal. This patriarchy is brahmanical in nature since it implies a model of oppression of women outlined in the brahmanical prescriptive texts, enforced by the power groups of society. Patriarchal codes prescribed by this structure ensure that the caste system can be reproduced without breaking the hierarchical order of closed endogamous circles, each different from and higher or lower than others. Furthermore, these codes for women differ according to the status of the caste group in the hierarchical social order with the most severe control over female sexuality preserved as an advantage of the higher castes. Finally, it invents an ideology of a chaste and patibrata wife who is valorized and concurrently composes a structure of rules and institutions based on the representation of an ideal woman that maintains both caste and gender inequality. This set of norms initially shaped the ideology of upper-caste gender norms but later on was emulated by the lower-castes who were seeking upward mobility. The motivation behind this lower-caste emulation of upper-caste gender norms was two-fold: firstly, patriarchy has always been an inherent feature of lower-caste social existence too, and secondly, unlike attempts to emulate or contest other distinctive social, cultural, economic, and political phenomena dominated by the upper castes, it was easier to control and restrict the life and work of the women of the lower orders following a brahmanical pattern in order to achieve social legitimacy.

Endogamy or control over women, however, was never declared as a norm for maintaining caste boundaries, but was instead rather projected as the custom of maintaining unities between families, traditions of the clans, or even more abstractly as cultural heritage. This was a clever tool for consolidating the entire structure of relations that produced the caste system, and the consequent patriarchy with its continuous coordination of systems of production and reproduction. The other important facet of the marriage system was to raise the girl child as the perfect bride to bear the responsibility to safeguard the prescribed marriage structure, the reproductive system, and perform the ritualized form of domesticity, which confined the women within the boundaries of the household, thus safeguarding their purity and that of the caste structure. These gendered aspects of daily existence and domestic practices were passed off as tradition, cultural practices and, most of all, as the pure and honourable way of living of the upper castes, which in turn ensured the continuation of the lineage system and a stratificatory social order. Rejecting the general form of upper-caste oppression, the implications of an endogamous marriage system were in most cases not sufficiently interrogated. As a result, the low-caste groups in their attempt to emulate the brahmanical model restricted the lives of their women, which in turn resulted in implicit acquiescence of a socio-genetic scheme of inequality. Here, brahmanical ideology was worth emulating for social mobility because it could successfully disguise the basic discriminatory form of social structure.

In this book I have thus focussed on those apparently routine aspects of daily existence for women such as maintaining a clean and healthy household, cooking nutritious food, teaching moral lessons to children, and above all leading the life of a perfect wife and mother that established an association between the caste structure and the centrality of women in maintaining that structure. The varied nature of these gendered practices along with many other transitional alterations upon which the caste structure rested, however, indicated the most important aspect of the caste arrangement: that caste is a social process, one that is historical and contextual rather than timeless. For example, in the context of colonial Bengal, education became one of the most significant factors in the constitution of an ideal that any upper-caste woman (and later on lower-caste women as well) was supposed to follow. It was considered to be the obvious mark of distinction between the high status and the low demeanour of a woman who was thereby the status definer of a caste group. To grant honour to women to establish their centrality in ensuring the welfare of a caste group had previously been unthinkable; however, the modification of the socio-political and religious boundaries that limited and also safeguarded the caste hierarchy actually demonstrated the otherwise vulnerable nature of the caste structure.

Additionally, this book has shown how social structures are affected by conflictual and assimilatory socio-political and economic changes that cannot be accounted for by any kind of absolutist interpretation or lethargic rationalism. Rationality and emotion in the form of despair, shame, pride, greed, and rage go hand in hand in processes of social construction in which social concepts like freedom, oppression, agency and status are neither undeviating nor intermittent. The caste structure, therefore, is not the result of any unchanging structuralist ideology; neither are its tenets based on a static Marxian rationale of class-based exploitation and the struggle of the masses.

Accordingly, I have acknowledged the effects of both idealization and materiality and the harmonious and/or discordant efforts to reassert or challenge the caste-based social order in colonial Bengal. Thus I have suggested that within a caste framework the idealized construction of women's existence should be seen as part of a complex route of identity formation, resulting out of an attempt either to consolidate or to ameliorate caste-based social status. In the process of highlighting the attempts at identity formation and social mobility of various caste groups, the book has contributed to understanding how ideal models are used to retain and remake the power of the both the influential and the defenceless, although varying in degrees. Thus I would want to emphasize that the importance of this book lies not only in offering a re-assessment of the previous work analysing the traditionalist/nationalist notion of 'ideal womanhood', but also in locating the origin of this ideal within Bengali discourse and its relationship to the socio-economic and religio-political norms against which the apparently ambiguous nature of the caste hierarchy is to be measured.

Finally, while the book has attended primarily to the re-employment of the ideal womanhood in colonial Bengal, it has implications for recognizing the pan-Indian potential veiled in localized manifestations of this tremendously influential model of womanhood. By a pan-Indian impact it is not claimed to project this ideal for all Indian women irrespective of their diverse differences based on language, culture, religion, politics and class structure, but rather to suggest that in transgressing all these boundaries, caste as a dogmatic and normative system exercises tremendous force in the dynamism of Indian society.

NOTE

1. The new ideal woman had to be reinvented as the embodiment of the reform-based new virtues that the native elites compulsorily went through. For example, literacy was the most important virtue among them. For a detailed discussion of the newly adorned virtues of native women see, for instance, Jayakrishna Mitra 1890.

References

PRIMARY

Bengali Sources

Dasi, Nagendrabala (Mustaphi).1904. 'Prayajania Prarthana', in *Bamabodhini Patrika,* Jaishtha: 191-92.
Devi, Rasasundari. 1956. *Amar Jibon* Calcutta: Jitendranath Mukhopadhyay.
Gupta, Purnachandra. 1885. *Bangali Bou.* Calcutta: A.K. Banerjee.
Gupta, Ramtanu. 1861. *Stri Sikhsha Pratham Bhag.* Calcutta.
Gupta, Rajani Kanta. 1896. *Aryakirti.* 5th ed. Calcutta: Sanskrita Press.
Mitra, Girindrabala. 1888. *Ramanir Kartabya.* Calcutta: Giribala Mitra.
Mitra, Jaykrishna. 1890. *Ramanir Kartabya.* Calcutta: Giribala Mitra.
Pal, Dhirendranath. 1883. *Strir Sahit Kathopakathan.* Calcutta: Baishnab Charan Basak.
Sastri, Shivanath. [1909] 2003. *Ramtanu Lahiri o Tatkalin Bangasamaj.* Calcutta: New Age Publishers.
—— 1885. *Grihadharma.* Calcutta: Girish Chandra Ghosh.

Official Records and Publications

The principal official sources used are the General and Education Proceedings of the Government of Bengal, housed in the West Bengal State Archives, Calcutta.
Bengal Library Catalogue (1881), I.
Census of India, 1931, vol. 5, part 1: 425. Registrar General of India and Census Commissioner, Delhi.
O'Donnell, C. J. ed 1893. *Census 1891*, vol. 3 (Bengal). Calcutta.
UK. Parliament. *Parliamentary Paper on Hindu Widows* 1821.

English Sources

Ibbetson, Denzil. [1883] 1974. *Punjab Castes* (reprint of the chapter on 'The Races, Castes, and Tribes of the People' in the Census of Punjab). Lahore: Mubarak Ali: 83.

Nesfield, Johh, C. 1885. 'Brief View of the Caste System of the North-western Provinces and Oudh, together with an Examination of Names and Figures Shown' in the *Census Report, 1882*, being an attempt to classify on a functional basis all the main castes of the United Provinces, and to explain their graduations of rank and the process of their formation. Allahabad: North-Western Provinces and Oudh Government Press.

Risley, H.H. 1891. rpt. *The Tribes and Castes of Bengal.* Calcutta.

—— 1908. *The People of India.* London: Thacker.

Journals and Newspapers

Amrita Bazar Patrika, 2 Jan 1905, vol. xxxvi: 12.

Anandabazjar Patrika, 1980-2006.

Asia Times, 21 June 2001.

Bamabodhini Patrika, 1270-1329 BS/1863-1922.

The Bengal Christian Herald, 1870.

Bharatbarsha, Nov-Dec 1943.

Bangadut (Calcutta), 13 June 1829.

Bengal Spectator, 16 March 1843.

Bramho Public Opinion, 1878-1880.

Calcutta Review. 1855, 25:49; 25:50; 1855, xxxiv; 1848, vol ix; no. xvii; 40:79, 93-94; 47:94; 1868.

Desh, 1958-1989.

Friend of India, 1820-59. Serampore.

Gandhabanik Samachar, 1329-1331 BS/1922-1924.

The Hindustan Times, 17 April 2007.

Indian Mirror, 1870-1879.

Korok Literary Magazine, 2005: pre-Autumn volume.

Kshatriya, 1321 BS/1914.

Liberal and New Dispensation, 1882-1884.

Mahishya Mahila, 1321-1329 BS/1914-1922.

Mahishya Samaj, 1323-1329 BS/1916-1922.

Nabyabharat, Feb-Mar, Dec 1893-Jan 1894.
Nutan Panjika, 1870-1871.
Paricarika, I, II June 1878.
Sadgope Patrika, 1335-1340 BS/1928-1933; 1388 BS/1981.
Samachar Chandrika, 8 June 1843; 23 November 1843; 4 February 1844; 6 October 1845.
Samachar Darpan, 23 November 1853.
Somprakash, 29 July 1878.
Subarnabanik Samachar,1323-1325 BS.
Tattvabodhini Patrika, 1834-1870.
Tili Bandhab, 1326 BS/1919.
Tilir Gaurab, 1324-1326 BS/1917-1919.

SECONDARY

Althusser, L. and E. Balibar. 1969. *For Marx*. Harmondsworth: Penguin Books.

Amin, Shahid, and Dipesh Chakrabarty, eds. 1996. *Subaltern Studies 9: Writings on South Asian History and Society*. Delhi: Oxford University Press.

Anand, Mulk Raj, ed. 1989. *Rammohun Roy, Raja, Sati, a Writeup of Raja Ram Mohan Roy about Burning of Widows Alive*. Delhi: B.R. Pub. Corp.

Bagchi, Amiya. 1972. *Private Investment in India 1900-1939*. Cambridge: Cambridge University Press.

Bagchi, Jasodhara. 1985. 'Positivism and Nationalism: Womanhood and Crisis in Nationalist Fiction in Bankimchandra's *Anandamath*', *Economic and Political Weekly* Review of Women Studies, 20, 43.

Bailey, F.G. 1957. *Caste and Economic Frontier: A Village in Highland Orissa*. Manchester: Manchester University Press.

Balagangadhara, S.N. 1994. *The Heathen in His Blindness: Asia, the West and the Dynamic of Religion*. Leiden: E.J. Brill.

Bandyopadhyay, Sekhar. 2004. *Caste, Culture and Hegemony: Social Dominance in Colonial Bengal*. Delhi: Sage.

——2001. 'Differentiation and Transience: History of Caste, Power and Identity in Bengal', in Sekhar Bandyopadhyay, ed., *Bengal: Rethinking History: Essays in Historiography*. Delhi: Manohar.

——1997. *Caste, Protest and Identity in Colonial India: The Namashudras of Bengal, 1872-1947*. Richmond, UK: Curzon Press.

—1994. 'From Alienation to Integration: Changes in the Politics of Caste in Bengal, 1937-47'. *Indian Economic and Social History Review*. 31, 3. July-September: 349-91.

—1992. 'Construction of Social Categories: The Role of Colonial Census', in K. S. Singh, ed, *Ethnicity, Caste and People*. Delhi: Manohar.

—1990. *Caste, Politics and the Raj: Bengal 1872-1937*. University of Calcutta: Dept. of History. Monograph No. 5: South Asia Books.

Banerjee, Sumanta. 2000. *Dangerous Outcastes: The Prostitute in Nineteenth-Century Bengal*. Kolkata: Seagull.

—1989. 'Marginalisation of Women's Popular Culture in Nineteenth-Century Bengal', in K. Sangari and S. Vaid, eds, *Recasting Women: Essays in Colonial History*. Delhi: Kali for Women: 127-79.

Banerjee, Swapna M. 2001. 'Child, Mother, and Servant: Motherhood and Domestic Ideology in Colonial Bengal', in Avril A. Powell and Siobhan Lambert-Hurle, eds, *Rhetoric and Reality: Gender and the Colonial Experience in South Asia*. Delhi: Oxford University Press.

—1998. 'Exploring the World of Domestic Manuals: Bengali Middle-Class Women and Servants in Colonial Calcutta', *Sagar* 3.1: electronic journal. At http://asnic.utexas.edu/asnic/pages/sagar/SAGAR3.r.html. (Accessed May 15, 2006)

Basu, Amrita. 1999. 'Women's Activism and the Vicissitudes of Hindu Nationalism'. *Journal of Women's History* 10, 4: 104.

Basu, Swaraj. 1994. 'The Colonial State and the Indigenous Society: The Creation of the Rajbansi Identity in Bengal', in Sekhar Bandyopadhyay, Abhijit Dasgupta, William van Schendel, eds, *Bengal: Communities, Development and States*. Delhi: Manohar.

Baxter, Christine. 1978. 'The Genesis of the Babu', in Peter Robb and David Taylor, eds, *Rule, Protest, Identity: Aspects of Modern South Asia*. London: Curzon Press.

Bayly, C.A., ed, 1996. *Empire and Information Intelligence Gathering and Social Communication 1780-1870*. Cambridge: Cambridge University Press.

Beetham, Margaret. 1996. *A Magazine of Her Own 1800-1914*. London: Routledge.

Béteille, André. 1991. *Society and Politics in India: Essays in Comparative Perspective*. Oxford: Berg.

Bhaba, Homi. 1994. *The Location of Culture*. London: Routledge.

Bhattarcharji, Sukumari. 1994. *Women and Society in Ancient India*. Kolkata: Basumati Corporation.

Bhattacharya, Tithi. 2005. *The Sentinels of Culture: Class, Education, and the Colonial Intellectual in Bengal, 1848-85.* Delhi: Oxford University Press.

Bose, Mandakranta. 2000. 'Textual Confrontations with Female Transgression in the Behula Legend', in Mariola Offredi, ed, *The Banyan Tree: Essays on Early Literature in New Indo-Aryan Languages.* Proceedings of the Seventh International Conference on Early Literature in New Indo-Aryan Languages, Venice, 1997, vol 1. Delhi: Manohar.

Borthwick, Meredith. 1984. *Changing Role of Women in Bengal 1849-1900.* Princeton: Princeton University Press.

Bouglé, Célestin. 1971. 'Introduction' by D. F. Pocock, trans., *The European Understanding of India.* Cambridge: Cambridge Univerisity Press.

Breckenridge, Carol A., and Peter van der Veer, eds. 1993. *Orientalism and the Postcolonial Predicament.* Philadelphia: University of Pennsylvania Press.

Broomfield, J.H. 1968. *Elite Conflict in a Plural Society: Twentieth-Century Bengal.* Berkeley: University of California Press.

Carroll, Lucy. 1989. 'Law, Custom, and Statutory Social Reform: The Hindu Widow's Remarriage Act of 1856', in J. Krishnamurty, ed, *Women in Colonial India: Essays on Survival, Work and the State.* Delhi: Oxford University Press.

Chakrabarti, Dilip K. 1997. *Colonial Indology: Socio-Politics of the Ancient Indian Past.* Delhi: Munshiram Manoharlal.

Chakrabarti, Kunal. 2001. *Religious Processes: The Puranas and the Making of a Religious Tradition.* Delhi: Oxford University Press.

Chakrabarti, Sambuddha. 1995. 'Changing Notions of Conjugal Relationships in Nineteenth-Century Bengal', in R. K. Ray, ed, *Mind, Body and Society.* Kolkata: Oxford University Press.

Chakrabarty, Dipesh. 1996. 'The Difference-Deferral of a Colonial Modernity: Public Debates on Domesticity in British India,' in David Arnold and David Hardiman, eds, *Subaltern Studies VIII: Essays in Honour of Ranajit Guha.* Delhi: Oxford University Press.

Chakraborty, Ratanlal. 1994. 'A Caste Movement in Mymensingh', in Sekhar Bandyopadhayay, Abhijit Dasgupta, Willem van Schendel, eds, *Bengal: Communities, Development and States.* Delhi: Manohar.

Chakravarti, Uma. 2003. *Gendering Caste: Through a Feminist Lens,* Kolkata: Stree.

——1989. 'Whatever Happened to the Vedic Dasi?' in K. Sangari and S. Vaid, eds, *Recasting Women*, Delhi: Kali for Women.

Chatterjee, Bankimchandra. [1884] 1946. *Devi Chaudhurani*, trans. S.C.Mitter. Kolkata.

——[1882] 1992. *Anandamath* (trs. unknown), Delhi: Orient Paperbacks.

——[1875] 1992. *Kamalakanta: A Collection of Satirical Essays and Recollections,* trans Monish Ranjan Chatterjee. Kolkata: Rupa.

Chatterjee, Indrani. 1990. 'Refracted Reality: The 1935 Calcutta Police Survey of Prostitutes'. *Manushi* 57 (Mar-April 1990): 26-36.

Chatterjee, Kumkum. 2005. 'The King of Controversy: History and Nation-Making in Colonial India', *American Historical Review* 110, 5.

Chatterjee, Partha. 1999. *The Partha Chatterjee Omnibus.* Delhi: Oxford University Press.

——ed, 1998. *Wages of Freedom: Fifty Years of the Nation-State.* Delhi: Oxford Univeristy Press.

——1993. *The Nation and Its Fragments: Colonial and Postcolonial Histories.* Delhi: Oxford University Press.

——1989. The Nationalist Resolution of the Women's Question', in K. Sangari and S. Vaid, eds, *Recasting Women: Essays in Colonial History.* Delhi: Kali for Women.

——1986. *Nationalist Thought and the Colonial World: A Derivative Discourse?* London: Zed.

Chatterjee Ratnabali. 1993. 'Prostitution in Nineteenth-Century Bengal: Construction of Class and Gender', *Social Scientist* 21: 244-46.

Chowdhury-Sengupta, Indira. 1998. *The Frail Hero and Virile History: Gender and the Politics of Culture in Colonial Bengal.* Delhi: Oxford University Press.

——1993. 'The Return of the Sati', *Resources of Feminist Research* 22, 3,4: 41-44.

Chowdhry, Prem. 1994. *The Veiled Women: Shifting Gender Equations in Hariyana 1880-1990.* Delhi: Oxford University Press.

Chunder, Bhola Nauth. [c 1846] 1978. 'Calcutta: Its Origin and Growth', reprinted in Alok Ray, ed, *Nineteenth-Century Studies,* 4. Calcutta: Calcutta Keepsake.

Cohn, Bernard S. 1992. 'Representing Authority in British India', in E. Hobsbawm and T. Ranger, eds, *The Invention of Tradition.* Cambridge: Cambridge University Press.

——ed. 1987. 'The Changing Status of a Depressed Caste', in *An*

Anthropologist among Historians and Other Essays. Delhi: Oxford University Press: 255-83.

—1983. 'Representing Authority in Victorian India', in E. Hobsbawn and T. Ranger, *The Invention of Tradition.* Cambridge: Cambridge University Press.

—1968. 'Notes on the History of the Study of Indian Society and Culture', in Milton Singer and B.S. Cohn, eds, *Structure and Change in Indian Society.* Chicago: University of Chicago Press.

Collet, Sophia Dobson. 1962. 'Editors' Note', in D.K. Biswas and P.C. Ganguli, eds, *The Life and Letters of Raja Rammohun Ray.* Calcutta: Sadharon Brahmo Samaj.

Comaroff, Jean, and John L. Comaroff. 1992 . 'Home-made Hegemony: Modernity, Domesticity, and Colonialism in South Africa', in K.Hansen, ed, *African Encounters with Domesticity.* New Brusnwick: Rutgers University Press.

Cooper, Frederick and Ann Stoler, eds, 1997. 'Between the Metropole and Colony: Re-thinking a Research Agenda', in *Tensions of Empire: Colonial Cultures in a Bourgeois World.* Berkeley: University of California Press.

Davidoff, Leonore, and Catherine Hall. 1987. *Family Fortunes: Men and Women of the English Middle Class 1780-1850.* Chicago: University of Chicago Press.

de Bary, W.T. et al., eds, 1988. *Sources of Indian Tradition.* New York: Columbia University Press.

Sara Delamont. 1978. 'The Contraditions in Ladies' Education', in Sara Delamont and Lorna Diffin, eds, *The Nineteenth Century Woman: Her Cultural and Physical World,* London: Routledge: 134-63.

Derrett, J.D.M. 1968. *Religion, Law and the State in India.* London: Faber and Faber.

Dharmapal. 1983. *The Beautiful Tree: Indigenous Indian Education in the Eighteenth Century.* Delhi: Oxford University Press.

Dharwadker, Vinay. 1993. 'Orientalism and the Study of Indian Literatures', in Carol A. Breckenridge and Peter van der Veer eds, *Orientalism and the Postcolonial Predicament.* Philadelphia: University of Pennsylvania Press.

Dirks, Nicholas B. 2001. *Castes of Mind: Colonialism and the Making of Modern India.* Princeton: Princeton University Press.

—. 1993. 'Colonial Histories and Native Informants: Biography of an Archive', in *Orientalism and the Postcolonial Predicament,* in

Breckenridge, Carol A. and Peter van der Veer, eds, Philadelphia: University of Pennsylvania Press.

—1987. 'Castes of Mind', *Representations* special issue: *Imperial Fantasies and Postcolonial Histories* 37 (Winter): 56-78.

Doniger, Wendy, and Brian K. Smith, trans, *The Laws of Manu*. London: Penguin, 1991.

Dube, Leela. 1988. 'On the Construction of Gender', in K. Chanana, ed, *Socialisation, Education and Women: Explorations in Gender Identity*. Delhi: Orient Longman.

—1986. 'Seed and Earth: Symbolism of Biological Reproduction and Sexual Relations of Production', in Leela Dube et al, eds, *Visibility and Power: Essays on Women in Society and Development*. Delhi: Oxford University Press.

Dube, S.C. 1990. *Indian Society*. Delhi: NBT.

Dumont, Louis. 1970. *Homo Hierarchicus: The Caste System and Its Implications*. London: Weidenfeld and Nicholson.

Dumont, Louis, and D.F. Pocock. 1957. 'Village Studies', *Contributions to Indian Sociology* 1: 23-41.

D'Souza, Victor. 1969. 'Measurement of Rigidity-Fluidity Dimension of Social Stratification in Six Indian Villages', *Sociological Bulletin* 18, 1.

Dutta, Krishna, and Andrew Robinson.1995. *Rabindranath Tagore: The Myriad-Minded Man*. New York: St. Martin's Press.

Embree, Ainslie T. 1962. *Charles Grant and British Rule in India*. London: Allen and Unwin. 'The Observations' were published in the *Parliamentary Papers* 1812-13, x paper 282, pp 1-112, and in *Parliamentary Papers* 1831-32, viii paper 734, General Appendix no 1, pp 3-92.

Forbes, Geraldine. 1996. *Women in Modern India*. Cambridge: Cambridge University Press.

Fox, Richard. 1996. 'Gandhi and Feminized Nationalism in India', in B. F. Williams, ed, *Women Out of Place*. Delhi: Sage.

— 1993. 'East of Said', in Michael Sprinker, ed, *Edward Said: A Critical Reader*. Oxford Blackwell: 144-56.

Frykenberg, Robert, E. 1989. 'The Emergence of Modern "Hinduism" as a Concept and as an Institution: A Reappraisal with Special Reference to South India', in Gunther-Dietz Sontheimer and Hermann Kulke, eds, *Hinduism Reconsidered*. Delhi: Manohar.

Fuller, Eugene. 1984. 'Educational Language Planning in a Navaho

Community,' *International Education Journal* 1, 1: 91-102.

Ghose, N. N. 1901. *Memoirs of Maharaja Nubkissen Bahadur*. Calcutta: K. B. Basu.

Ghurye, G.S. [1932] 1950. *Caste and Race in India*. Mumbai: Popular Prakashan.

Glucksmann, Miriam. 1974. *Structuralist Analysis in Contemporary Social Thought: A Comparison of the Theories of Claude Lévi-Strauss and Louis Althusser*. London: Routledge and Kegan Paul.

Goldelier, Maurice. 1977. *Perspectives in Marxist Anthropology*. Cambridge: Cambridge University Press.

—. 1972. *Rationality and Irrationality in Economics*. New York: Monthly Review Press.

Gough, K. 1963. 'Indian Nationalism and Ethnic Freedom', in David Bidney, ed, *The Concept of Freedom in Anthropology*. The Hague: Mouton.

Gupta, Dipankar. 2000. *Interrogating Caste: Understanding Hierarchy and Difference in Indian Society*. Delhi: Penguin.

—1997. 'Continuous Hierarchies and Discrete Castes', in Dipankar Gupta, ed, *Social Stratification*. Delhi: Oxford University Press.

Habib, Irfan. 1995. *Essays in Indian History: Towards a Marxist Perception*. Delhi: Tulika.

—1965. 'Distribution of Landed Property in Pre-British India', *Enquiry* l, 2: 21-75.

Hatcher, Brian. 2001. 'Sanskrit Pandits Recall Their Youth: Two Autobiographies from Nineteenth Century', *Journal of the American Oriental Society* 121, 4 (October).

Harlan, Lindsey, and Paul, B. Courtright. 1995. *From the Margins of Hindu Marriage*. Delhi: Oxford University Press: 190.

Hatalkar, V.G. 1973. 'M.G. Ranade', in S.P. Sen, ed, *Historians and Historiography in Modern India*. Calcutta: Institute of Historical Studies.

Hutton, J.H . [1947] 1963. *Caste in India: Its Nature, Function and Origin*. Bombay: Oxford University Press.

Inden, Ronald. 1990. *Imagining India*. Oxford: Blackwell.

—1976. *Marriage and Rank in Bengali Culture*. Delhi: Vikas.

Jha, H. 1977. 'Low-Caste Peasants and Upper-Caste Zamindars in Bihar, 1921-1925: An Analysis of Sanskritisation and Contradiction between Two Groups', *Indian Economic and Social History Review* 14, 4.

Khastagir, Amitabha. 2006. *Brahmoism: From Foundation to Confluence: An Anthology of Essays*. Kolkata: Brahmo Sammilan Samaj and Blue Pencil.
King, Richard. 1999. *Orientalism and Religion: Post-Colonial Theory, India and 'The Mystic East'*. London: Routledge.
Kishwar, Madhu and Ruth Vanita. 1984. 'The Burning of Roop Kanwar', *Race & Class* 30, 1, 59-67.
Kolenda, Pauline. 1976. 'Seven Kinds of Hierarchy in *Homo Hierarchicus*', *Journal of Asian Studies*, 35, 4 (August).
Kosambi, D. D. 1986. 'Caste and Class in India', in A.J. Syed, ed, *D. D. Kosambi on History and Society: Problems of Interpretation*. Mumbai: Department of History, University of Bombay.
—1962. *Myth and Reality: Studies in the Formation of Indian Culture*. Bombay: Popular Prakashan.
Lawson, Thomas. E., and Robert N. McCauley. 1993. 'Crisis of Conscience, Riddle of Identity: Making Space for a Cognitive Approach to Religious Phenomena', *Journal of the American Academy of Religion* 41, 2 (Summer).
Leopold, Joan. 1974. 'British Applications of the Aryan Theory of Race to India, 1850-70', *The English Historical Review* 89, 352: 578-603.
Leslie, Julia. 1996. 'Myth and Myth-Making: Continuous Evolution in Indian Tradition', *SOAS Collected Papers in South Asia*. London Curzon.
—1992. 'Suttee or Sati: Victim or Victor?' In Julia Leslie, ed, *Roles and Rituals for Hindu Women*. Delhi: Motilal Banarsidass.
—1989. The Perfect Wife: The Orthodox Hindu Woman According to the *Stridharmapaddhati* of *Tryambakayajvan*, Oxford University South Asian Studies Series. Delhi: Oxford University Press.
Lévi-Strauss, C. 1969. *The Elementary Structures of Kinship*, rev. ed, trans. James Bell, John R. von Sturmer and Rodney Needham. London: Eyre & Spottiswoode.
—1966. *The Savage Mind*. Chicago: Chicago University Press.
Luke, Carmen. 1989. 'Pedagogy, Printing and Protestantism: The Discourse on Childhood', in P. L. Smith, ed, *SUNY Series in the Philosophy of Education*. Albany: State University of New York Press.
Lynch, Owen. 1969. *The Politics of Untouchability: Social Mobility and Social Change in a City of India*. New York: Columbia University Press.
Madan, T. N., ed, 1992. *Religion in India*. Delhi: Oxford University Press.

Mairs, Nancy. 1996. *Carnal Acts: Essays*. Boston: Beacon Press.

Mani, Lata. 1998. *Contentious Traditions*. Berkeley: University of California Press.

——1989. 'Contentious Traditions: The Debate on Sati in Colonial India', in K. Sangari and S. Vaid, eds, *Recasting Women: Essays in Colonial History*. Delhi: Kali for Women: 88-126.

Marriot, McKim. 1970. Review of *Homo Hierarchicus*, *American Anthropologist* new series, 72, 2: (April): 468-69.

Marshall, Peter. 1970. *The British Discovery of Hinduism in the Eighteenth Century*. Cambridge: Cambridge University Press.

Meillasoux, Claude. 1973. 'Are There Castes in India?' *Economy and Society* 2,1.

Mencher, John, 1974. 'The Caste System: Upside Down or the Not So Mysterious East', *Current Anthroplogy* 15, 4: 469-78.

Menon, Visalakshi. 2003. *Indian Women and Nationalism: The U.P. Story*. Delhi: Shakti Books.

Milner, Andrew. 1994. *Contemporary Cultural Theory*. London: UCL Press.

Moffatt, Michael. 1979. *An Untouchable Community in South India: Structure and Consensus*. Princeton: Princeton University Press.

Mukherjee, Ramkrishna, 1957. *The Dynamics of a Rural Society*. Berlin: Akademie Verlag.

Mukherjee, Rudrangshu. 2006. 'City with a Past' in 'Soul City: A Symposium on the Many Facets of Calcutta'. *Seminar* (March).

Mukherjee, S.N. 1987. 'Bhadralok and Their *Dals*—Policies of Social Factions, 1820-1856', in Pradip Sinha, ed, *The Urban Experience: Calcutta*. Calcutta: Riddhi.

——1977. *Calcutta: Myths and History*. Calcutta: 20.

——1975. '*Daladali* in Calcutta in the Nineteenth Century', *Modern Asian Studies*. 9, 1: 59-80.

——1970. 'Class, Caste and Politics in Calcutta, 1815-1838', in Edmund Leach and S.N. Mukherjee, eds, *Elites in South Asia*. Cambridge: Cambridge University Press.

Murshid, Ghulam. 1984. *Reluctant Debutante*. Rajshahi: Rajshahi University Press.

Nagar, S. 2006. *The Image of Chastity*. Delhi: B.R. Corp.

Naidu, B.N. 1996. *Intellectual History of Colonial India: Mysore 1831-1920*. Jaipur: Rawat.

Nandy, Ashih. 1975. 'Sati: A Nineteenth-Century Tale of Women,

Violence and Protest', in V.C. Joshi, ed, *Rammohun Roy and the Process of Modernization in India*. Delhi: Vikas.

—1998. *Exiled at Home: Comprising at the Edge of Psychology; The Intimate Enemy; and Creating a Nationality*. Delhi: Oxford University Press.

Nicholas, F. Gier. 1995. 'Hindu Titanism', *Philosophy East and West* 45:1 (Jan): 73-96.

Niyogi, Chandreyee. 2006. *Reorienting Orientalism*. Delhi: Sage.

O'Hanlon, Rosalind, and David Washbrook. 1994. 'After Orientalism: Culture, Criticism, and Politics in the Third World', in *Comparative Studies in Society and History*. 34, 1 (January): 141-67.

Omvedt, Gail. 1994. *Dalits and the Democratic Revolution: Dr Ambedkar and the Dalit Movement in Colonial India*. Delhi: Sage.

Östör, Äkos, Fruzzetti, Lina, and Burnett Steve, eds. 1982. *Concepts of Person: Kinship, Caste, and Marriage in India*. Cambridge: Harvard University Press.

Pandey, G. 1983. 'Rallying Round the Cow: Sectarian Strife in the Bhojpuri Region, *c*. 1888-1917', in R. Guha, ed, *Subaltern Studies 2: Writings on South Asian History and Society*. Delhi: Oxford University Press.

Quigley, D. 1994. 'Is a Theory of Caste Still Possible?' In M. Searle-Chatterjee and U. Sharma, eds, *Contextualising Caste*. Oxford: Blackwell: 25-48.

Radhakrishnan, Sarvepalli. [1927] 1988. *The Hindu View of Life*. London: Unwin.

Ray, Rajat Kanta, ed. 1999. *Mind, Body and Society*. Kolkata: Oxford University Press.

—1984. *Social Conflict and Political Unrest in Bengal, 1875-1927*. Delhi: Oxford University Press.

Raychaudhuri, Tapan. 1988. *Europe Reconsidered*. Delhi: Oxford University Press.

Rocher, Rosane. 1995. 'Weaving Knowledge: Sir William Jones and Indian Pundits', in Garland Cannon and Kevin R. Brine, eds, *Objects of Enquiry: The Life, Contributions, and Influence of Sir William Jones (1746-1794)*. New York: New York University Press: 51-79.

—1993. 'British Orientalism in the Eighteenth Century: The Dialectic of Knowledge and Government', in Carol. A. Breckenridge and Peter van der Veer, eds, *Orientalism and the Postcolonial Predicament*. Philadelphia: University of Pennsylvania Press.

Roy, Kumkum. 2002. 'Goddesses in the Rg Veda: An Enquiry', in Nilima Chitkopekar, ed, *Invoking the Goddess: Gender Politics in Indian Religion*. Delhi: Shakti Books

—1994. *The Emergence of Monarchy in North India 800-400 BC: As Reflected in the Brahmanical Tradition*. Delhi: Oxford University Press.

Rukmini, T.S. 1999. *Hindu Diaspora: Global Perspectives*. Montreal: Concordia University Press.

Sanyal, Hiteshranjan. 1992. 'Popular Culture, Community, Power: Three Studies of Modern Indian Social History', *Studies in History* 8, 2 (1992): 309-23.

—1982. *Literary Sources of Medieval Bengali History: A Study of a few Mangalkavya Texts.* Calcutta, Centre for Studies in Social Sciences.

Sarkar, Smriti Kumar. 1994. 'Caste, Occupation and Social Mobility: A Study of the Kansaris in Colonial Bengal', in Sekhar Bandyopadhyay, Abhijit Dasgupta and Willem van Schendel, eds, *Bengal's Communities, Development and States*. Delhi: Manohar.

Sarkar, Sumit. 1997. *Writing Social History*. Delhi: Oxford University Press.

—1992.' Popular Culture, Community Power: Three Studies of Modern Indian History.' *Studies in History* 8, 2: 309-23.

—1985. *A Critique of Colonial India*. Kolkata: Papyrus.

Sarkar, Sushobhan. 1999. *Bengal Renaissance and Other Essays*. Delhi: Granth Shilpi.

Sarkar, Tanika. 2011. 'Holy Infancy: Love and Power in a Low Caste Sect in Bengal', *South Asian History and Culture* 2, 3 (July): 337-57.

—2001. *Hindu Wife, Hindu Nation: Community, Religion and Cutural Nationalism*. Delhi: Zubaan.

Sastri, Sibanath. 1907. *Ramtanu Lahiri, Brahman and Reformer: A History of the Renaissance in Bengal*. Berkeley: University of California Libraries.

Savarkar, V.D. 2003. *Hindutva: Who Is a Hindu?* Delhi: Hindi Sahitya Sadan.

Senart, E. 1975. *Caste in India: The Facts and the System*, trans E. Denison Ross. London.

Sengupta, Shayamalendu. 1990. *A Conservative Hindu of Colonial India: Raja Radhakanta Deb and His Milieu (1784-1867)*. Delhi: Navrang.

Sharma, R.S., ed. 1994. *A Comprehensive History of India, AD 985-1206*, vol 4, pt. 1. Delhi: People's Publishing House.

Silverberg, James, ed. 1968. *Social Mobility in the Caste System in India.* The Hague: Mouton.

Sinha, Mrinalini, ed. 2000a *Mother India.* Ann Arbor: University of Michign Press.

——2000b *Colonial Masculinity: The 'Manly Englishman' and the 'Effeminate Bengali' in the Late Nineteenth Century.* Manchester: Manchester University Press.

Sinha, Pradip. 1978. *Calcutta in Urban History.* Kolkata: Firma KLM.

——1962. *Nineteenth-Century Bengal: Aspects of Social History.* Kolkata: Firma KLM.

Singer, Milton, 1965. 'The Social Organization of Indian Civilization', *Diogenes* 2, 45.

Singh, Yogendra. 1997. *Social Stratification and Change in India.* Delhi: Manohar.

Smith, Vincent A. 1958. *The Oxford History of India,* 3rd ed. Oxford: Clarendon Press.

——1919. *Oxford History of India.* Oxford: Oxford University Press.

Srinivas, M.N. 1994. *Religion and Society among Coorgs of South India.* Bombay.

——1989.*The Cohesive Role of Sanskritization and Other Essays.* Delhi: Oxford University Press.

——1968. 'Mobility in the Caste System', in Milton Singer and B.S. Cohn, eds, *Structure and Change in Indian Society.* Chicago: Aldine Publishing Company.

——1966. *Social Change in Modern India.* Berkeley: University of California Press.

——1962. *Caste in Modern India and Other Essays.* Mumbai: Orient Blackswan.

Stokes, Eric. 1978. *The Peasant and the Raj: Studies in Agrarian Society and Peasant Rebellion in Colonial India.* Cambridge: Cambridge University Press.

Stietencron, H. von. 1997. 'Hinduism: On the Proper Use of a Deceptive Term', in Gunter D. Sontheimer and Hermann Kulke, eds, *Hinduism Reconsidered.* Delhi: Manohar: 11-28.

Tambiah, S.J. 1973. 'From Varna to Caste Through Mixed Unions', in Jack Goody, ed, *Character of Kinship.* Cambridge: Cambridge University Press.

Taniguchi, S. 1994. 'The Rajbanshi Community and the Changing Social Structure of Land Tenure in Koch Bihar Princely State', in

S. Taniguchi, et al, eds, *Economic Changes and Social Transformation in Modern and Contemporary South Asia*. Tokyo: Hitotsubashi University.

Thapar, Romila. 2004. *Early India: From the Origins to AD 1300*. Berkeley: University of California Press.

2000. 'Interpretations of Indian History: Colonial, Nationalist, Postcolonial' in P.R. de Souza, ed, *Contemporary India: Transitions*. Delhi: Sage.

—1993. *Interpreting Early India*. Delhi: Oxford University Press: 60-88.

—1989. 'Perspective in History, in *Sati: A Writeup on Raja Rammohan Roy about Burning of Widows Alive*. Delhi: B.R. Publishing Corporation.

—1985. 'Syndicated Moksha', *Seminar* 313 (Sept).

Tharu, Susie, and K. Lalita, eds, 1991-93. *Women Writing in India: 600 BC to the Present*, 2 vols. Delhi: Oxford University Press.

Uberoi, Patricia. 2006. *Freedom and Destiny: Gender, Family and Popular Culture in India*. Delhi: Oxford University Press.

—1994. ed. *Family, Kinship, and Marriage in India*. Delhi: Oxford University Press.

Walsh, Judith E. 2005. *How to Be the Goddess of Your Home: An Anthology of Bengali Domestic Manuals*. Delhi: Yoda Press.

—2004. *Domesticity in Colonial India*. Delhi: Oxford University Press.

—2001. 'The Virtuous Wife and the Well-Ordered Home', in Rajat Kanta Ray, ed, *Mind, Body, and Society*. Calcutta: Oxford University Press.

Washbrook, D. 1975. 'The Development of Caste Organisation in South India, 1880 to 1925', in C.J. Baker, and D.A. Washbrook, eds, *South India: Political Institutions and Political Change 1880-1940*. Delhi: Macmillan.

Yalman, Nur. 1969. 'The Flexibility of Caste Principles in a Kanyadan Community', in Edmund Leach, ed, *Aspects of Caste in South India, Ceylon and North West Pakistan*. Cambridge: Cambridge University Press.

Zelliot, E.1973. 'Learning the Use of Political Means: The Mahars of Maharashtra', in R. Kothari, ed, *Caste in Indian Politics*. Delhi: Orient Longman.

Bengali

Bandyopadhyay, Bhabanicharan. 1936. *Kalikata Kamalalay*. Kolkata.

Bandyopadhyay, Brajendranath, ed, 1994. *Sangbad Patre Sekaler Katha*. Kolkata.

Bandyopadhyay, Chandicharan. 1990. *Vidyasagar*. Kolkata: Standard Publishers.

Bandyopadhyay, Iswarchandra. 1891. *Vidyasagarcharit*. Kolkata: The Calcutta Library.

Basu, Swapan, 1978. *Sati*. Calcutta: published by author.

Biswas, Taraknath. 1987. *Bangiya Mahila*. Kolkata: Rajendralal Biswas.

Chatterjee, Bankimchandra, ed, 1885. *Kabita Sangraha*, vol 1. Kolkata: 121-22.

——1984. *Bankim Rachanabali*, 13th ed. Kolkata: Sahitya Sangsad.

Chaudhuri, Nirad C. 1988/1396 BS. *Atmaghati Bangali*. Kolkata: Mitra and Ghosh.

Choudhury, Sirajul Islam. 1993. *Dwijati Tattver Saotyamithya*. Dhaka: Bidyaprakash.

Datta, Tirthapati. 1994. *Vidyasagar Rachanabali*, vol 1. Kolkata.

Deb, Chitra. 2004. *Thakurbarir Andarmahal*. Kolkata: Ananda Publishers.

Dey, Susheel Kumar, ed, 1952. *Bangla Prabad: Chara o Chalti Katha*. Kolkata: A. Mukherjee.

Devi, Soudamini. 1912 'Pitrismriti', *Prabashi* 1908.

Dutta, Pranakrishna. 1981. *Kolikatar Itibirtta*. Kolkata.

Ghosh, Benoy. 1963. *Samayik Patre Banglar Samajchitra*. vols 1-4. Calcutta: Bengal Publishers.

Ghosh, L.N. 1983. *Kolkatar Babu Brittanta*, trans, Suddhadan Sen. Kolkata: Aryan.

Mullick, Pramathanath. 1935. *Sachitra Kalikatar Itihas*. Kolkata.

Raychaudhuri, Girijaprasanna. 1888. *Grihalakshmi*, 2nd ed. Kolkata: Gurudas Chatterjee.

Seth, Harihar. 1934. *Prachin Kolikata*. Kolkata.

Sinha, Kaliprasanna. 1977. *Hutom Penchar Noksha*. Kolkata: Basumati Corporation.

Index